ŚAṄKARA SOURCE-BOOK

VOLUME I

ŚAṄKARA ON THE ABSOLUTE

ŚAṄKARA ON THE ABSOLUTE

A ŚAṄKARA SOURCE-BOOK

VOLUME I

by

A.J. ALSTON

SHANTI SADAN
LONDON

First Edition 1980
Reprinted 1981, 1987

Second Edition 2004

29 Chepstow Villas
London W11 3DR

www.shanti-sadan.org

ISBN 0-85424-055-1

Printed and bound by
J W Arrowsmith Ltd., Bristol BS3 2NT

PREFACE TO SECOND EDITION

The present volume is the first of a series of six which aims to bring together the most important texts of Śaṅkara in a systematic and digestible form. They have been extracted from the commentaries in which they were for the most part embedded and re-arranged in topics, so that the six volumes into which they are divided broadly speaking cover six basic themes of religious philosophy, namely (I) The Absolute, (II) God and the World, (III) God and the Soul, (IV) Polemics, (V) Spiritual Discipline and the rôle of Revelation and (VI) the Spiritual Path itself, culminating in this case in 'Enlightenment' or 'Liberation'.

The bibliography for all six volumes is included at the end of each volume, followed by a conspectus of the contents and main topics covered in the Source Book as a whole. The main index is reserved for Volume VI, Śaṅkara on Enlightenment, together with an index of the extracts used from Śaṅkara's writings.

Apart from some introductory historical matter, appearing mostly at the beginning of the opening volume, the work consists mainly of groups of Śaṅkara's texts in translation, interspersed only by a few passages from the anthologist designed to draw attention to the main features of the material to come, somewhat in the manner of programme notes at a concert. Explanations designed to help the non-specialist reader have been placed in notes at the end of each chapter, along with a few discussions and references which will mainly be of interest to the specialist. The work is based only on texts of well-established authenticity, namely the Commentaries, including those on Gauḍapāda and the Bhagavad Gītā, plus the Upadeśa Sāhasrī.

PREFACE

The work is dedicated with the greatest reverence to our spiritual Teacher, the late Hari Prasad Shastri, founder of Shanti Sadan, who demonstrated to his pupils by his own life that the texts of Śaṅkara are not merely an interesting and historically important exposition of the ancient upanishadic teaching, but are also, when properly approached, a sure means to a direct intuition into one's own true nature as the Self of all. It was he who originally instructed me to collect Śaṅkara's texts under topics, and the work has been carried out from first to last with the help and guidance of Dr. A.M. Halliday, the present Warden of Shanti Sadan.

For this second edition I have only made a few minor corrections to the translations. The burden of scanning the text for computerized presentation, and the setting up of the Notes pages and the Index in greatly improved format, has been undertaken by Michael Halliday, and all the taxing duties of a copy-editor have been carried out by Anthony Collins, with help from Stephen Cross, Paul Houghton, June Rathbone and Julie Thomas. To these colleagues I am indeed grateful.

A. J. ALSTON
LONDON 2004

CONTENTS

page

Preface v

Sanskrit transliteration x

Chapter

I. Sources of Śaṅkara's Doctrine: His Life and Works

1. A Doctrine of Transcendence 1
2. Vedas: Saṃhitās, Brāhmanas, Upanishads 2
3. The Smṛti: Viṣṇu-worship and Śiva-worship 7
4. The Bhagavad Gītā 13
5. The Brahma-Sūtras and their Background: Bhartṛprapañca 15
6. The True Tradition: Gauḍapāda, Draviḍa, Brahmanandin, Sundara Pāṇḍya 22
7. Doctrine of Illusion before Śaṅkara: Māyā Vāda and Avidyā Vāda 32
8. Śaṅkara's Date, Life and Works 39
9. Śaṅkara's School 46

Notes to Chapter I 51

II. The Doctrine of Nescience

1. The Nature and Results of Nescience 62
2. Nescience as Non-Comprehension and False Comprehension 84

CONTENTS

Chapter *page*

3. The Self and the Not-Self: Non-Discrimination and Mutual Superimposition 90

4. The Standpoint of Nescience and the Standpoint of Knowledge 104

Notes to Chapter II 114

III. Knowledge of the Absolute

1. The Absolute is already known in a general way 120
2. The Absolute is not known as an object 129
3. The Path of Negation 141
4. Going Beyond the Mind 161

Notes to Chapter III 173

IV. The Absolute as Being, Consciousness and Bliss

1. The Definition of the Absolute as 'Reality, Knowledge, Infinity' 180
2. The Absolute as the Self-Existent Principle 196
3. The Absolute as the Self-Luminous Principle 209
4. The Absolute as Bliss 235

Notes to Chapter IV 247

List of General Abbreviations 255

CONTENTS

The General Index and the Index to texts cited are published at the end of Volume VI.

TRANSLITERATED SANSKRIT WORDS

The following table gives the most elementary indications of the value of the vowels that are variable in English (but regular in Sanskrit) and of the unfamiliar symbols and groupings of letters found in transliterated Sanskrit words. It is not intended as an accurate guide to correct pronunciation, for which see M. Coulson, *Sanskrit* (Teach Yourself Books), 4-21.

a	=	u in but
ā	=	a in father
ai	=	uy as in buy
au	=	au in audit (or French au)
c	=	ch in chant
ch	=	ch aspirated (said with extra breath)
ḍ	=	d in drake
e	=	ay in hay (better, French é elongated)
h	=	immediately after a consonant aspirates it without altering the value. (bh, ph, etc.)
ḥ	=	strong h
i	=	i in hit
ī	=	ea in eat
jñ	=	ja or gya (as in big yard)
ṃ	=	m before b, p, v, y and at the end of a word; elsewhere = n
ṅ	=	n in king
ṇ	=	n in tendril
ñ	=	n (except in jñ, q.v.)
o	=	o in note
ṛ	=	ri in rich
s	=	s in such
ś	=	sh in shut
ṣ	=	sh in shut
ṭ	=	t in try
u	=	u in put
ū	=	oo in boot

CHAPTER I

SOURCES OF ŚAṄKARA'S DOCTRINE: HIS LIFE AND WORKS

1. A Doctrine of Transcendence

Śaṅkara Bhagavatpāda (*circa* 700 AD), or Śaṅkara Ācārya as he later came to be called, was the man who produced, through his commentaries, the earliest surviving synthesis of the teachings of the main Upanishads, the Bhagavad Gītā and the Brahma Sūtras. The highest result and final aim of the study of the upanishadic texts according to traditional methods was for him 'Brahma-vidyā', variously rendered in English as 'enlightenment', 'God-realization' or 'realization of the Absolute'. For Śaṅkara enlightenment implied that the individual awoke to a sense of his perfect identity with the Absolute, the principle of Being and Consciousness that illumines the body and mind but is not identified with them or subject to any form of limitation, or to pain or extinction.

Not everyone who is called to the task of realizing his latent spiritual powers is ready for a path leading to the transcendence of all the finite elements in the personality. To some it suggests the prospect of impoverishment or extinction. Hence it is understandable that at a later time other Teachers, such as Rāmānuja, Nimbārka and Vallabhācārya, should have arisen and made a different synthesis of the upanishadic teaching, regarding the highest result of it as a condition in which the soul retained its individuality, but remained in perpetual proximity with and adoration of the Lord of the Universe, conceived in personal form and understood as the great whole of which the individual worshipper was an infinitesimal part. But Śaṅkara adhered to the principle of transcendence that had been enunciated in the earliest Upanishads. 'That which is not seen by the eye, but which beholds the activities of the eye — know that that, verily, is the Absolute (brahman) and not what people here adore'.[1] He could not accept that deliverance from the bondage of illusion and plurality had been attained as long as the notion of any difference between the worshipper and the object of his worship remained. Hence he regarded the theistic teachings of the ancient texts as provisional doctrine, aimed partly at introducing the student to the pure transcendent principle through clothing it in forms which he could readily conceive, and partly at preserving him from the grosser errors of materialism and spiritual negligence. He did not regard them as statements of the final truth. It is on account of his strict adherence to the principle of transcendence that Śaṅkara's writings have been regarded as providing the classical formulation of the Indian wisdom. He alone could account for *all* the upanishadic texts. None of the pantheistic and theistic commentators who followed him were able to give satisfactory explanations of the negative texts which deny all empirical predicates of the Absolute. And yet, as we shall see, a tradition (sampradāya) which judged these negative statements to be the key texts of the entire Veda had existed long before Śaṅkara's day.

2. Vedas: Saṃhitās, Brāhmaṇas, Upanishads

Śaṅkara was primarily a commentator. The student of his writings needs to know something of the works on which he composed commentaries and something, too, of earlier works which influenced his own views. He wrote commentaries not on 'books' in our sense of the word, but on bodies of texts memorized and handed down the generations by 'families' or 'schools' of priests. The hymns of the ancient Aryans of the Punjab, dating from perhaps the middle of the second millennium BC, constituted the Ṛg Veda. Addressed, say, to Varuṇa, god of the heavens, to Indra, the storm-god, or to Agni, the deity of fire (cp. Latin *ignis*) who carried the oblations up to the gods in heaven, they would often ask in simple-hearted fashion for material boons. Though Śaṅkara shows some knowledge of these hymns, they were of little practical concern to him, as he was a monk who had given up the householder's ritual.

Later the sacrifices grew more intricate. The formulae used in the big sacrifices were codified as the Yajur Veda and handed down by special schools of priests (such as the Taittirīyakas, Kāṭhakas, Vājasaneyins, etc.) who specialized in carrying out the main ritualistic acts in the big sacrifices, each of which had to be accompanied by the murmuring of a benedictory formula. Meanwhile some of the hymns of the Ṛg Veda were re-arranged, with additions, in a special form for singing, and in this form were known as the Sāma Veda. Śaṅkara refers to schools of priests who specialized in this discipline too, such as the Tāṇḍins, Talavakāras and others. For long, these three bodies of texts (saṃhitās) must have constituted the whole recognized Veda. Later a fourth collection of texts, a mixed bag consisting partly of ancient incantations and charms but including some noble 'cosmological hymns' in a later vein, gained Vedic status as the Atharva Veda. Schools of priests began to specialize in the memorization and transmission of these texts also.

Gradually the 'required learning' of the various schools of priests was extended to include a whole range of new matter, embodying new speculations about the symbolic significance of various elements of the ritual, as well as legends of various kinds and scraps of cosmology. According to the texts of this period, advantages flow from a knowledge of occult 'correspondences', and in this connection distinctions were made between 'the plane of the ritual' (ādhiyajña), 'the plane of the gods' (ādhidaivika), 'the plane of the external world' (ādhibhautika) and 'the plane of the individual' (ādhyātmika). The texts conveying this new material were called Brāhmaṇas, and the various Brāhmaṇas went by the names of the schools of priests who evolved them. Thus the Aitareya school of Ṛg Veda priests had their Aitareya Brāhmaṇa, the Taittirīyaka priests of the Yajur Veda had their Taittirīya Brāhmaṇa and so on. The priests of this phase tended to regard themselves as able to dominate the gods through the instrument of the ritual. The old Ṛg Vedic deities who had been believed to grant boons in return for ritual offerings lost status in comparison to more abstract creator-gods, such as Brahmā and Prajāpati (sometimes identified), to whom new powers were ascribed.

With the passage of time, some of the priests from the various schools began to retire from the villages into solitary spots in the forest to practise single-minded meditation on the ritual and its symbolic significance. New texts for memorization came to be incorporated as a result of this practice, known as Āraṇyakas or texts-from-the-forest. And the most sacred parts of these texts were known as 'Upanishads', texts that could only be heard 'sitting in proximity', that is, removed from worldly intercourse and sitting at the feet of a Teacher who considered you worthy to hear them.

The Upanishads were known as the Vedanta or end-part of the Veda. And Śaṅkara is called a Vedantin because he is primarily a commentator on the Upanishads and other works expressing the upanishadic wisdom. Because he interpreted the upanishadic wisdom from the standpoint of strict non-dualism (advaita), according to which reality is not only bereft of all plurality but bereft even of internal distinctions, his system was known as Advaita Vedanta. By a further refinement, it came to be characterised as Kevala Advaita Vedanta (the Non-Dualistic Vedanta of Transcendence) to distinguish it from the Viśiṣṭādvaita system of Rāmānuja (c.1100 AD), who also interpreted the Upanishads as teaching non-dualism, but a theistic form of non-dualism, which permitted real internal distinctions in the Absolute, such as those between the conscious and the non-conscious, the individual soul and his Lord and so forth.

Already in the Brāhmaṇas we find the view that the world of plurality comes forth from unity and returns back into it. The world is said to come forth from Brahmā or Prajāpati, either directly through his own self-dismemberment or through intermediaries sprung from him and operating under his control. But in the course of their 'metaphysical brooding' in the forests (to say nothing of their metaphysical jousting in the royal courts) the sages whose teachings were fragmentarily recorded in the Upanishads, who were not all of the priestly caste, penetrated to a more abstract and ethereal realm. Their most profound utterances concern not the creator-deity (Brahmā, masculine) but the Absolute (Brahman, neuter), conceived as the impersonal (or supra-personal) *ground* in and through which manifestation takes place, itself bereft of all finite characteristics. The profundity, the age-long appeal, one might almost say the modernity of the upanishadic wisdom, lies in the fact that in their moments of deepest inspiration the upanishadic sages broke through to a realization of the transcendence of the Absolute. They knew that it could not be known as an object among objects through the medium of thought and its logical distinctions, but that as a result of a suitable discipline it could be apprehended in immediate intuition, carrying a conviction of identity that was beyond verbal expression. 'He "attains" the Absolute in the sense that he is the Absolute'.[2]

While the doctrines of the upanishadic sages vary very considerably in their details, the main line of teaching is, to use Śaṅkara's own phrase, a spiritual 'monism' (ekatva-vāda). All is one, and that one an eternal mass of homogeneous light. But as one fire breaks up into many sparks without losing its unity, so does the one Self (ātman) of all assume the form of the objects of the world and enter into living beings as their 'living soul' without forfeiting its essential unity. If the forms that go to make up the world are a 'mere activity of speech'[3] this means that the notion that they constitute a genuine plurality of completely distinct entities is due to the habit of referring to them by different names, when the truth is that they are nothing but manifestations of the one real principle, Being. If objects are real (satya), they are less real than the Self in that they owe their existence to the latter, while concealing its fundamental unity and homogeneity beneath their facade of plurality and variety.[4]

The individual upanishadic sages voiced their sublime intuitions in the language of myth and symbol. As a traditional commentator and apologist, committed to the task of presenting all the texts as harmonious expressions of a single view, Śaṅkara was sometimes forced to translate the vivid imagery of the sages into the paler but more precise language of conceptual thought. Further, he had to subject their formulae to a degree of systematization. The sages of the Upanishads merely condemned the world and its finite objects as paltry and insignificant (alpa) in comparison with the Infinite (bhūman).[5] In their most inspired moments, however, they had spoken of the Absolute in purely negative terms as beyond all human predication. Śaṅkara saw that *all* the intuitions of the earlier sages could be taken into account and presented as forming a single system, if all plurality was regarded as totally illusory from the standpoint of the highest truth. He held that the upanishadic texts which smack of dualism, pluralism or theism are mere provisional affirmations, of practical utility to the student. For what is non-dual by nature can only be communicated through texts which first assert its existence clothed in recognizable empirical characteristics and then subsequently deny these empirical characteristics. This was already a recognized principle amongst those who knew the true tradition (sampradāya-vid) for interpreting the Upanishads before Śaṅkara's day,[6] so he was not introducing anything new in applying it. It has been thought that the technique may originally have been borrowed from the early Teachers of the Mahāyāna, who used it in their interpretation of Sūtra texts attributed to Buddha.

3. The Smṛti: Viṣṇu-Worship and Śiva-Worship

Śaṅkara, in common with most of his co-religionists, distinguished between the texts of the Veda (Śruti), regarded as eternal and inviolable, and the 'derivative' texts called 'Smṛti', traditional Sanskrit lore that was regarded as authoritative because derived directly or indirectly from Vedic authority, but also as fallible because of human origin, and therefore subject to correction when it could be shown to contradict the Veda. For Śaṅkara the most important Smṛti texts were the Law Books (Dharma Śāstra), notably those ascribed to Manu, Yājñavalkya, Gautama and Āpastamba, the two Epics (the Mahābhārata and the Rāmāyaṇa) and certain Purāṇas. Śaṅkara only refers very occasionally to the Rāmāyaṇa or to the Mahābhārata, apart from the Twelfth Book (the Śānti Parvan) and the Gītā. He attributes the Mahābhārata and all the Puranic texts he knew of collectively to Vyāsa. It is not possible to draw conclusions about his spiritual affiliations from stray identifications of his quotations from the Purāṇas made by modern translators, as the verses he quotes are sometimes to be found in several different works.[7] The Viṣṇu Purāṇa, however, would appear to predominate. There are no references to the Bhāgavata Purāṇa, the finest text of them all and the closest to Śaṅkara in spirit and metaphysical outlook. It was probably composed shortly after his day and partly under the influence of his own writings and perhaps of those of his earliest followers.[8]

These Smṛti works, especially the Epics and Purāṇas, embody what amounts to a new form of religion that had already begun to rise and spread before 300 BC, and which for a long time flourished under Brahminical patronage in more or less amicable partnership with the strictly Vedic form of worship, and which then gradually, during the course of the Middle Ages, virtually came to supplant it. Greatly simplifying, and omitting all reference to the importance of Brahmā at an earlier stage, we may speak of it as the religion of Viṣṇu-worship (Vaishnavism) and Śiva-worship (Shaivism).

(I. 3) SOURCES OF ŚAṄKARA'S DOCTRINE

We have seen that already before the upanishadic period the Vedic priests had begun to lose respect for the ancient Vedic gods. As living presences the deities were forgotten, while the priests occupied themselves with the meticulous performance of complicated ritual from which material benefits were expected eventually to flow. This mentality persisted in certain Brahminical circles. It was attacked in the Gītā.[9] And it was represented in Śaṅkara's own day by the Pūrva Mīmāṃsakas, the professional technicians of the Vedic ritual, towards whom he was not sympathetic.

But not all the upper castes retained their interest in Vedic ritual. It must be remembered that, particularly after Alexander's invasion (327-325 BC), the north Indian plains had been regularly exposed to barbarian conquest. Some of the invaders settled and extended their patronage to Buddhism and Jainism and other religions which rejected caste. The Brahmins and their upper caste co-religionists responded by broadening the basis of their own support. Non-Aryan cults had always flourished among the humbler sections of society, and gradually many of them came to be adopted, in modified form, by the upper castes themselves. The Brahmins developed the legendary parts of their own traditions and absorbed some elements from local and non-Aryan cults. The outcome was a new body of religious tradition focused on the old Vedic deities Viṣṇu and Śiva now elevated by their worshippers to the status of supreme deity. Unlike Vedic ritualism, the new cults were predominantly devotional in character. Honour, not to say reverence and adoration, was restored to the deity. It is convenient to speak of those votaries of the new sects who accepted the old Vedic caste system and observed the code of the Law Books, the Smṛti *par excellence*, as 'Smārta' Vaishnavas or Shaivas, to be distinguished from those Vaishnava and Shaiva sects which rejected the Vedic traditions outright. The new cults evolved their own forms of ritual, mainly consisting in image-worship (pūjā) in temples, a form of religion unknown in the Vedic texts. New meditative techniques for gaining contact with the deity on the mental plane were also adopted. Amongst these may be included the practice of repetition of the Name of God with a rosary in such formulae (mantra) as 'Om namo Vāsudevāya' or 'Om namaḥ Śivāya', both attested before Śaṅkara's day. The final goal of such worship was usually some form of intimate association with the deity after death, in his 'heaven' or 'world', together with perhaps a foretaste of this beatitude here below.

Śaṅkara's writings provide the earliest surviving synthesis of the upanishadic wisdom with the Vaishnava and Shaiva teachings of the Smṛti. Hence he is not unjustly regarded by his followers as 'a storehouse of compassion and Vedic, Smṛti and Purāṇa lore'. He did not regard the more recent practices taught in the Smṛtis, such as temple worship or repetition of the Name of God, as forming part of the discipline of the monk who had embarked on the upanishadic path to liberation.[10] But he held them to be efficacious for the preliminary purification of the mind. And it appears that his own impulse to search for the Absolute on the upanishadic path may well have owed something to a pious upbringing in a Smārta Vaishnava environment. There is little in his commentaries to connect him with Śiva-worship. But he invokes Nārāyaṇa, equatable with Viṣṇu, at the beginning of his Gītā commentary in what the sub-commentator Ānandagiri calls an obeisance to his chosen deity (iṣṭa-devatā). And part of the verse in which he does so appears in the course of his statement of the doctrine of the Pāñcarātra school of Vaishnavas in his commentary on Brahma Sūtra II.ii.42. He there says: 'There are parts of this (Pāñcarātra Vaishnava) doctrine which we do not deny. We do not deny that Nārāyaṇa is the supreme Being, beyond the Unmanifest Principle, widely acknowledged to be the supreme Self, the Self of all.... Nor do we see anything wrong if anyone is inclined to worship the Lord (bhagavān) vehemently and one-pointedly by visits to His temple and the rest, for adoration of the Lord is well-known to have been prescribed (as a preliminary discipline) in the Veda and Smṛti'. Here the Nārāyaṇa of the early

Pāñcarātras is equated with the supreme Self of the Upanishads.

We find further confirmation of Śaṅkara's connection with the early Pāñcarātras in the introduction to his Gītā commentary. He there suggests that at the beginning of the world-period (kalpa) two separate groups of mind-born 'sons of Brahmā' were projected, to whom the Lord, called Nārāyaṇa, communicated a practical knowledge of the two-fold Vedic wisdom. To the 'Prajāpatis', Marīci and the rest, He communicated a practical knowledge of the ritualistic and ethical aspects of the Vedic path (pravṛtti-dharma). To others, such as Sanaka and Sanandana, He communicated the practical mastery of the path of renunciation of worldly duties and withdrawal from all action, including ritual. In the Gītā itself (IV.1ff) the imperishable yoga is said to have been taught by the Lord to Vivasvat, by Vivasvat to Manu, by Manu to Ikṣvāku and by him to the king-sages. Inasmuch as Śaṅkara deviates from this account of the original transmission of the eternal wisdom at the beginning of the world-period in the introduction to his Gītā commentary, he must have held the alternative account given in that introduction in high regard. But there seems to be at least some presumption that the latter was based on early Pāñcarātra tradition. For the account of the Pāñcarātra traditions in the Nārāyaṇīya section of the Śānti Parvan of the Mahābhārata, from which Śaṅkara quotes fairly frequently throughout his works, speaks twice of the 'mind-born sons of Brahmā'.[11] The second passage says: 'Marīci, Aṅgiras, Atri, Pulastya, Pulaha, Kratu and Vasiṣṭha — these seven beings are mind-born sons of Brahmā. It is they who have the best knowledge of the Veda, and they are the true Teachers of the Veda (veda-ācārya). They have been projected to function as "Lords of Creation" (prajāpati) with responsibility for the supervision of the active aspect of the spiritual law (pravṛtti-dharma). Hereby is manifest the eternal path for men of action... On the other hand Sana, Sanat-Sujāta, Sanaka, Sanandana, Sanat-Kumāra, Kapila and Sanātana are also spoken of as (another set of) seven ṛṣis and mind-born sons of Brahmā. Having attained to knowledge, they follow the spiritual law in its aspect of renunciation from action (nivṛtti-dharma)'.

There are other circumstances which combine to suggest that Śaṅkara had affinities with the worshippers of Viṣṇu Nārāyaṇa. He refers to Kṛṣṇa as Nārāyaṇa several times in his Gītā commentary, although the name Nārāyaṇa does not occur in the Gītā text.[12] He identifies the being whom Gauḍapāda calls 'the best of men' (Kārikā IV.1) with Nārāyaṇa, interpreting 'the best of men' to mean 'the supreme Spirit (puruṣottama)'.[13] And Śaṅkara's pupil Sureś-vara, who represents Śiva in a subordinate rôle to Viṣṇu at Naiṣkarmya Siddhi IV.76 and opens the work with a salutation to Viṣṇu under the name of Hari, elsewhere quotes the same verse that Śaṅkara had attributed to the Pāñcarātras and placed at the head of his Gītā commentary, and remarks that Nārāyaṇa is the best form under which to worship the supreme Self, as the supreme Self is represented under this form not only in the Smṛtis but also in the Veda itself.[14] The Vivaraṇa attributed to Śaṅkara on the Yoga Sūtra Bhāṣya of Vyāsa salutes Viṣṇu in its opening and closing bene-dictory stanzas even though Vyāsa's Bhāṣya, at least in some manuscripts, salutes Śiva.[15]

It is true that Śaṅkara often explains away references to the personal aspect of the Lord Kṛṣṇa or Viṣṇu in his Gītā commentary, interpreting them as references to the impersonal, or rather supra-personal, Absolute (brahman) of the Upanishads. Yet there was undoubtedly a devotional component in his spiritual personality, capable of breaking out into poetic metaphors at any time. When the Gītā speaks of the 'lamp of wisdom'(X.11), Śaṅkara elaborates the metaphor and speaks of the lamp as 'filled with the clear oil of devotion', 'fanned by the breezes of ardent longing for Me (Kṛṣṇa)', as having 'intelligence purified by celibacy and other observances for its wick' and 'a dispassionate mind for its base', and as being 'protected by the chimney of an imagination that is withdrawn from sense-objects and unstained by attachment and aversion' and 'shining with the right-insight that springs from constant one-pointed meditation'. Here, as elsewhere in Śaṅkara's writings, knowledge and devotion, jñāna and bhakti, are fused. Though we cannot say for certain that any of the devotional hymns attributed to Śaṅkara are genuine, there can be little doubt that he had the capacity for composing devotional poetry of a high order.

Whether Śaṅkara also worshipped Śiva as well as Viṣṇu must be accounted doubtful in the present state of our knowledge. We have seen that there is little evidence of it in his commentaries. But we have the verse commentary called the Mānasollāsa Vārttika attributed to his pupil Sureśvara on the Shaiva hymn called the Dakṣiṇāmūrti Stotra attributed to himself. On the one hand, the authenticity of the commentary is doubtful, and even if it could be proved there would still be, as its learned editor remarks, nothing in it to connect Śaṅkara with the hymn. Indeed, the absence of any eulogistic references to Śaṅkara is unparalleled in Sureśvara's certainly authentic works. On the other hand, certain features of the commentary do suggest that Sureśvara may have been its original author. And there is a passage in the Brahma Sūtra Commentary of the early post-Śaṅkara author Bhāskara, in which he appears to be recalling the image of a perforated pot inverted and placed over a light, that occurs in the hymn, and attributing it to Śaṅkara.[16] If the Mānasollāsa and the Dakṣiṇāmūrti Stotra really are works of Sureśvara and Śaṅkara respectively this would point to a sojourn in Kashmir, as both speak the language of Kashmiri Shaivism in places. Thus whereas Śaṅkara's connection with Vaishnavism is certain and emphatic, his connection with Shaivism is highly problematic, and, if it existed at all, may have occurred in Kashmir.

The more developed and independent form of Shaivism associated with the name 'Tantra' had already begun to flourish before Śaṅkara's day. Although certain Tāntrika hymns have come down falsely associated with his name, there is no trace of the influence of Tāntrika ideas in his commentaries. Tāntrika ritual was 'anti-Vedic' in the sense of being specifically designed to supplant the Vedic ritual and meditation. Certain branches of it included woman-worship, in both its loftier and cruder forms. Śaṅkara attacked the orgiastic variety of Tāntrika worship as sinful according to Vedic law.[17]

4. The Bhagavad Gītā

The second 'starting-point' of the Vedanta on which Śaṅkara wrote a commentary was the Bhagavad Gītā. We may pass over the difficulties experienced by modern scholars in accounting for the origin of this most famous of all Indian spiritual classics with the remark that for Śaṅkara it was a miraculous transmission of the very words and teachings of the Lord (īśvara) Himself, who periodically took embodied form through His Māyā to restate or re-introduce the eternal spiritual law.[18] We shall see that Śaṅkara in fact identified the Lord (Viṣṇu, Vāsudeva, Kṛṣṇa, Nārāyaṇa, Hari) with the Absolute (brahman) of the Upanishads.

The Gītā tries to preserve what was great and profound in the upanishadic teaching, while at the same time making it available to a wider circle, to householders living in the world as well as to monks retired to the forests. The upanishadic doctrine that liberation arises through an intuitive knowledge of one's identity with the world-ground (brahma-nirvāṇa) is allowed to stand.[19] But the upanishadic path of renunciation of worldly life and solitary meditation on the Absolute in its 'unmanifest' (transcendent) aspect that leads to it is declared 'hard'.[20] The easier path which the Gītā teaches as its special contribution is that of disinterested action (karma-yoga) leading to and culminating in one-pointed devotion to the Lord conceived in manifest or 'personal' form (bhakti-yoga). The devotion called for in the Gītā is perhaps more intense and certainly more intimate in flavour than the devotion envisaged in the Upanishads, if we except the Śvetāśvatara. It implies an active life fulfilling one's social duties in the faith and conviction that one participates in the nature of God as the great whole of which one is oneself an infinitesimal 'ray' or 'part'. God is conceived in forms that inspire deep awe and reverence, and one's love of Him is expressed in service of His creatures. Such a life culminates in 'entry' into God and final cessation of transmigratory life. The circumstance that no accounts of 'sporting' with the Lord in the after-life are found in the Gītā, whereas there is a reference to the upanishadic conception of 'reaching Brahman through a knowledge of Brahman',[21] confirms Śaṅkara's contention that the path taught by the Gītā culminates in realization of one's identity with the suprapersonal Absolute, that devotion, when complete, passes beyond all subject-object relationships to a realization of one's identity with the one Spirit that pervades all.[22] This interpretation exalts realization that in one's true nature one is identical with God in His true nature (jñāna) over the mere participation in the life of the Lord that is the goal of devotion (bhakti). It must be confessed that some passages in the Gītā seem to exalt the personal God (puruṣa, puruṣottama) over an impersonal world-ground (brahman).[23] Here we probably have to reckon with the Indian propensity for eulogy, which prompts the author of the Gītā to exalt devotion to a personal deity over dissolution of the individual in the world-ground not as his final word but simply as a means to recommend devotion to those who need it. But in any case the goal of absorption in the supreme Brahman is a constant theme in the Gītā, and in one verse Kṛṣṇa asserts that He is Brahman.[24] In his Gītā commentary, Śaṅkara does in some cases have to bend the texts to make them conform to a systematic view. But the flexibility of his own system shows to advantage in this commentary, as he is able to do justice to the Gītā's peculiar contribution to Indian spirituality, the doctrine of disinterested action culminating in total self-dedication to the Lord, without abandoning, in the manner of Rāmānuja and the later sectarian Vedanta commentators, the great metaphysical teachings of the Upanishads that, in the end, the Absolute transcends all empirical categories.

5. The Brahma-Sūtras and their Background: Bhartṛprapañca

Apart from his commentaries on individual Upanishads and on the Gītā, Śaṅkara also wrote a substantial commentary on the third 'starting-point' of Vedanta tradition, the Brahma Sūtras. No accurate chronology is possible in this realm. The relevant Upanishads were probably composed gradually over the period of about 700-300 BC. The earliest Upanishads being compilations, some of the material they include may have originated somewhat earlier. And the latest of all, the Māṇḍūkya, must be placed considerably later than 300 BC, as its terminology seems in places to show the clear influence of Mahāyāna Buddhism.[25] The Bhagavad Gītā, in the form we have it, may be placed tentatively about 200 BC, as it appears to quote two of the later classical Upanishads, the Kaṭha and the Śvetāśvatara, while bearing a certain family resemblance in style and content to the latter. This leaves the Brahma Sūtras, which, on the evidence of references in the Buddhist and Jaina writers, have to be placed, in their completed form, in the first half of the fifth century AD.[26] It may be, however, that the Brahma Sūtras were put together gradually over a long period of time and only acquired the polemical portions that brought them to the notice of the Buddhists and Jainas at a late stage of their development. For example, they refer to Kāśakṛtsna who lived before the second century BC, and Professor Ingalls and other scholars have held that the core of them may well go back before the Christian era. The Advaita Teacher Gauḍapāda must have composed his Kārikās a little after the Brahma Sūtras had assumed their completed form. The date of the other pre-Śaṅkara author to be mentioned in the present section, Bhartṛprapañca, is uncertain, but Śaṅkara's pupil Sureśvara treats him in a way that suggests that he was probably a near-contemporary of Śaṅkara himself.

In judging of Śaṅkara's attitude towards the Brahma Sūtras we have to remember that the texts of the Upanishads can be divided into two classes, later called the Meditation Section (upāsanā kāṇḍa) and the Knowledge Section (jñāna kāṇḍa) respectively. The texts of the Meditation Section are closely related to the early ritualistic sections of the Veda. It will be recalled that the earliest Upanishads lie embedded in the Brāhmaṇas, compilations of traditional lore by priests, but embodying in their Āraṇyaka and Upanishad sections teachings suitable for those engaged in meditation on the symbolic significance of the ritual while living in retirement in the forest. Here the meditator performs prescribed meditations, usually on themes connected with the ritual, which bring him some stated reward, sometimes in this life, sometimes in the next, and sometimes in the form of identification with a deity that has been meditated upon, often the deity presiding over a particular ritual. The Brahma Sūtras treat even the path leading to realization of the Absolute as a path of this kind, based on prescribed meditations on the Vedic ritual allied to performance of certain parts of it. Śaṅkara accepts that this discipline may lead to liberation, through translation to the 'World of Brahmā' (brahma-loka) followed by absorption in the Absolute at the end of the current world-period. From Śaṅkara's own standpoint, however, the only texts of the Upanishads which led directly to realization of the Absolute in the present life were those which ignored the ritual and gave a metaphysical statement of the true nature of man. These are the texts which came later to be known as the Knowledge Section (jñāna kāṇḍa). With the guidance of Gauḍapāda and other members of his own tradition, Śaṅkara went back behind the Brahma Sūtras to these upanishadic texts as his true source of inspiration.

The needs that called the Brahma Sūtras into existence were partly exegetical, partly apologetic: the Sūtras were partly concerned with the explanation of the upanishadic texts, partly with their defence. As the classical Upanishads grew into being gradually over a period of four hundred years or more, it is not surprising that they showed variations and inconsistencies and that the need was felt to find a means of exhibiting them as all contributing to one unified doctrine. Evidently the Sāṅkhya philosophers had already tried to impose their own dualistic view on the texts of the Upanishads, uprooting them from their setting amidst the ritualistic texts and forcing them to conform to their own quasi-rationalistic system. The Brahma Sūtras endeavour to show that the texts of the Upanishads can be integrated with the remainder of the Vedic texts to form a single unified body of teaching. The texts were interpreted through a monistic world-view, according to which the objects of the world, as well as the body, mind and soul of the individual, all relate to the Absolute from which they proceed, like drops of water to the ocean or sparks to fire.

Apart from the natural desire to be able to view the revealed texts as a unitary body of teaching, however, there was also the need to supply a rallying-point for the forces of Vedic orthodoxy. By the end of the upanishadic period, the old Vedic religion, rooted in the practice of making daily offerings to invisible deities by placing them in a duly consecrated fire, but soaring from this humble level to the heights of upanishadic mysticism, was beginning to lose ground to the Buddhists and Jainas, who protested against the iniquities of caste and the cruelty of Vedic animal sacrifice, and to the new Hindu cults, the sects worshipping Śiva and Viṣṇu, which were often indifferent to caste restrictions and offered their followers the stimulus of the worship of a visible form of the deity in a temple. Some texts in the Purāṇas attest that by the early centuries of our era Brahmins were abandoning the memorization of the Veda and the practice of its rituals, and, neglecting the methods prescribed in the Upanishads for realizing union with the Absolute (brahman), were applying themselves to the worship of the popular deities.[27]

Meanwhile, secular philosophy was developing and attracting new adherents. Partly under the stimulus and example of the Buddhists and Jainas, technical philosophy amongst the Hindus abandoned its Vedic roots and assumed the form of the construction of quasi-rationalistic systems. For example, the earliest thinkers known by the name of Sāṅkhyas had drawn their inspiration from, and in turn contributed to, upanishadic speculation. But the references to the Sāṅkhyas in the Brahma Sūtras show that by the time the latter came to be composed the Sāṅkhyas had given up the monistic doctrines of the upanishadic sages, which had been rooted in their intuitive experience of the fundamental unity of all in the Absolute. At the base of the new system lay not an act of spiritual intuition but an act of intellectual separation, the discrimination (viveka) of Spirit from nature, and it was held that final and eternal liberation from pain arose, not from the spiritual intuition of the ultimate unity of all, but from the mere intellectual understanding of the system of the world as described in the Sāṅkhya philosophy. The Sāṅkhya teacher Vṛṣagaṇa, who must have lived well before the completion of the Brahma Sūtras, specifically claimed that the final knowledge that brought about liberation came through inference.[28]

Another Hindu school, the Vaiśeṣikas, went further along the path of secularism and produced a more elaborate system of intellectual constructions. The radical distinction attained by the Sāṅkhyas between the conscious and the non-conscious, a truly creative feature of their system which helped pave the way for the strict Advaita view, is lost in the Vaiśeṣika world-view, and the human soul is treated as an object and as a substance in which consciousness inheres as a mere quality that has to be called forth into manifestation by the contact of the senses with the objects of the external world. The external world itself was conceived at first as made up of many substances, and later as atomic in structure. It lacked the organic unity of the 'Nature' of the Sāṅkhyas, and the fact that the separate atoms combined together to form a world-system was attributed to occult (adṛṣṭa) forces beyond man's power to explain. This system was also 'intellectualist' in the sense that it taught that liberation arose through a mere intellectual grasp of its own doctrines, from which understanding an indifference to selfish activity would automatically follow, leading eventually to escape from reincarnation, since the latter was nothing more than the nemesis of our selfish acts.

The Vaiśeṣikas were originally primitive scientists, and the connection of their system with God and with liberation from rebirth has a somewhat artificial air, since it is clear that it was partly imposed by the need to conform with prevalent beliefs. This is less true, however, of the theism of those who practised meditation independently of the traditions of the Upanishads with a view to release, and who adopted a form of the Sāṅkhya system as the intellectual framework for their own teaching, namely the Yoga school of Patañjali. This school, too, tried to represent itself as in conformity with orthodox tradition. But in fact it pursued release through its own independent path of abstract meditation (dhyāna), breath-control, adoption of special bodily postures and other techniques. The Sāṅkhyas, Vaiśeṣikas and adherents of the Yoga system are the three Hindu schools attacked in the Brahma Sūtras, though attention is also paid there to the Buddhists and Jainas and to those forms of the worship of Viṣṇu and Śiva which neglected Vedic traditions.

Thus the Brahma Sūtras represent a reaffirmation of the values of the old Vedic religion and the mysticism of the Upanishads in face of the rejection of the Vedas by the Buddhists and Jainas, the rationalism of the Sāṅkhyas and Vaiśeṣikas, and the indifference to the Vedic methods of salvation evinced by the Yoga school and the new theistic sects. They constitute a prolongation in four 'Books', consisting in all of 555 short phrases (sūtra), of the sixteen Books of the Mīmāṃsā Sūtras. The latter were designed to state the main rules explaining the ritualistic section of the Veda in a compact form which could be memorized, and the Brahma Sūtras perform a similar service for the texts of the Upanishads. They attack the claims of the Sāṅkhyas to explain the Upanishads in terms of their own dualistic doctrine.[29] They speak of the world as a modification (pariṇāma) of the one root-principle of all, the Absolute (brahman) or supreme Self (ātman).[30] They distinguish between the supreme Self and the individual soul, its mere ray, minute in size.[31] They proclaim the belief that, directly or indirectly, all the texts of the Veda 'harmonize' and co-operate to point to the fact that all is but a modification of the one supreme principle.[32] They point out the self-contradictory character of the teachings of the Sāṅkhyas, Vaiśeṣikas, Buddhists and Jainas, and criticize the Pāñcarātra sect of Vaishnavas and the Pāśupata sect of Shaivas.[33] They sketch the emergence of the elements at the time of creation and their withdrawal at the time of dissolution of the world as envisaged in the Upanishads, and consider the nature of the embodied soul in its states of waking, dream and dreamless sleep.[34] They deal in some detail with the after-life of those who perform Vedic rituals, both of those who do and who do not perform meditations to accompany them.[35] They teach that escape from rebirth comes through knowledge of the Absolute and that the latter comes as a result of practising the meditations enjoined in the Upanishads, preferably (though not necessarily) accompanied by the daily performance of the Vedic ritual. They argue that the enlightened man may remain as pure consciousness after the death of the physical body or else may elect voluntarily to assume a new body.[36]

The Brahma Sūtras only carried systemization to a point where it had to go further. On many important points of doctrine, such as the relation of the world to the Absolute, or the relation of the soul to its bodies and organs on the one hand and to the Absolute on the other, or the nature of the liberated man, alternative views are cited and often compromise formulae are found, the aim being to leave a place for various views without choosing.[37] Sometimes the Gordian knot is cut by a mere appeal to the infallibility of the Veda, even where contradictions in its texts are left unresolved. One passage, for instance, which apparently implies that the Absolute undergoes a real modification to assume the form of the world, poses the following dilemma. Either the Absolute modifies entirely into the world (in which case it would not be the Absolute), or else it has parts (in which case the texts that deny that it has parts would be contradicted). The reply given is that it has to be accepted that the Absolute modifies in part to form the world and yet remains partless, as that is what the texts say.[38] This irrational appeal to authority is the sort of thing that failed to satisfy the commentators who followed. They wanted to represent the Vedanta as a coherent system and sought for the deeper principles explaining the harmony of the texts.

One attempt to harmonize the texts was the doctrine of 'difference and non-difference' (bhedābheda-vāda). Before Śaṅkara, Bhartṛprapañca had applied this doctrine to the explanation of the Bṛhadāraṇyaka Upanishad, and after Śaṅkara's day it was applied by Bhāskara, with modifications, to the explanation of the Brahma Sūtras and the Gītā. On this view, the Absolute as unmanifest cause is somehow both different and non-different from the same Absolute as manifest effect, namely the world, even as the water of the sea is both different and non-different from the waves and the foam. The logic of this system denies the law of contradiction in its ontological application, the law that a thing cannot both have and not have the same characteristic at the same time. This method of argumentation forms a basis for harmonizing any body of texts, as it denies the possibility of outright contradictions anywhere. But it was obviously quite unacceptable to Śaṅkara. Of the many objections he raised against it, one typical one is that by applying to the Absolute, which is said in the Veda to have no parts, the same logic that held for the objects of the world, which do have parts, the system was contradicting the Veda.[39] To expect to be able to treat the Absolute as an object among objects, obeying the laws that apply to objects, was to forget that the Upanishads teach that it is transcendent.

Śaṅkara himself followed a different tradition for the harmonization of the texts, and one that preserved the transcendence of the Absolute to the full. He appealed to the maxim of 'those who know the true tradition' (sampradāya-vid) that 'That which is beyond plurality is communicated by means of false attribution (adhyāropa) followed by subsequent denial'.[40] The Absolute has no empirical characteristics. But when the student is first told this he does not understand and thinks that in that case the Absolute cannot exist. Belief in the existence of the Absolute is then inculcated through statements showing it in relation with the phenomenal world, as its material cause or controller, or in its relation to the individual as the overseer (anumātṛ) or the witness (sākṣin) of his experiences. Eventually, however, the student has to lose his obsession with the objects of the world altogether and realize that only the Absolute exists. When this stage is reached, the texts attributing to the Absolute any relationship with the world are negated through texts which deny all relation. The texts of the Upanishads are thus harmonious in the sense that they form a ladder of graded teaching which has to be climbed rung by rung until the final truth is known.

6. The True Tradition: Gauḍapāda, Draviḍa, Brahmanandin, Sundara Pāṇḍya

The Teacher who best represented this tradition in the eyes of Śaṅkara was Gauḍapāda,[41] author of four 'Books' of 'Kārikās' (mnemonic verses) on the short Māṇḍūkya Upanishad. Unlike the authors of the Brahma Sūtras, Gauḍapāda insists very strongly on the illusory or phenomenal character of the world, and claims that in this he is only following an earlier tradition for the interpretation of the upanishadic texts. The existence of earlier followers of the Upanishads who held this view is confirmed by Bhartṛhari,[42] late fifth century, who writes: 'The adherents of the Upanishads

(Vedantins) hold that only the substratum is real, while subject, object and act of empirical cognition are all imagined'. Gauḍapāda says: 'Those who are experts in the upanishadic wisdom look upon this world as if it were a cloud-city seen in a dream'.[43] The sages who have gone beyond fear, attachment and anger have the direct experience of the truth of non-duality, in which all plurality and illusion vanishes.[44] Where the Upanishads speak of the Absolute as related to the world like clay to pots or fire to sparks, they are only using a device to bring home the ultimate absence of any world and of any differentiation anywhere.[45] For the texts speaking of duality are merely an indirect way of affirming the existence of the non-dual reality, and are due to be negated by other texts later.

It is today no longer possible to deny that Gauḍapāda was to some extent indebted to the great dialecticians and mystics of the early Mahāyāna. The doctrines and terminology of the Laṅkāvatāra Sūtra appear as early as the second book of the Kārikās, while the last book, which begins with a salutation to the Buddha and ends with a standard Buddhist phrase referring to him,[46] is composed in the technical terminology of the Buddhists almost throughout. Here Gauḍapāda expresses agreement with the school of Buddhist Absolutists (i.e. the Mādhyamikas) who teach the doctrine that nothing can come into being (ajāti-vāda).[47] He then proceeds to develop the thesis on lines laid down by the Mādhyamikas but with arguments from the Vijñāna Vādins also thrown in. Finally he sums up by saying: 'It is from the Mahāyāna that we have to learn what things have to be avoided and what are to be sought after and cherished'.[48] While it is no surprise to learn that there is a tradition that Gauḍapāda studied under a Buddhist Teacher called Bakka,[49] it is difficult to see eye to eye with those who hold that the Fourth Book of the Kārikās was originally an independent Buddhist tract. In relation to the Mādhyamikas, the author preserves his 'us and them' stance even when expressing agreement with them (tair anumodāmahe vayam, IV.5). And with his characteristic acumen Saccidānandendra Svāmin has pointed out that the phrase 'ajam, anidram, asvapnam' occurs in three of the different Books, namely at I.16, III.36 and IV.81.[50] This suggests common authorship and authorship by a Vedantin. For no Buddhist philosophers have relied, in the manner of Gauḍapāda, on the examination of the three states of consciousness, waking, dream and dreamless sleep, to support the doctrine that Reality is non-dual, unborn, free from the sleep of ignorance (anidram) and devoid of the dream of (consequent) misconception (asvapnam).

Three important principles used by Gauḍapāda and Śaṅkara for the interpretation of the upanishadic texts are, however, found in the earlier Mādhyamika teaching. First, there is the principle that the transcendent is conveyed indirectly by attributing empirical characteristics to it that are subsequently denied.[51] Secondly there is the principle that 'The enlightened ones (Buddhas) taught the spiritual truth through resort to two standpoints, that of the surface-truth (saṃvṛti-satya) and that of the final truth (paramārtha)' and 'One cannot teach the supreme truth except on the basis of the surface-truth'.[52] And thirdly the principle that, on the basis of the distinction between the two truths, the traditional texts may be divided into those, called nītārtha, which express the fundamental truth in terms of negations, and the rest, called neyārtha, which are not to be taken literally at their surface value but have to be interpreted as indirectly supporting the fundamental texts.[53]

It seems clear that Gauḍapāda thought that the Buddhist works which he so freely quoted were only restating the old upanishadic wisdom enunciated by Yājñavalkya, but in a clearer, more systematic form, better suited to the philosophic climate of his own day. Both the Mādhyamikas and Gauḍapāda appeal to a special form of yoga that takes those who practise it successfully to an experience that lies beyond the distinction of subject and object. Thus Nāgārjuna's commentator Candrakīrti says: 'Objects are only perceived through the distorted double-vision (timira) of nescience. Their true nature (ātman) is perceived by the masters through the yoga-of-non-vision (adarśana-yoga)'.[54] This answers to the (originally Buddhist) yoga-of-no-contact (asparśa-yoga) taught by Gauḍapāda,[55] and to his 'experts in the upanishadic wisdom who look upon the world as if it were a cloud-city seen in a dream'.[56] Gauḍapāda's doctrine, like Nāgārjuna's, makes provision for two levels of truth.[57] In each case it is an exegetical doctrine, asserting that wherever traditional texts accord reality to the empirical world, this amounts to a provisional accommodation to the viewpoint of the student, a deliberate distortion of the truth to a form which the student can understand and from which he can be led progressively to higher conceptions. Perhaps the distant origins of this way of thinking may be traced back to Yājñavalkya in the Bṛhadāraṇyaka Upanishad, where he declares that the Absolute is the 'truth of truth' and says 'Now there is the teaching "Not this, not this", for there is nothing higher than this, that He is "not this"'.[58] The Upanishads, too, in their own way, distinguish between a higher knowledge and a lower knowledge.[59] Through the lower knowledge (aparā vidyā) one knows only the texts and the rituals. One requires the higher knowledge (parā vidyā) in order to apprehend 'the Imperishable' in direct intuition. Compare also such a text from the Viṣṇu Purāṇa as, 'The feelings and talk of "I" and "mine" both constitute nescience; one cannot speak of the final truth, which is beyond the range of words'.[60]

We may say, then, Gauḍapāda clearly considered that Buddhist dialectic, Buddhist methods of textual interpretation and Buddhist yoga were all powerful aids in attaining practical realization of the ancient upanishadic wisdom. And we know that Śaṅkara considered that Gauḍapāda was one of the few who had the keys to the true interpretation of the upanishadic texts. Why is it, then, that Gauḍapāda warmly acknowledges his debt to the Mahāyāna, while Śaṅkara is hostile to Buddhism in every aspect and explains most of Gauḍapāda's references to Buddhism away? The answer to this question seems to lie in historical developments that occurred between the time of Gauḍapāda and Śaṅkara. We have seen that the two Teachers probably flourished about 500AD and 700AD respectively, and were thus separated by an interval of about two hundred years. In this period many changes took place. The mystical inspiration that sustained the Mahāyāna Teachers of earlier centuries seems to have waned, and the leading Buddhist thinkers of the new period, speaking generally, tended to abandon the higher knowledge in their enthusiasm for the problems of logic and epistemology.[61] Giving up the pursuit of the Supreme Wisdom (prajñā-pāramitā) that lies beyond empirical knowledge and is mediated by the yoga-of-non-vision, they threw themselves into technical enquiries into the mere form of empirical knowledge. The shift of interest among professional philosophers from mystical to purely epistemological questions was not confined to the Buddhists. The Vedanta was not prominent during the period, and after the time of Bhartṛhari, fifth century, who treated linguistic and grammatical problems in the context of a metaphysical monism based on Vedic authority, the chief developments on the Hindu side, too, were in the technicalities of logic and theory of knowledge, conceived as empirical disciplines. Attitudes hardened, for, as Gauḍapāda observes, mysticism unites while conceptual thinking divides.[62] The nominalism of the Buddhist logician Diṅnāga is answered by the realist logic of the Hindu Naiyāyika Uddyotakara and the Mīmāṃsakas Kumārila and Prabhākara, while the Buddhists reply through Dharmakīrti and Dharmottara. The typical Buddhist for Gauḍapāda was the author of the Laṅkāvatāra Sūtra or Nāgārjuna: the typical Buddhist for Śaṅkara was Dharmakīrti, and *mutatis mutandis* one might compare the transition from the Laṅkāvatāra Sūtra to Dharmakīrti to the transition from St Bonaventura to Kant. By the time of Śaṅkara, the period of cross-fertilization between the Vedanta and the Mahāyāna was over, and it fell to the Vedanta alone to impart new life and new forms to the ancient spiritual tradition.

One may also ask whether Śaṅkara explained away most of the

references to Buddhism in the Fourth Book of Gauḍapāda's Kārikās deliberately or simply through ignorance. Professor S. Mayeda has spoken of 'intentional misinterpretation'.[63] But it seems hard to believe that Śaṅkara would intentionally misinterpret the man whom he more than once spoke of as 'the knower of the true tradition'. The question seems to turn on the degree of acquaintance that Śaṅkara had with the earlier Mahāyāna texts. Professor Nakamura has affirmed that his statement of Sautrāntika and Vijñāna Vāda positions was greatly superior to that of either Bhāskara or Rāmānuja. But the earlier Japanese writer, Yamakami Sogen, found it full of errors all the same.[64] Indian authorities have generally regarded Śaṅkara's knowledge of Buddhism as inferior to that of Kumārila.[65] Professor Mayeda supports his contention with references to the use of Buddhist technical terms in Śaṅkara's commentary to the Kārikās and elsewhere. But the technical terms involved seem to be only of a fairly general and elementary kind. And one is still left wondering whether Śaṅkara had any opportunity for studying the earlier Mahāyāna texts in sufficient depth to enable him to realize the extent of Gauḍapāda's borrowing.[66] Did he have any access at all to the earlier texts from which Gauḍapāda was quoting? Or was he dependent for his statement of Buddhist positions on contemporary Buddhist sources, eked out by an astute use of scraps of earlier Buddhist doctrine retained in Brahminical oral tradition? After all, his prime concern was the protection of upanishadic Advaita from the attacks of Buddhist and other opponents of the Veda of his own day, and not the restitution of ancient Buddhist texts in the manner of a modern philologist.

Gauḍapāda, however, was not the only Teacher to whom Śaṅkara appealed as a predecessor who knew the tradition. There were also Draviḍa and Sundara Pāṇḍya, who will be assumed here to have been different people, though they have sometimes been identified.[67] No attempt will be made in the remarks that follow to build up a true picture of their views according to the fragments resurrected by scholars. Mention will only be made of those fragments which show that Śaṅkara and other Advaitins were able to quote them as predecessors who were already interpreting the Upanishads on Śaṅkara's lines before Śaṅkara's day.

Thus Śaṅkara quotes a phrase from Draviḍa which reads, 'The validity of the Veda stems from the fact that its function is to negate'.[68] According to a well-informed modern scholar of the school of Rāmānuja, the maxim goes back to the grammarian Vararuci. The latter conceived grammar as the science that corrected speech-errors, and Draviḍa extended the principle to the Vedanta as the science which corrected error in general.[69] The Vedanta, that is to say the Upanishads, teaches that the Self is self-evident and yet not known in its true nature. So the function of the Vedanta is to negate the misconceptions about the Self. Rightly interpreted and understood, the texts put an end to the false superimpositions that obscure the Self, and so leave it to shine in its true nature. And again, according to Ānandagiri,[70] Draviḍa taught that the Veda was able to fulfil its office of communicating the transcendent through the process of negating later what had first been proposed provisionally. Thus the texts of the Veda are 'harmonious' because the philosophically profounder ones negate the provisional ones. In the teachings of Prajāpati to Indra set out in the Eighth Book of the Chāndogya Upanishad, on which Draviḍa wrote a commentary, we find an upanishadic example of this process where the Teacher leads his pupil to a succession of new and profounder standpoints.

But there is another and even more important point on which Śaṅkara followed Draviḍa and which helped to shape the entire arrangement of his system. For Draviḍa also taught that the content of all other texts had ultimately to be negated in favour of the supreme text 'That thou art'.[71] Śaṅkara's pupil Troṭaka tells us that Draviḍa interpreted even this text as fundamentally a negation,[72] an interpretation that brings it into line with Śaṅkara's own.[73] The text brings no new knowledge, but removes the obstruction of ignorance so that the self-luminous Self can shine in its own true nature.

Draviḍa told a famous story to illustrate the operation of the text 'That thou art' that has come down in various slightly different versions. According to one version, a certain prince was lost in the forest as a child and brought up in a family of hunters as a hunter. On the death of his father he was found in the forest by one of the ministers and told 'Thou art the king'. On this he suddenly remembered his true identity and rejected his former belief that he was a hunter. The text 'That thou art' operates in the same way. When properly assimilated through the traditional discipline, it awakens the hearer to his true nature as the supreme Self and puts an end to his sense of identity with the finite personality. It does not inject any new knowledge but causes one to recognize one's true nature as the infinite Self and thereby negates finitude. Since Śaṅkara refers to Draviḍa as a knower of the tradition (āgama-vid),[74] Draviḍa himself must have been following a more ancient tradition when he placed the text 'That thou art' at the summit of all as the means to communicate the final truth to the student, while at the same time treating it as fundamentally of the nature of a negation.

Like Gauḍapāda and Śaṅkara, and unlike the author of the Brahma Sūtras, Draviḍa saw the need of insisting on the illusory character of the world if the texts of the Veda are to be given a coherent interpretation. According to Sarvajñātman and Madhusūdana Sarasvatī, two later writers of Śaṅkara's school, this was also true of Brahmanandin, a yet earlier commentator on the Chāndogya Upanishad on whose work Draviḍa commented, who is referred to by Sarvajñātma Muni as 'a member of our school'.[75] Madhusūdana attributes to Brahmanandin the view that the world must be illusory because it is an effect. It can be shown logically that nothing that is either real or unreal can be produced. The unreal is quite evidently not subject to production. But the real is not subject to production either, for it is already in being. Nor can one say that the real can be produced in the sense of 'brought into manifestation', for if it were ever produced or brought into manifestation at all, it would always be being produced or brought into manifestation. For any character of a real thing is constant. Thus the texts in the Veda which speak of creation are intelligible only if the whole process is taken as illusory, and it is this line of reasoning which gives the key to the interpretation of the Chāndogya Upanishad text, 'A modification is a name, a mere activity of speech'.[76] If Brahmanandin resorted to the illustration of foam coming forth from water to explain the rise of the world in the Absolute, this did not mean that he took the process to be real. He was merely giving an example that would prevent grosser misconceptions on the part of the pupil. Brahmanandin first spoke of the world as a modification of the Absolute and then gradually denied all modifications until he had brought home to the pupil that all modification was illusory. In this way he preserved the transcendence of the Absolute. Such, at any rate, was the impression that the teachings of Brahmanandin and Draviḍa made on Advaitins of later times.

Another predecessor who must have taught Advaita on Śaṅkara's lines is Sundara Pāṇḍya. Śaṅkara quotes three of his verses at the end of his commentary on Brahma Sūtra I.i.4. The doctrine here implies that our power to act and our power to know are not genuine properties of the true Self. A man falsely identifies himself with his body, senses and mind, and in a looser sense with his property, relatives and friends. When these identifications are broken, the Self shines forth in its true nature, and such a man has nothing further to do. Similarly, 'knowership' is no more a property of the Self than 'agency'. It is only my ignorance of my own true Self that sets up the notion 'I am a knower and will destroy my ignorance through knowledge and will realize the Absolute'. For in fact I am the Self, void of all distinctions whatever, including that of being a knower. And if 'knowership' depends on the false identification of the Self with the body, senses and mind, it follows that the existence of instruments of knowledge and means of proof must also depend on this false identification likewise. With the realization of one's true Self, there is no more empirical knowledge and no play of the instruments of knowledge and means of proof.

It was these Teachers, then, with Gauḍapāda at their head, who provided the true keys to the upanishadic wisdom. In an eloquent passage at the end of his commentary on Chāndogya Upanishad VIII.xii.1, Śaṅkara draws attention to the plight of the philosophers of his day who strove to know the truth through mere theorizing. They remained bound to the wheel of repeated births and deaths, haunted by a sense of their proximate extinction, unable to rise to an intuition of their own true immortality. The case of the worldlings who lacked powers of reflection and threw themselves into the search for sense-pleasures was naturally worse. The truth, Śaṅkara goes on to say, is 'intuitively savoured only by those exceedingly venerable monks of the Paramahaṃsa order who have given up all desires for anything external, who depend on nothing outside their own Self, who have risen above the whole system of caste and stages of life (āśrama) and who are solely preoccupied with the knowledge proclaimed in the Upanishads. And this truth... has been formulated in four chapters of verses by one (i.e. Gauḍapāda) who followed the true tradition. And even today it is only they who teach it and no one else'.

7. Doctrine of illusion before Śaṅkara: Māyā Vāda and Avidyā Vāda

We have seen that the view that the world of multiplicity is an illusion is *implicit* in some of the texts of the Upanishads and that it must be drawn out and made explicit if the texts are to be presented as forming a unified body of teaching. And we have also seen that there is evidence that there were other Vedantic teachers besides Gauḍapāda before Śaṅkara's day who may have interpreted the Upanishads along these lines, and have noted that Gauḍapāda himself refers to Vedantic predecessors. Thus the view of Bhāskara and others that the doctrine that the world of plurality is an illusion is not implicit in the upanishadic texts and was read into them by Śaṅkara under the influence of the Mahāyāna is, to say the least, an over-simplification. Nevertheless, the fact remains that there is today a well-nigh unanimous opinion amongst academic scholars that the Brahma Sūtras teach that the Absolute undergoes a real modification to assume the form of the world. Śaṅkara's own writings leave the impression that he thought that the Upanishads and the Gītā were being misrepresented by the commentators in his own day and that one had to go back to Gauḍapāda and Draviḍa to find the true tradition. In this context it is relevant to note that the works of Gauḍapāda and Śaṅkara are full of what one might call the imagery of illusion, in particular of repeated references to such illusions as the rope taken for a snake, the piece of nacre mistaken for silver, the two moons seen by the man of squint-eyed vision, the mirage, the post mistaken for a man in the dark, the illusion (māyā) conjured forth by the magician and so forth. This imagery is continually used in the early Mahāyāna classics to illustrate how all plurality is an illusion. In the surviving pre-Śaṅkara Brahminical literature, these illustrations are commonly used by philosophers when they are defining erroneous cognition as opposed to right cognition. But we do not find them used, in the manner of Gauḍapāda, Śaṅkara and the Buddhists, to dismiss the whole world of plurality as a mere instance of illusory cognition. Apart from the doubtful case of the use of the word 'māyā', no scholar appears to have produced any instance of this illusion imagery being applied in the Upanishads or the Mahābhārata, including the Gītā, to the world as a whole. Śaṅkara, however, maintains that his doctrine is only a representation of what the Veda and the Smṛtis, properly understood, teach with a single voice. Without discounting the possibility that certitude about the illusory character of the world of plurality first arose in Mahāyāna circles, let us glance at the pre-Śaṅkara Brahminical literature apart from Gauḍapāda, Draviḍa and Sundara Pāṇḍya to see if we can find further instances of a belief in the illusory character of the world.

It has been seen that Śaṅkara was probably educated in a Vaishnava environment. We can point to two surviving pre-Śaṅkara Vaishnava works which in certain passages dismiss the world as an illusion and which combine, in a way very reminiscent of Śaṅkara himself, the yearning of the mystic for dissolution in the Absolute with the yearning of the devotee to worship a God endowed with personality and lofty attributes.

The Paramārtha Sāra is a short work combining Advaita Vedanta with devotion to Viṣṇu that must have been composed before the sixth century AD,[77] although it seems to show acquaintance with the Māṇḍūkya Upanishad and possibly with Gauḍapāda. There is no proof that Śaṅkara knew it or was directly influenced by it, but it does supply evidence that many of his typical doctrines were already circulating amongst Hindus well before his own day. The text roundly affirms that the whole world is a mere illusion, and the images of the mirage, the double-vision of the moon, the silver erroneously perceived in what is really nacre and the rope-snake all occur.

As in the Paramārtha Sāra, so in the Viṣṇu Purāṇa, texts implying theism, pantheism and acosmism occur side by side. But there is no lack of texts prefiguring Śaṅkara's own view. Viṣṇu, also referred to as Hari and Nārāyaṇa, is declared to be both the Self (ātman) and the supreme Lord (parameśvara).[78] He has no particular form and can be experienced only as 'that which exists'.[79] The real is what does not change, and what changes has no reality.[80] Only consciousness truly exists.[81] Consciousness alone is real, all else unreal: but within the unreal there exists a 'realm of experience'.[82] The highest truth is the complete absence of all difference or plurality, expressed by the term 'non-duality'.[83] When Viṣṇu appeared as the child Kṛṣṇa, it was through a special illusion (māyā).[84] The basic result of nescience is the rise of the false feeling 'I am this' and 'This is mine'.[85] Liberation is dissolution (laya) in the Absolute.[86] Meditation on the Absolute impersonally conceived, if one cleaves to it persistently in thought and will, amounts to devotion (bhakti).[87] Through meditation (bhāvanā) one achieves identity with the Absolute. Then the devotee cries: 'Because the Infinite One is everywhere, He is also present as my 'I'. All proceeds from Me. I am all. In Me, the eternal One, all exists'.[88] He forgets his empirical self and has no more empirical experience. His idea is, 'I am the Imperishable, the Infinite, the Highest Self'.[89] Thus in the Paramārtha Sāra and the Viṣṇu Purāṇa, as in Śaṅkara, we find a fusion of the devotional approach to the Absolute with the mystical. In each case, the Absolute (brahman), the Lord (īśvara) and Viṣṇu (Vāsudeva, Nārāyaṇa or Hari) are treated as one and the same entity. We have to reckon some of the texts of Vaishnava worshippers along with the three recognized 'starting-points' (prasthānatraya) of the Vedanta — the Upanishads, Brahma Sūtras and Gītā — as having had a formative influence on Śaṅkara's views.

The familiar charge that Śaṅkara imported 'the doctrine of Māyā' (māyā-vāda) from the Buddhists via Gauḍapāda may thus by now be regarded as a bit dated. Śaṅkara never refers to himself as a 'Māyā Vādin' and is in fact somewhat sparing in his use of the word Māyā. No more than fifty instances of its use have been found in the upanishadic commentaries all told, and the long Chāndogya and Bṛhadāraṇyaka Upanishad commentaries total two and three usages respectively.[90] The term 'māyā' occurs not once in any technical or theological sense in the prose section of the Upadeśa Sāhasrī, which is supposed to be a complete, if brief, exposition of the main tenets of Śaṅkara's Advaita, nor in the whole of the Naiṣkarmya Siddhi of Śaṅkara's pupil, Sureśvara, which is supposed to fulfil the same function. On the other hand the commentary to the theistic work, the Gītā, contains between thirty and forty instances, which shows that the theistic connotations of the word were relatively strong in Śaṅkara's mind.

The 'theistic' connotations of the term māyā derive from the Veda and Smṛti. Various conceptions of the 'māyā' of the gods and demons are to be found in the Ṛg Veda. By the time of the Śvetāśvatara Upanishad and Mahābhārata the sages have passed from polytheism to monotheism, and 'Māyā' or 'Māyā-śakti' has become the mysterious creative power through which the Lord, though remaining one, manifests in the form of a universe which appears to consist in a plurality of different objects. Scholars today tend to assure us that the term 'Māyā' did not at this stage yet stand for a mere illusion that did not exist. The forms of Māyā, we are told, were conceived as real projections, and yet there was a delusive element in the whole process in that the individual soul was led to conceive himself as an isolated being among other isolated beings and to lose sight of the fact that, in essence, he was nothing other than a ray of the Lord from whom the whole display proceeded. The term māyā only occurs on four occasions in this sense in the classical Upanishads on which Śaṅkara commented,[91] three of which occur in the Śvetāśvatara Upanishad. At Śvetāśvatara Upanishad IV.10 the Lord is said to be a magician and the world of Nature to be His magic (māyā). For our present purposes, it is only of passing interest to observe that the verse has been pronounced to be an interpolation (on metrical grounds) by a modern philologist.[92] Vedantins of Śaṅkara's school take the Lord as magician to be a kind of mass hypnotist who brings about the appearance of a world that does not really exist. Rāmānuja[93] refers to the passage specifically and denies that the magic referred to in the Vedas and Smṛtis is invariably that of the mass hypnotist performing the rope-trick. There are demons, for instance, equipped with magic powers (māyā) capable of inflicting an all-too-real evil.[94] Modern philologists have tended to accept Rāmānuja's view of the Śvetāśvatara texts mentioning māyā rather than Śaṅkara's.[95] The imagery of the work as a whole suggests that its author regarded the world as real and not as an illusion, and even the 'interpolated' verse contains a reference to 'beings' as 'parts' of the Lord.

In the Epics and Purāṇas, however, the term māyā came to be more frequently used, and the delusive aspect of the māyā of the Lord came to be more strongly emphasized. Thus Kṛṣṇa declares in the Gītā that, though unborn in reality, He appears to take birth in bodily form through His Māyā.[96] Again, in the Viṣṇu Purāṇa[97] the Lord addresses His own personified 'Great Māyā' as 'a nescience (avidyā) by whom the whole world is deluded'. In the Nārāyaṇīya section of the Mahābhārata, Nārāyaṇa says to Nārada, to whom He has revealed Himself: 'This which you see as Me, O Nārada, is only an illusory appearance (māyā) that I have projected'.[98] Thus the ground was prepared for the use of the term 'māyā' by Gauḍapāda and Śaṅkara to express the totally illusory character of the world-appearance.

Like the term māyā, the term nescience (avidyā) was used in different senses before Śaṅkara's day. In one specialized sense it was a synonym for the Nature (Prakṛti) of the Sāṅkhyas or the Cosmic Māyā-śakti of the Lord. In this sense, it did not necessarily betoken a total illusion. Of more interest to Śaṅkara, however, was its use to refer to the erroneous confusion of the Self with the not-self that was widely regarded in his day as the prime cause of self-interested action and thus of continued rebirth in the world of suffering.[99] For the Hindu realists, the Sāṅkhyas, Vaiśeṣikas, Naiyāyikas and Pūrva Mīmāṃsakas, the confusion of the Self with the not-self which led to continued worldly experience and pain was a confusion of two reals. If intellectual discrimination between the two were achieved, the not-self was in no way abolished. It was claimed, however, that the practical result of this discrimination was the end of that self-interested activity that perpetuated rebirth and suffering.

For Gauḍapāda and Śaṅkara the not-self was unreal. From an initial failure to apprehend the true nature of the soul as infinite arose the positive wrong apprehension of it in various finite forms,[100] as non-apprehension of the rope is the necessary pre-condition for the false notion that the rope is a snake. These finite forms constitute the not-self. Enlightenment arises through awakening to the true nature of the Self through the upanishadic discipline, which *effaces* the not-self as knowledge of the rope effaces the illusory snake.

We know, however, from Śaṅkara's younger contemporary Maṇḍana Miśra, that even before his day there must have been Advaita Vedantins using the term nescience in somewhat the sense he used it, as Maṇḍana outlines the attack made on such a theory by Śaṅkara's Mīmāṃsaka predecessor, Kumārila Bhaṭṭa.[101] The Mīmāṃsaka, as Vedic ritualist, does not want to admit the existence of God as the conscious and intelligent creator of the world, as such a conscious creator might be able to interfere with the operation of the rigid laws governing the hidden future results of rituals that it was the Mīmāṃsaka's business to explain and defend. He must therefore refute the God of the Advaita Vedantin. Kumārila first argues that if the Lord, in His true nature, is pure and homogeneous consciousness, as the Advaitin maintains, then He cannot undergo real modifications to assume the form of the world without acquiring impurity. To this the Advaitin is assumed to reply that the world is a product of nescience, a mere dream which does not affect the true nature of the Lord. 'If this is so' asks Kumārila, 'who promotes nescience, seeing that the Lord is pure, and that there exists, on the Advaitin's premises, no other being apart from Him?' If nescience were inflicted on the Lord by another we would have duality, which would contradict Advaita; yet if nescience were natural to the Lord it could never be extirpated. Or again, if it could be extirpated, this would be due to the supervening of some new and adventitious factor, and the existence of any adventitious factor cannot be admitted by the non-dualist. Hence the whole conception of nescience as the cause of the world-appearance is unintelligible and one cannot appeal to it to defend one's conception of God as a creator who is unsullied by His creation.

It is worth while recording briefly Maṇḍana's answer to Kumārila's objection and contrasting it with Śaṅkara's, as this will throw light on Śaṅkara's conception of the rôle of a Vedantic Teacher. For Maṇḍana the problem is primarily an intellectual one. An intellectual objection has been raised against Advaita doctrine and it has to be met with arguments on the intellectual plane. On the plane of intellectual discussion, nescience has to be regarded as a kind of entity that can be referred to by a word, an object that can be known and classified and assigned its place in a system. On these terms, it is difficult to state a theory of nescience that avoids circularity of argument. For example, to avoid the absurdity of the Absolute being afflicted with nescience, Maṇḍana, following precedent, declares that nescience inheres in and afflicts the individual soul. But the individual soul is itself an illusory appearance and an effect of nescience. So where did nescience inhere to bring the soul into being? Some, replies Maṇḍana, say that because the soul and nescience are both beginningless, the problem of which comes first does not arise. Others say that the problem does not arise because it is of the very nature of an illusion to be unintelligible, and if it were not unintelligible it would not be an illusion. All this, incidentally, makes it clear that the 'theory of nescience' had been propounded and defended against attack by Advaitins well before Śaṅkara's day. Śaṅkara refers to Kumārila's objection[102] and answers it, in a completely different way, on the plane of spiritual experience. When the final truth is known, there is no nescience, no external world, no other souls and no God apart from one's own Self as infinite, unbroken consciousness. The oft-quoted remarks of the fourteenth-century Advaitin Vidyāraṇya Svāmin about Māyā[103] are a fair representation of Śaṅkara's view of nescience. From the standpoint of the ordinary man it is a fact. From the standpoint of reason it is inexplicable. From the standpoint of the highest truth and the experience of the enlightened man it is negligible (tuccha).

8. Śaṅkara's Date, Life and Works

Śaṅkara's personal pupil Sureśvara mentions the Buddhist philosopher Dharmakīrti by name,[104] and it is generally believed that Śaṅkara's statement of the Vijñāna Vāda doctrine in his commentary to Brahma Sūtra II.ii.28 implies some direct acquaintance with Dharmakīrti's works.[105] Dharmakīrti is known to have taught in the middle of the seventh century AD. But the free-lance Advaitin Maṇḍana Miśra quotes from Śaṅkara,[106] and was himself in all probability referred to by the Buddhist Śāntarakṣita,[107] whose Tattva Saṅgraha must have been written by 763.[108] So Śaṅkara must have taught *circa* 700 AD. K. Kunjunni Raja has produced a well-informed summary of the arguments for a later date.[109] But he appears to overlook or underrate the importance of the evidence from Maṇḍana.

We have no reliable knowledge of the details of Śaṅkara's life. The standard account is that of the Śaṅkara Digvijaya of Mādhava, which cannot be early as it quotes a seventeenth century author.[110] According to this work, Śaṅkara was born of Nambūdarī Brahmin parents at Kālaṭī in the beautiful land of Kerala, deep in the south-west corner of India. Leaving home while yet young, he travelled north to the banks of the Narmadā. Here he met his Teacher Govinda, and studied the Vedanta texts with him for three years. From the Narmadā he journeyed to Vārāṇasī, where he assembled a band of pupils and expounded the Brahma Sūtras according to Govindapāda's explanations. Next he passed up the Ganges beyond Hardwar into the Himalayan region. For some time he stayed at Badrikāśrama on the banks of the Alaknanda River, the supposed haunt of Gauḍapāda, an earlier Teacher of his line. Here he is said to have re-established the worship of Viṣṇu in the local temple by diving into a deep icy pool to rescue the stone image, and to have made permanent arrangements for the maintenance of temple worship there by Nambūdarī Brahmin priests. He inhabited the 'cave of Vyāsa' near Badrikāśrama and composed some of his commentaries there.

Later he travelled the length and breadth of India, holding debates with Vedic ritualists (Mīmāṃsakas), Buddhists and orgiastic worshippers of the Tāntrika cults. He is said to have founded the Jyoti Maṭh monastery near Badrikāśrama in the north, and also monasteries at Śṛṅgerī in the south, at Purī in the east and at Dvārakā in the west. According to a dearly-cherished tradition, he performed the funeral rites of his mother, even though technically not competent to do so as a wandering monk. Eventually he returned to the Himalayas and disappeared from amidst his pupils after revealing to them that he was an incarnation of the deity Śiva.

The idea that Śaṅkara was a Brahmin from the south who taught and wrote mainly in the north, who gathered many pupils about him, who won fame travelling about and engaging in debates and who was a devotee of Viṣṇu can be supported from the surviving writings of Śaṅkara himself and his early followers. His personal pupil Sureśvara tells us that he was a 'lordly ascetic who walked with a single bamboo-staff', from which we conclude that he was a complete renunciate (parivrājaka) who had thrown away his sacred thread and abandoned all connection with ritual. We are told at the same place that he was descended from Ṛṣi Atri, from which we conclude that in lay life he must have been a Brahmin.[111] That he hailed from the south is shown by Sureśvara's further reference to him as a 'Drāviḍa',[112] as well as by the fact that he conceived of writing as performed through incisions into palm leaf that were later filled with ink. This was the practice in the south, whereas in the north the ink was applied at the time of writing, often on birch-bark.[113] On the other hand the geographical indications to be found in his writings seem all to point to the north. The towns he mentions all occupy the Ganges plain from Patna to Hardwar.[114] He can speak of the *feel* of the Ganges.[115] And his pupil Sureśvara speaks of the Himalayan and Vindhya ranges[116] and refers contemptuously to men of the south.[117] Some of Śaṅkara's texts lend colour to the idea that he might have written and taught in the Himalayan regions. For instance, he refers to the melting of snow and hail,[118] he takes as one of his examples 'I have seen a Himalayan peak',[119] and he refers to the practice of keeping warm by a fire.[120] Śaṅkara's references to a Guru are hard to evaluate,[121] but they could be taken as supporting the tradition that he was a pupil of a Teacher of Gauḍapāda's line.

The picture drawn in the Śaṅkara Digvijaya of Śaṅkara travelling far and wide and gaining fame as a Teacher and debater can also be supported from the same sources. All his early followers refer to the large number of his pupils. His words are said to have 'crushed the views of the secular philosophers'.[122] On the other hand, the view of the author of the Śaṅkara Digvijaya that Śaṅkara was an incarnation of the deity Śiva receives no support from contemporary sources. On the contrary, a certain predilection for Viṣṇu has been detected in Śaṅkara's own writings and in those of his immediate pupils and followers which militates against the possibility of any contemporary belief that he was an incarnation of Śiva.[123] For instance, Śaṅkara himself identifies Hari and Nārāyaṇa (names of Viṣṇu) with the Absolute in his Brahma Sūtra commentary, but does not mention Śiva in this way. When he wishes to illustrate the processes of worship of a deity in the course of the same commentary, he does so seven times from Viṣṇu-worship but never once from the worship of Śiva. When he comes to criticize the philosophical theories of the theists of his day, he praises the followers of Viṣṇu for worshipping Nārāyaṇa, whom he identifies with the Absolute, but he can find nothing to say in defence of the worshippers of Śiva at all. His pupils and early followers salute either Viṣṇu or the Absolute in their benedictory stanzas, and there is even an introductory verse in the

Pañcapādikā which contrasts Śaṅkara, the ascetic and Teacher who had the mere name of Śiva, with the real Śiva, remarking, incidentally, that he did not wear ashes smeared over his body like Śiva and his ascetic devotees.[124] Probably we should assume that the belief that Śaṅkara was an incarnation of Śiva first arose at a much later date when Śaṅkara was an established classic but already a distant legendary figure, and that it arose originally among circles devoted to Śiva and spread from them to the people at large.

But if his early followers did not regard him as an incarnation of the deity, they certainly regarded him as a Teacher of quite exceptional importance and magnitude. They tell us he was surrounded by flocks of pupils who were already liberated in life (sadyo-mukta).[125] They assure us that he had totally destroyed their own ignorance.[126] They call him a 'noble-minded man who had swept away all the impurities from his heart'[127] and who was 'devoted to the welfare of all living creatures',[128] and speak of him as 'The holy commentator who was the glory of the knowers of the Absolute and who took birth solely out of philanthropic feeling and with a view to promote the knowledge of truth'.[129] The last text, especially, may have been a factor in the later rise of the belief that he was an incarnation of Śiva.

Although Śaṅkara was evidently a monk who renounced the world, he was not quite without interest in worldly accomplishments. For instance, he refers to the tale of the blind men feeling the elephant, which is preserved in the secular and not the sacred literature of the Hindus.[130] And when he comes to describe the plight of man in the toils of rebirth, he is able to produce an occasional purple passage in the loaded style of the romance-writers of his day.[131] He uses the image of a sculptor pouring a cast into a mould.[132] He also refers to the practice of an actor being dressed differently for successive rôles[133] and remarks that talent for painting may be inherited.[134] He notes that alterations can be produced in flowers and fruits by the culture of seeds,[135] and that the shape and cavities of the heart can be observed when animals are dissected (Taitt. Bh. I.6), and has incidentally given the first circumstantial account of the Indian rope-trick, one that tallies to a surprising extent with modern reports.[136] Śaṅkara commanded a good prose style. Certain passages in his commentaries suggest that he had the capacity to write beautiful devotional poetry if he had wished, but in the verse part of the Upadeśa Sāhasrī, the only surviving verse work of certain authenticity, the beauty derives from the content rather than from the form throughout.

As far as his own spiritual attainments are concerned, Śaṅkara observes an engaging reticence. Nevertheless, there is one passage which 'tradition views as an allusion to his own direct experience of ultimate truth'.[137] It reads: 'For if a man... has the conviction in his own heart that he has direct knowledge of the Absolute and is also supporting a physical body at the same time, how can anyone else cause him to deviate from that conviction?'[138]

In assessing the extent of Śaṅkara's literary output, authenticity questions are important and should be faced by the modern student. It is clearly a mistake to accept indiscriminately all that has come down under his name. On the one hand certain devotional works, occasionally of a high order, were composed by later Teachers of his school and eventually attributed to his name, probably because their authors left them anonymous. On the other hand, once his fame had become established and linked through his name with the divinity Śiva, works of Shaiva sects and syncretistic works bearing both Shaiva and Vedantic characteristics, some of them not of a very high order, were deliberately and falsely assigned to his name for the sake of prestige. Even the best of the inauthentic Vedanta works, like the Viveka Cūḍāmaṇi, are a source of confusion if taken as a guide to Śaṅkara's actual views. This is because Vedanta doctrine was gradually developed and altered by his successors under pressure of new criticisms from opposing schools. Once the doctrine had tended to become standardized by works like the Vivaraṇa of Prakāśātman (probably not later than the tenth century)[139] which abound in definitions, the temptation to read the new formulae back into Śaṅkara's genuine texts became irresistible. And the tendency was greatly strengthened and re-inforced by the existence of works such as the Viveka Cūḍāmaṇi and others in which the later formulae occur and which are ascribed to Śaṅkara's name.

The groundwork for securing criteria for distinguishing between the authentic and inauthentic works has been done by Professor Hacker.[140] The authenticity of the Commentaries (Bhāṣya) on the Brahma Sūtras and on the Bṛhadāraṇyaka, Chāndogya, Taittirīya, Īśa, Aitareya, Kaṭha, Praśna and Muṇḍaka Upanishads is not questioned by the vast majority of authorities. Amongst works formerly considered doubtful in some quarters, modern research, largely following Professor Hacker's methods, has removed all reasonable doubt as to the authenticity of the commentaries on the Bhagavad Gītā[141] and on the Māṇḍūkya Upanishad with Gauḍapāda's Kārikās,[142] as also of the two commentaries on the Kena Upanishad.[143] It appears also that there is no reason to doubt the authenticity of the commentary on the Adhyātma Paṭala of the Āpastamba Dharma Sūtra, while the case for or against the Vivaraṇa on Vyāsa's Yoga-Bhāṣya appears to be so far unproved. This work will be left out of consideration here because it expounds a system which in his Advaita works Śaṅkara emphatically rejects. Hacker drew attention to certain terminological puzzles in Śaṅkara's works that could be solved if it were assumed that he passed from the Yoga school to Vedanta, but the hypothesis has not found universal acceptance.[144]

Likewise excluded (and it is very important to exclude them if one wants clarity about what Śaṅkara actually said) are such popular favourites as Viveka Cūḍāmaṇi, Ātma Bodha, Svātmanirūpaṇa, Aparokṣānubhūti and Śata Ślokī, which belong to an altogether later age. It is also unsafe to use any of the devotional hymns attributed to Śaṅkara's name as guides to his doctrine. For instance, the two of them with the best *prima facie* claims to authenticity are the Dakṣiṇā

Mūrti Stotra with a commentary ascribed to Sureśvara and the Hymn to Hari with a commentary ascribed to Ānandagiri. Both works, however, have dubious features. The Dakṣiṇā Mūrti Stotra illustrates the operation of Māyā in its opening verse with the simile of 'a city seen in a mirror', which is the language not of Advaita Vedanta but of Kashmiri Shaivism,[145] and twice uses the term 'sphuraṇa', which apparently does not occur in Śaṅkara's commentaries.[146] The Hymn to Hari is also doubtful because it repeatedly characterizes the Absolute as bliss, a term which scarcely figures in the one independent work of proved authenticity, the Upadeśa Sāhasrī, and also because at verse 43 the commentator says that the author is descended from Ṛṣi Aṅgiras, whereas Sureśvara tells us that Śaṅkara was descended from Ṛṣi Atri.[147] In fact the only verse work which it is safe to rely on as a source for Śaṅkara's doctrine is the verse section of the Upadeśa Sāhasrī. This section of the work is arranged in nineteen 'chapters', which are placed, apart from the first and last, not in any order of subject-matter but in ascending order of length, which suggests that it may be a compilation, probably not by the author himself. The work as it stands opens and ends with a benedictory stanza, but the seventeenth and eighteenth chapters also begin and end with benedictory stanzas, which suggests that they, at least, were originally independent works. However, references in Bhāskara's Gītā commentary to the fifth and eighteenth chapters under the heading 'Upadeśa Grantha' show that the work must have assumed its present form in or near Śaṅkara's own life-time.[148] In view of the fact that Jñānottama, a commentator on Sureśvara's Naiṣkarmya Siddhi who probably wrote before 1300 AD,[149] speaks of 'the Upadeśa Sāhasrikā *and other* independent works of the Teacher (of Sureśvara)'[150] we must acknowledge that some of the other independent works attributed to Śaṅkara must be ancient and may be authentic. But the fact remains that the Upadeśa Sāhasrī in both its verse and prose sections is the only independent work that has so far been established as genuine by satisfactory criteria.

The present anthology is accordingly based on the Commentaries to the Brahma Sūtras, the Gītā, the Kārikās of Gauḍapāda and to the Adhyātma Paṭala of the Āpastamba Dharma Sūtra, and on the individual commentaries to the classical Upanishads. Professor Hacker has pointed out that the commentary to the Śvetāśvatara Upanishad enfolds two separate opening formulae in its long introductory passage.[151] While it is therefore possible that what we have there is a genuine commentary heavily worked over by a later hand, any attempt to use the work is bound to raise more problems than it solves. On the other hand the authenticity and importance of both the verse and prose parts of the Upadeśa Sāhasrī may be taken as well proved,[152] so they will be laid under contribution.

9. Śaṅkara's School

The anecdotes about Śaṅkara's pupils contained in the traditional biographies hardly seem worthy of credence today, but it is clear that we do have some of the actual works that were written by his direct pupils and early followers. The Vārttikas (verse sub-commentaries) on his Bṛhadāraṇyaka and Taittirīya Upanishad commentaries attributed to his personal pupil Sureśvara are clearly genuine, as is the short general summary of Advaita doctrine called the Naiṣkarmya Siddhi by the same author. There are grounds for thinking that the Śruti Sāra Samuddharaṇa attributed to Troṭaka was indeed the work of a personal pupil,[153] and the same could be said of the short Hastāmalaka Stotra. But the case of the Pañcapādikā, a large-scale sub-commentary on the Brahma Sūtra commentary which was probably never completed and of which only a fragment beyond the part on the first four Sūtras has survived, is more dubious. The benedictory stanzas salute a Teacher 'whose fame (or wealth) was the commentary' and 'in whose mouth the commentary was brought to life' or perhaps 'was *again* brought to life (prati-labdha-janma)'. On the latter interpretation it would be possible to think of the author of the Pañcapādikā either as the pupil of a pupil or early follower of

Śaṅkara, which would help to account for the extraordinary degree of development to which Śaṅkara's views are subjected in the course of the work, or else as an immediate pupil who took the commentary down from dictation.

Sureśvara and the author of the Śruti Sāra Samuddharaṇa, then, were direct pupils of Śaṅkara, and the author of the Pañcapādikā was either a direct pupil or an early follower. The Sruti Sāra Samuddharaṇa does little more than rehearse some of Śaṅkara's basic teachings in simple language. Sureśvara, though a much more independent and inspired author, did not depart enough from the main line of Śaṅkara's teaching to stand out as the founder of a particular branch of Śaṅkara's school. The author of the Pañcapādikā, however, was a more systematic thinker than either Śaṅkara or Sureśvara. He was more concerned with definition than Śaṅkara, and less keenly aware than Sureśvara that the empirical means of knowledge and proof are due to fade away completely under the floodlight of spiritual illumination. His definitions, developed, multiplied and moulded into more precise form by Prakāśātman in or before the tenth century, have come to form the basis of Advaita Vedanta as a dogmatic system.

Another important contributor to post-Śaṅkara Advaita Vedanta was Maṇḍana Miśra, who, as we have seen, was probably a younger contemporary of Śaṅkara. He took up for discussion several points in the theory of nescience which had already been discussed by Advaitins of Śaṅkara's day but which were of small interest to Śaṅkara, such as the theory of error, the problem of the reality-grade of nescience and the problem of what nescience conceals and whom it deludes. Another problem that troubled Maṇḍana was that whereas the supreme upanishadic texts proclaimed non-duality, sense-perception appears to affirm plurality and differences. Maṇḍana supplied *a priori* arguments to show that perception of difference *must* be illusory, thereby laying the foundations of that 'critique of difference' that was to bulk large in the writings of Vimuktātman, Ānandabodha, Śrī Harṣa, Citsukha, Madhusūdana Sarasvatī and other famous later dialecticians of the school.

In his Bhāmatī sub-commentary to Śaṅkara's Brahma Sūtra commentary, not composed much later than the end of the ninth century,[154] Vācaspati Miśra writes with his characteristic eclecticism, occasionally paying respect to the views of Śaṅkara and the author of the Pañcapādikā, but interweaving this with much that derives ultimately from Maṇḍana. It now appears that, contrary to popular belief, he may quite possibly have written *after* Prakāśātman, without being directly acquainted with the latter's work.[155] In any case, the opposition between Vācaspati and Prakāśātman has been somewhat exaggerated by later writers. In some texts Vācaspati approximates closely enough to Prakāśātman's world-view, even if in others he departs from it, usually under the influence of Maṇḍana. On practical points, it is Prakāśātman who is often closer to Śaṅkara and Sureśvara, partly because Maṇḍana and Vācaspati were householders.

More important than the opposition between Vācaspati and Prakāśātman, however, is the opposition between Gauḍapāda, Śaṅkara, Troṭaka and Sureśvara on the one hand and (with Maṇḍana added) all the writers of the school who followed them on the other. The first group were only concerned to offer provisional theories about the nature of God, man and the world which would be useful to the student while he pursued the path leading to transcendence, which is in the end a path of negation in which all that has at first been taught is finally denied. This was already one recognized path in Śaṅkara's day, as the verses of Gauḍapāda and the fragments from Draviḍa and Sundara Pāṇḍya show, and Śaṅkara thought it was the only true one. Others, however, while groping towards this path, became entangled in theorizing and polemics. We have listed above a few of the typical theoretical problems that troubled Maṇḍana but which Śaṅkara passed over. Śaṅkara's followers, generally speaking, took up these problems somewhat in the style of Maṇḍana, accepting, rejecting, developing or modifying his views.

A prominent view, mentioned by Maṇḍana and accorded great weight and importance by the author of the Pañcapādikā and by Prakāśātman, is that one cannot account for the facts of experience unless one assumes, beyond the ignorance and erroneous cognition of the individual, a cosmic principle of nescience, a power (śakti) which undergoes transformation (pariṇāma) in the manner of the Nature of the dualistic Sāṅkhyas to assume the form both of the objective world and of the cognitions of the creatures who inhabit that world. The concept of a cosmic nescience stems, no doubt, from the Smṛti texts, and was acknowledged to do so by Śaṅkara. But he paid little heed to it, because for him the only important purpose of the Vedic and Smṛti texts was to destroy that more fundamental ignorance which afflicts the individual and causes him to identify himself with the body and the mind. But the later authors of his school began to *speculate* about cosmic nescience in order to arrive at a world-view that they could defend against the world-views of rival schools. Having accepted a cosmic nescience they had to decide in what it rested, accord it its correct reality-grade, find out whether it was different from or the same as the Māyā of the ancient texts, above all *prove its existence* by all the arguments that ingenuity could devise. Advaita Vedanta, which in the hands of Gauḍapāda, Śaṅkara and Sureśvara had remained basically a system for raising the student above the realm of individual experience through the instrumentality of the upanishadic texts administered by a Teacher who enjoyed an intuitive conviction of their truth, tended amongst Śaṅkara's followers after Sureśvara and Troṭaka to become a group of competing speculative systems, in the formation of which hypothetical reasoning (tarka) unchecked by practical experience (anubhava) was given free rein. Free appeal to all the empirical means of knowledge (pramāṇa) is made to establish the existence of a cosmic nescience, which gains in reality-status as a result. A reaction is noticeable in certain authors, notably Sarvajñātma Muni and Prakāśānanda, who voluntarily contract the range of the various means of empirical knowledge (pramāṇa) in order to re-assert the claims of the Absolute that stands beyond them.[156] These authors tend to revert to something like the phenomenalism of Gauḍapāda and the irrationalism of Sureśvara.

To speak thus, however, is to generalize from the literature only. We know that Śaṅkara's teaching has survived in its pure form as there are men who have attained enlightenment through it even today. In a sense, too, Śaṅkara's later followers who 'intellectualized' the doctrine were only performing again the service previously performed by Gauḍapāda and Śaṅkara themselves, that of restating the upanishadic teaching in language intelligible to men of their own day. As philosophy in India grew more abstract and complicated, the Advaitins of Śaṅkara's school kept pace. But the starting-point of any enquiry into Advaita Vedanta must surely be the work of Śaṅkara himself. And the glance we have taken at developments in his school after his death should be enough to convince us of the need for adhering very strictly to his own texts of proven authenticity, and for avoiding the temptation to seek light on his views from the writings of his followers after Sureśvara.

NOTES TO CHAPTER I

(List of abbreviations, pp 255-257; Bibliography, pp 258-276)

1 Kena I.7 (or I.6).

2 Bṛhad. IV.iv.6, freely rendered.

3 Chānd. VI.i.4.

4 Bṛhad. I.vi.3.

5 Chānd. VII.xxiii.1, xxiv.1.

6 Bh.G.Bh. XIII.13, trans. Shastri, 349. Such teachings may be traced as at least implicitly present in Sundara Pāṇḍya, cp. Kuppuswami Shastri in J.O.R.M., Vol.I., 6.

7 Hazra, 20, Note 31.

8 Gail, 9-16; Hacker, *Prahlāda*, 125 and 126.

9 Bh.G. II.41-49.

10 Śaṅkara refers to repetition of the Name in describing the Pāñcarātra discipline at B.S.Bh. II.ii.42 and in describing the practices appropriate for widowers and outcastes at B.S.Bh. III.iv.38. Probably it is included under the term 'other practices' in describing saṃrādhana at B.S.Bh. III.ii.24, and understood as a preliminary purifying practice. Elsewhere in his writing 'japa' and 'svādhyāya' probably refer exclusively to the repetition of Vedic mantrams and the syllable OM, and not to the 'repetition of the Name' in the modern sense. Despite Swāmī Ātmānanda, 135, the japa-yajña of Bh.G. X.25 is surely the Brahma-yajña or daily repetition of part of the Veda mentioned at Ś.B. XI.v.6.1ff. and not 'repetition of the Name'. See Jośī, T.L., 68. At B.S.Bh. I.iii.33, Śaṅkara quotes Y.S. II.44, and Swāmī Gambhīrānanda's translation of B.S.Bh. (p.228) suggests repetition of the Name. But the classical commentaries and sub-commentaries to Y.S. II.44, including the Vivaraṇa attributed to Śaṅkara, do not bear such an interpretation out. They take japa and svādhyāya as

repetition of Vedic mantrams or OM. Cp. Citsukha, 530, vedānta śatarudrīya-praṇavādi-japam budhāḥ svādhyāyam āhur.

11 M.Bh. XII.340.34 and 340.68-74, G.P. Ed., Vol.III., 709f.

12 Bh.G.Bh. I.1. (introduction) twice, II.21, V.29, VII.15, VII.19, IX.22, XI.9, XIV.26, XV.7, XV.16 and XV.17. See Darśanodaya, 508. Budhakar (see Bibliog.) connects Śaṅkara with the Bhāgavatas, not the Pāñcarātras, but brings much evidence to connect him with Vaishnavism. See also Hacker, *Kleine Schriften*, 205-12.

13 Hacker, W.Z.K.S.O., IX, 1965, 150.

14 Sureśvara, B.B.V. III.vii.40.

15 Hacker, *Śaṅkara der Yogin*, W.Z.K.S.O., 1968/9, 124.

16 Bhāskara's B.S.Bh., 7. Note the introduction of the image at Bṛhad. Bh. I.v.17, trans. Mādhavānanda, 161.

17 Ānandagiri *ad* B.S.Bh. III.iv.II. See Hacker, *Texte*, 114, Note 2 and Madhusūdana *ad* Sarvajñātman, III.18.

18 Bh.G.Bh. I.1 (introduction).

19 Bh.G.Bh. II.72, V.24-26.

20 XII.5.

21 VIII.24.

22 Bh.G.Bh. XIII.10, sā (bhaktiś) ca jñānam.

23 E.g. Bh.G. XIV.27, 'I am the foundation (pratiṣṭhā) of Brahman', also XII.2, XV.18.

24 X.12. Of course by the theistic commentators this text has been taken to mean 'I, the personal God, am everything, including the impersonal Brahman'.

25 Nakamura, *Indian Philosophical Thought*, Vol.III, 593, kindly Englished for me by Trevor Leggett.

26 Nakamura, *The Vedanta Philosophy*, 40-74.

27 Gonda, *Religions*, I, 260.

28 Frauwallner, G.I.P., I, 380.

29 Book I, *passim*.

30 B.S. I.iv.26.

31 B.S. II.iii.19-32.

32 B.S.Bh. I.i.4.

33 In the first two quarters or sections of the second Book.

34 B.S. III.ii.1-10.

35 Third Book.

36 B.S. IV.iv.4-7 and 12-14.

37 Gonda, *Inleiding*, 227.

38 B.S. II.i.26-27.

39 Bṛhad. Bh. V.i.1, trans. Mādhavānanda, 559f.

40 Bh.G.Bh. XIII.13. Cp. Note 6 above.

41 See the references to him at B.S.Bh. I.iv.14 and II.i.9, also at Chānd. Bh. VIII.xii.1 *ad fin*, on which last cp. Pandey, 30. If one confined one's attention to the maṅgalācaraṇas of the last three books of the verse section of the U.S. and of the Māṇḍūkya commentary, one might be tempted to agree with Pandey that Gauḍapāda was Śaṅkara's personal Guru. But this seems to be negatived by the chronology and the contrasted attitude to Buddhism of the two Teachers. Bhāvaviveka was a contemporary of Dharmapāla and active about 550AD and familiar with Gauḍapāda's Kārikās: Śaṅkara was familiar with Dharmakīrti, who wrote about 650AD. The hypothesis that Gauḍapāda might have been a ciraṃjīvī (yogī who lived for an abnormal span) and Śaṅkara's personal Teacher seems unlikely

in face of the fact that Śaṅkara's commentary to his Kārikās converts their warm *approbation* for Mahāyāna teaching into keen *disapprobation*. Possibly, therefore, some of the maṅgal-ācaraṇa verses refer to Gauḍapāda and others to Śaṅkara's personal Teacher, presumably of Gauḍapāda's line. Further, at G.K.Bh. 1.9 and 1.12 he gives alternative interpretations, suggesting uncertainty as to Gauḍapāda's meaning and hence separation from him in time. Cp. A. Venkatasubbiah in *Indian Antiquary*, Oct. 1933, 192.

42 Bhartṛhari, *Vākyapadīya*, III.iii.72.

43 G.K. II.31.

44 G.K. II.35. Cp. Sac Ś.Ś.P.B., I, 15, Eng., 20.

45 G.K. III.15.

46 G.K. IV.1 and IV.99. For the Buddhist references passed over by Śaṅkara in his commentary, see the annotated trans. of the G.K. in Bhattacharya, Ā.Ś.G. The word 'tāyin' at G.K. IV.99 is not classical Sanskrit but Buddhist hybrid Sanskrit, see Edgerton's *Buddhist Hybrid Sanskrit Grammar and Dictionary*, *sub verbo*. Its true meaning was known to Hindu literati of Śaṅkara's day, cp. Bhāravi XV.20, where Mallinātha glosses 'tayanti rakṣantīti'. On the meaning of 'This was not uttered by the Buddha', cp. Bhattacharya, *op.cit.*, 213-217, and Darśanodaya, 32f.

47 G.K. IV.5.

48 G.K. IV.90.

49 Jhalakīkara, 3rd. Ed., 808, gauḍapādasya tu bakkanāmā bauddho guruḥ.

50 Sac, *Misconceptions*, 6. See also Venkatasubbiah *loc. cit.*, 193, who, likewise, emphasizes the importance of the avasthā-traya doctrine as part of Gauḍapāda's contribution to the interpretation of the Upanishads.

51 Candrakīrti, *Prasannapadā*, 264,7: śrūyate deśyate cāpi samāropād anakṣaraḥ.

52 Nāgārjuna, *Mādhyamika Kārikās*, XXIV.8 and 10.

53 Murti, C.P.B., 254.

54 Candrakīrti, *Prasannapadā*, 265.

55 G.K. III.39 and IV.2. Cp. Bhattacharya. Ā.Ś.G., 94ff. The term 'asparśa yoga' has only been found in Buddhist works, cp. Ā.Ś.G., 94ff. and 305 and Mayeda in Brahma Vidyā (Adyar Library Bulletin), Vols 31-2, 1967/8, 93.

56 G.K. II.31, quoted above.

57 G.K.IV.74. Nāgārjuna, M.K. XXIV.10, vyavahāram anāśritya paramārtho na deśyate / paramārtho anāgamya nirvāṇam nādhigamyate.

58 Bṛhad. II.iii.6.

59 Muṇḍ. I.i.4.

60 V.P. VI.vii.100.

61 Cp. Biardeau, *Encyclopédie*, 106, 'Avec Diṅnāga... la rupture avec le bouddhisme mystique s'accomplit en même temps que la prise de conscience des principes épistémologiques du bouddhisme philosophique'.

62 G.K. III.17-18.

63 Mayeda, *loc. cit.*, 92.

64 Sogen, 126-142, cp. 161-169.

65 E.g. M.M. Umesha Mishra, writing in Jhā, *Pūrva Mīmāṃsā*, Critical Bibliography section, 22.

66 Cp. Vetter, W.Z.K.S.O. 1968/9, 411.

67 Cp. *Pañcapādikā* Editor's English Introduction, xix f.

68 G.K.Bh. II.32, cp. Sac, Ś.Ś.P.B., I, 20, Eng., 28.

69 *Darśanodaya*, 124.

70 Ṭīkā to G.K.Bh. II.32.

71 Ānandagiri's ṭīkā to Sureśvara, B.B.V. II.i.506.

72 Troṭaka, Ś.S.S. 106.

73 E.g. B.S.Bh. I.ii.6, trans. Gambhīrānanda, 115.

74 G.K.Bh. II.32.

75 Sarvajñātma Muni, III.217ff. See also Madhusūdana's Sāra-saṅgraha Vākhyā on this passage and Sac, Ś.Ś.P.B., I, 22f., Eng., 30f.

76 Chānd. VI.i.4.

77 Hacker, W.Z.K.S.O., IX, 1965, 154.

78 V.P. I.ii.28.

79 I.xix.79. Cp. Kaṭha II.iii.13.

80 II.xii.41.

81 II.xii.43.

82 II.xii.45.

83 II.xvi.18.

84 V.iii.12.

85 VI.vii.12.

86 VI.viii.1.

87 On this, see Hacker, *Prahlāda*, 95f.

88 I.xix.85-86.

89 I.xx.1 and 2

90 R.T. Śāstrī, 58.

91 Bṛhad. II.v.19, Śvet. I.10, IV.9 and 10.

92 Johnston, 27.

93 *ŚrīBhāṣya* I.i.1, Ed. Abhyaṅkara, 102.

94 He quotes V.P. I.xix.20.

95 Oldenberg, *Upanishaden*, 241; Strauss, 71; von Glasenapp, *Einführung*, 183; Gonda, *Inleiding*, 126; Maṅgaladeva Śāstrī, 207f.

96 Bh.G. IV.6.

97 V.P. V.i.70.

98 M.Bh. XII.339.45.

99 Īśvara Kṛṣṇa, Kārikā 55; Vyāsa, Y.S. Bhāṣya II.5; Vātsyāyana, N.Sū. Bhāṣya IV.ii.1; V.P. VI.vii.10-12.

100 Cp. G.K. I.13-15.

101 Maṇḍana, B.Sid., 10. Kumārila Ś.V., *Sambandhākṣepa Parihāra* section, verses 84-86 (text, 663).

102 B.S.Bh. IV.i.3, trans. Gambhīrānanda, 821. Or see the present work below, Vol.III, Chap.VIII, section 4, Extract 9, note 187.

103 Vidyāraṇya, P.D. VI.130.

104 Sureśvara, B.B.V. IV.iii.753.

105 K. Kunjunni Raja in *Brahma Vidyā* (Adyar Library Bulletin) Dec. 1960, 134f. Cp. Vetter, W.Z.K.S.O. 1968/9, 411. The apparent quotations from Dharmakīrti at U.S. (verse) XVIII.142 and 143 are problematic, see Mayeda's Notes to his translation of the U.S. *ad loc.*

106 Maṇḍana, B. Sid., Editor's Introduction, xlvii.

107 See Abhinava Raṅganātha's Comm. on Veṅkaṭanātha

Vedāntācārya, Vol.II, 403. Cp. Hacker, *Vivarta*, 35f. and Nakamura, *Proceedings of the Okuryana Oriental Research Institute*, Yokohama, 1956, 7.

108 Frauwallner in W.Z.K.S.O., Vol.V, 1961, 141ff.

109 K. Kunjunni Raja, *loc.cit.*

110 B.D. Upādhyāya, *Śrī Śaṃkarācārya*, 12.

111 B.B.V. VI.v.22 and 23.

112 N. Sid. IV.44. The term 'Drāviḍa' is the Sanskrit form of the English word Tamil, but it was more broadly used to cover most of the Indian lands south of the Narmadā River.

113 Bṛhad. Bh. IV.iv.25. I owe the interpretation of the significance of this text to the kindness of my former Sanskrit teacher, Professor T. Burrow of Oxford. It is confirmed at Renou and Filliozat, Vol.II, 712.

114 Sahasrabuddhe, 193.

115 B.S.Bh. II.iii.22 *ad fin.*

116 B.B.V. I.iv.629.

117 N. Sid. III.93.

118 B.S.Bh. II.iii.14, III.i.8.

119 Bṛhad. Bh. IV.iii.6.

120 Bh.G.Bh. IX.29.

121 They only occur at the beginning and end of the seventeenth and eighteenth chapters of the verse section of the U.S. and at the end of the nineteenth chapter, at the end of the G.K.Bh. and at the beginning of the Taitt. Bh. The reference to 'this supreme Guru' in the benedictory verses at the end of the G.K.Bh. should probably not be taken to mean 'Guru's Guru' in view of the presence of the word 'this' (amum) and for the reasons

mentioned at Note 41 above.

122 Sureśvara, T.B.V. I.2.

123 Hacker, 'Relations of Early Advaitins to Vaishnavism' (in English) W.Z.K.S.O. IX, 1965, 147ff.

124 P.P., 6.

125 Troṭaka, Ś.S.S. 178.

126 *Ibid.*, and cp. Sureśvara, N. Sid. IV.76.

127 Sureśvara, B.B.V. I.iv.607.

128 Sureśvara, N. Sid. IV.19.

129 P.P., 97, trans. Venkataramiyah, 66.

130 Chānd. Bh. V.xviii.2.

131 E.g. at Kaṭha Bh. II.iii.1.

132 U.S. (verse) XIV.3.

133 B.S.Bh. II.i.18.

134 Bṛhad. Bh. IV.iv.2, trans. Mādhavānanda, 491.

135 Bṛhad. Bh. IV.iii.7, *ibid.*, 438.

136 G.K.Bh. I.7. The first known brief reference is at Vasubandhu, *Viṃśatikā*, 19.

137 Hiriyanna, *Outlines*, 381, footnote 2.

138 B.S.Bh. IV.i.15, *ad fin.*

139 Cammann, 8: the chronology of early post-Śaṅkara Advaita is, however, very confused. One cannot argue from Vācaspati's date as it is simply not known. The authenticity of the *Nyāya-sūcīnibandha*, hitherto regarded as the key, has now been questioned: see S.A. Srinivasan's Introduction to his Critical Edition of Vācaspati's *Tattvakaumudī*, 54-63 (quoted Rüping,

13). See also Note 154, below.

140 The fundamental work is the article 'Eigentümlichkeiten der Lehre und Terminologie Śaṅkaras'. Among Hacker's other papers, the significance of colophons is examined in 'Śaṅkarācārya and Śaṅkarabhagavat-pāda', and the first inflections of Śaṅkara's concepts amongst his immediate followers *Untersuchungen über Texte des frühen Advaita Vāda*, I. See Bibliography for details.

141 Mayeda in W.Z.K.S.O. IX, 1965, 155-197.

142 Mayeda in 'Brahma Vidyā' (Adyar Library Bulletin) Vols. 31-2, 1967/8, 73ff.

143 Mayeda in I.I.J. No.10, 1967, 35-55.

144 'Śaṅkara der Yogin und Śaṅkara der Advaitin' in W.Z.K.S.O., Vol XII/XIII, 1968/9, 119-148.

145 L.N. Sharma, 113.

146 Hacker was correct in pointing out its absence in the B.S.Bh., as the subsequent publication of a *Brahma Sūtra Bhāṣya Word-Index* by T.M.P. Mahadevan has proved. Elsewhere, the present writer has only found 'sphuran' at Bṛhad. Bh. II.i.15, (ed. Bhāgavat, 109, line 4). Sphuraṇa is shown by the word-index to Mayeda's edition to be absent from the U.S. It seems improbable that it would occur twice in a short genuine work by Śaṅkara.

147 Sureśvara, B.B.V. VI.v.23.

148 Mayeda, Śaṅkara's U.S., Introduction, 67f. Cp. also V. Rāghavan in W.Z.K.S.O. XI, 1967, 137f.

149 Sureśvara, N.Sid., Editor's (Hiriyanna) Introduction, xxxv f.

150 Sureśvara, N.Sid., Bombay Ed. with Comm. of Jñānottama, 9.

151 The second occurs at the end of the passage, G.P. Ed., 68 (top line).

152 By Mayeda, in J.A.O.S, Vol. 85, 1965, No.2, 178ff.

153 Hacker, *Texte*, 30ff.

154 As Jayanta Bhaṭṭa, writing c.890, shows familiarity with the work of Vācaspati's Guru, Trilocana. See G. Oberhammer, W.Z.K.S.O., VIII, 1964, 132, footnote 4.

155 This is because when Prakāśātman defines the term 'vivarta' (*Vivaraṇa*, 653) he has to go back to the pre-Śaṅkara grammarian Bhartṛhari's definition to shape his own formula, which suggests that there was no current Advaita definition in his own day. On the other hand, when Vācaspati attacks Advaita Vedanta in his pre-Vedanta works written from the standpoints of other schools, he equips the Advaitins with a clearly defined distinction between vivarta and pariṇāma. At *Bhāmatī*, I.ii.21 he brings out the contrast with the help of the classical similes, spider and web for pariṇāma, rope-snake for vivarta. See Hacker, *Vivarta*, 40 and 44ff. and Cammann, 126, footnote 1.

156 Cp. Hacker, *Vivarta*, 53f.

CHAPTER II

THE DOCTRINE OF NESCIENCE

1. The Nature and Results of Nescience

Śaṅkara's doctrine has been well summed up in the following verse which circulates among the Teachers of his school. 'This universe of plurality is verily an illusion. The reality is the undifferentiated Absolute and I am that. The proof of this is the Upanishads, the great Teachers who have realized the truth of the upanishadic doctrine, and one's own personal experience'.[1]

Śaṅkara's doctrine of nescience has to be viewed in this context. Attempts have been made to represent it as a mere theological device for eliminating contradictions in the upanishadic texts. For example, if some texts say that the Absolute is without internal distinctions and others say that it undergoes modification to assume the form of a diversified world, then the contradiction can be eliminated if the texts which speak of diversification are relegated to the standpoint of nescience. It is true that the doctrine of nescience does have this theological function. But it is primarily concerned with human experience; and it must be remembered that from Śaṅkara's own point of view the texts themselves have little value unless they lead to a cancellation of the illusion under which one feels identified with the individual body and mind. As interpreted by the Advaita tradition, the texts of the Veda proclaim that man, in his true nature, is identical with the one Spirit that sustains all, and which is infinite, eternal, raised above all differentiation and change, beyond all limitation and suffering, of the nature of perfect peace. It is ignorance or 'nescience' (avidyā) which obscures this truth, reduces man to the level of an acting, suffering individual, and paints before him a world of multiplicity and illusion, an abode of change, limitation and suffering, and keeps him revolving on the wheel of repeated births and deaths called 'saṃsāra'. The eternal truth lies embedded in the Vedic texts. But it requires a Teacher who has himself had personal experience of the truth to communicate it to a student. Whatever intellectual insight the student may attain, the Spirit will not shine forth manifestly in his heart in its true nature until all attachment and other psychological defects have been weeded out. And to attain this end he requires the loving guidance of a Teacher.

From an original failure to apprehend the true nature of the Self (agrahaṇa) there arise positive wrong conceptions (anyathāgrahaṇa),[2] even as from failure to apprehend the true nature of the rope there arise erroneous superimpositions (adhyāsa, adhyāropa) of different images, such as those of a snake or stick or patch of water on the ground. From failure to apprehend the true nature of the Self arises, by way of unwitting superimposition or projection, a not-self. And then comes that 'failure to discriminate' (aviveka) the Self from the not-self which is the proximate cause of our self-identification with the body and mind and thus of our painful experiences in the realm of saṃsāra.

Śaṅkara conceived of nescience as operating in much the same way as earlier Hindu philosophers had conceived of errors of sense-perception occurring in everyday life.[3] Nescience thus conceived is 'of the form of memory' (smṛti-rūpa) and depends on the unwitting revival of the impressions (saṃskāra, vāsanā) of previous experience. The snake for which the rope is mistaken results from images derived from previous experiences, stored in seed-like form and capable of manifestation upon an appropriate stimulus. In this way Śaṅkara can, on occasion, represent the world as no more than the outcome of the revival of images derived from the past acts and experiences of its denizens.[4]

In an atheistic creed like Buddhism, past actions together with their 'seeds' may well suffice to account for the continuation of the world, without appeal to a God as Creator or Controller or even to permanently subsistent souls as authors of those actions. But the Upanishads, the Bhagavad Gītā and the Brahma Sūtras, on which the Vedanta is based, all affirm the existence of a supreme Lord (īśvara, parameśvara) who projected the world, who entered it as the principle of life, and under whose control it evolves. There are aspects of the world as it appears before us in the waking state, such as its size and order and harmony, as also the inter-relation of the experiences of souls which each possess only limited and mutually exclusive trains of knowledge, and the free 'descent' (avatāra) of the supreme deity into the world as Vāsudeva or in other forms, which cannot be explained as the mere outcome of the activity of the mass of individual souls with their puny personalities and limited powers.[5] If we wish to explain the order inherent in the common objective world of waking experience, we cannot make do with mere action and its impressions and seeds. We have to assume a Creator and Controller or 'Lord' (īśvara), from whom it is projected and under whose guidance and control it evolves.

Śaṅkara recognizes that in the Upanishads, the Mahābhārata and the Purāṇas, the unmanifest seed-form of the activity of the various creatures is known by a variety of different collective names, chief of which he instances akṣara, avidyā, avyākṛta, māyā, prakṛti, bīja, nidrā, tamas and śakti. Thus the unmanifest seed of activity and experience left by the deeds of creatures in previous world-periods, which evolves in part into the manifest world, may be known as avidyā or nescience. And in this special sense the word avidyā may be synonymous with the words māyā, prakṛti and śakti. For most of Śaṅkara's followers, this was the chief sense of the word avidyā, sanctioned by the Epics and Purāṇas and traceable here and there in Śaṅkara's texts. And it has long been traditionally regarded as being what Śaṅkara himself normally understood by the term, particularly as certain works which make free use of the word in this sense have been ascribed to his name.[6] Nescience (avidyā, ajñāna) has in this way been set up as a power (śakti) which undergoes transformation or evolution (pariṇāma) to assume the form of the objects of the world, and the 'mutual superimposition' of the Self and the not-self through which the individual soul imagines itself to be limited and bound is affirmed to be the result of the activity of this cosmic power.[7]

If we keep strictly to Śaṅkara's own texts, however, we find the 'seed of the world' (jagad-bīja), this unmanifest name and form traditionally known by various names such as māyā, prakṛti, avyākṛta and others, is itself a superimposition resulting from nescience (avidyā-kalpita).[8] It is not that the superimpositions of the individual depend on the activity of a cosmic power presided over by the Lord. On the contrary, the whole notion of an objective world and of a divine controller governing it makes sense only from the standpoint of the waking experience of an individual experiencer, which itself depends on superimposition, as we shall see.

But if nescience consists only in failure to apprehend the Self in its true nature followed by superimposition of a not-self and subsequent failure to discriminate the Self from the superimposed not-self, what happens to the traditional theistic world-view mentioned above? Can other souls exist? Can there really be a world exterior to the perceiver and a divine projector and controller of it, as some of the Vedic texts seem to maintain? To understand Śaṅkara's attitude to such questions we have to remember that for him the distinction between the standpoint (dṛṣṭi) or state (avasthā) of nescience or ignorance of the Self and the state of enlightenment (bodha) or knowledge of the Self (ātma-vidyā) is fundamental. In the state of nescience, everything perceived is a reality in exactly the form in which it is perceived, unless and until it is negated by some correcting-cognition. But when nescience is destroyed through the discipline of Vedanta and the grace of the enlightened Teacher, then the ignorant one awakens to his true nature as infinite Being and Consciousness. There is then no possibility of any further super-imposition, any more than one can again take a rope for a snake once the rope has been clearly perceived as such. A semblance of empirical experience may, however, continue until the fall of the physical body; in this phase the enlightened one perceives his embodied state but is not deluded into belief in plurality.

Śaṅkara speaks of nescience not as a power (śakti) but as a state (avasthā), an undesirable state or passion (kleśa) which afflicts the individual.[9] He was not speaking about anything he conceived to be real but merely constructing a hypothesis that would account for our everyday experience in such a way as to do justice to the metaphysical truth revealed in the Upanishads and confirmed in the experience of the enlightened man. For instance, if there is empirical experience at all or sense of 'I' and 'mine', then, if we are to account for it in the light of the final truth as revealed initially in the upanishadic texts and finally confirmed in direct intuition, it can only be spoken of as being due to nescience.[10] If there is action and the accompanying notion that the Self is subject to experiencing the moral consequences of its actions in future births, then these can only be due to nescience. Likewise embodiment, agency, bondage, power to have experience of objects, mortality and propensity to experience sense-illusions can only be due to nescience. So also, in a wider sense, the whole universe (prapañca), even distinction (bheda) itself and the experience of distinction, is due to nescience.

But if 'plurality' and 'other souls' are only illusions appearing before an ignorant individual, where does nescience lie? Whom does it afflict? Is it one or many? Śaṅkara maintains that in truth there is no nescience, so that if the student or opponent raises the question of the nature or conditions of nescience at all, it amounts to no more than a complaint that he, personally, is afflicted with nescience. He then proceeds to argue that if anyone knows that he is afflicted with nescience he must know nescience as an object, in which case it cannot belong to him, the subject who knows it. The Self only appears to be deluded, and only appears to be later liberated. It is not that time is a reality and that liberation is a real event involving a real change taking place at a fixed point in time. Nor can we say that nescience is anything real or that the Self undergoes a change from bondage to liberation, as if the latter were two separate real states.[11]

If, says Śaṅkara, you demand to know to whom this 'not-being-awake-to-the-Self' (aprabodha) belongs, we reply, 'To you who ask this question'.[12] True, in some passages the Upanishads teach that you are not really afflicted with nescience as you are yourself the Lord (īśvara), the supreme Self. But if you were awake (prabuddha) to this, you would see that in truth no nescience exists anywhere for anyone.

Śaṅkara argues in a rather similar way in his Gītā Commentary.[13] First he asserts that nescience does not afflict the true Self. Then he brings forward a pupil who wants to know what it does afflict if it does not afflict the Self. It afflicts, he is told, whatever it is perceived to afflict. To ask further 'What is that?' is a useless question, since one cannot perceive nescience at all without perceiving the one afflicted by it. Śaṅkara so conducts the remainder of the argument that the pupil has to admit that, because he cannot help *perceiving* the one afflicted with nescience, he cannot himself *be* the one afflicted with nescience. Thus bondage is an illusion and enlightenment does not imply any real change of state. Enlightenment does not so much destroy nescience as reveal that it never existed.

TEXTS ON THE NATURE AND RESULTS OF NESCIENCE

1. This 'being-the-Self-of-all' is the highest state of consciousness of the Self, His supreme natural state. But when, before this, one feels oneself to be other than the Self of all, even by a hair's breadth, that state is nescience (avidyā). Whatever states of consciousness, of the nature of not-self, are set up by nescience, they are not the supreme state, any of them. In comparison with these states, 'being-the-Self-of-all', being all, within and without, is the highest state of the Self. Therefore, when nescience falls away and knowledge attains its summit, 'being-the-Self-of-all' supervenes, and this is liberation....

The results of these two, knowledge and nescience, are 'being-the-Self-of-all' and 'being-of-a-limited-nature' respectively. Through knowledge one becomes the Self of all. Through nescience one becomes finite. One becomes cut off from others. Being cut off, one finds oneself opposed. Being opposed, one is struck, overpowered, stripped. This happens because, being in the realm of the finite, one becomes different (from others). But when one is the all, how can one be different from others that anyone could oppose him? And if there were no opposition, how could he be struck, overpowered and stripped?

This, therefore, is the essence of nescience. It causes one to conceive what is the Self of all as not the Self of all. It sets up (the appearance of) other things over against the Self, which do not really exist. It makes the Self to be finite. Hence desire arises for what one is separated from. Because one is separated and feels desire, one resorts to action. From action follow consequences (phala),[14] this is what is being affirmed....

Thus the essence of nescience has been indicated, together with its results. And the result of knowledge (vidyā) has also been shown implicitly to be 'becoming-the-Self-of-all', as it is the opposite of nescience. And this nescience is not a property (dharma) of the Self. Therefore, when knowledge increases, nescience automatically diminishes. And when knowledge reaches its zenith, one becomes established in 'being-the-Self-of-all' and nescience ceases entirely, as the erroneous notion of a snake in a rope ceases altogether when the rope is determinately known. And so it has been said, 'When all has become one's own Self, then through what could one see what?'[15] Therefore nescience is not a natural property of the Self. For what is a natural property of anything can never be eradicated, like heat and light in the case of the sun. Therefore there can be liberation from nescience.[16]

❖

2. Nescience is the notion that there is the distinction 'action, its factors and results'. It is constantly active in the Self. This nescience has been active from beginningless time in the form of such notions as 'My act', 'I am the agent', 'I will do this and act for this end'. When knowledge of the Self arises in the form 'I alone exist, not an agent, not an act, not a result, and no one else whatever exists apart from me', it puts an end to nescience because it puts an end to the notion of difference which is the

cause of engaging in action.[17]

❖

3. *Objection:* If one were to hold that in all bodies there is only the one Lord and no other experiencer apart from Him, then either the Lord Himself would be the one subject to transmigration (saṃsāra) or else there would be no transmigration at all on account of the absence of anyone else apart from the Lord to be subject to it. Now, neither of these positions is tenable, because they would render the Vedic revelation about bondage and liberation and their causes useless, and because they are contradicted by perception and by other means of knowledge. For instance, transmigratory experience, in the form of pleasure and pain and what lead to them, is directly known through perception. And because the world is seen to contain distinctions, we infer that there must be transmigration, (experience in which is) determined by merit and demerit (earned in earlier births). But if the Lord and the Self (of man) were one and the same, all this would be inexplicable.

Answer: No. For the matter is explicable when it is realized that knowledge (jñāna) and absence of knowledge (ajñāna) are different. 'Wide apart and leading in different directions are these two, ignorance (avidyā) and that which is known as knowledge (vidyā)'.[18] And the results of knowledge and ignorance are declared to be contradictory as 'the good' and 'the pleasant' respectively... And the Veda, the Smṛti and popular wisdom alike show that ignorance and its effects should be removed through knowledge... We learn from ordinary worldly reasoning, 'Those men who have *knowledge* of the presence of snakes, spiky grass and (concealed) wells are able to avoid them. But some who do not know of such traps, through ignorance, fall into them. Behold the great advantages of knowledge!'[19]

And thus, we argue, the ignorant one, who thinks that his physical body and other components of his personality *are* his own true Self, applies himself to acts of merit or demerit prompted by desire and aversion and the like, and thus continues to be reborn and to die. But those who perceive the Self separate from the body and the rest, lose attachment and aversion and the like, and from this they cease to engage in acts of merit and demerit and are liberated. This fact cannot be contraverted by argumentation.

This being so, the Lord alone is the Knower of the Body and is the one who *appears* to undergo transmigratory experience on account of distinctions set up by illusory external adjuncts (upādhi) introduced by nescience (avidyā), whence arises, for example, the notion that the Self is of the nature of the body and the rest (mind, senses, etc.). For the well-known impulse of all living beings to identify their Self with the body and other elements of the not-self is certainly something introduced by nescience. Just as, when a post is mistaken for a man, the attributes of the man are not really introduced into the post nor the attributes of the post into the man, so, in the same way, the attributes of consciousness are not really introduced into the body (when the body is mistaken for the Self), nor the attributes of the body into consciousness. Being of the nature of pleasure or pain or delusion are not attributes that really pertain to the Self any more than old age or death do, being notions introduced by nescience in just the same way.[20]

Now an objector might reason as follows. Your claim is wrong, he might say, because the example cited does not agree with the case in hand. The post and the man are both knowable objects. They can be mutually superimposed on one another through nescience by anyone who has known them previously. But the body and the Self are respectively object known and knower. To say that they can be mutually superimposed on one another does not agree with the example cited. So it follows that knowable attributes of the body (are not superimposed and therefore) do really belong to the knower, the Self.

But this objection is wrong, because it would follow that consciousness and other such properties could not belong to the Self. The body and the rest are knowable objects. If their attributes, such as pleasure, pain and delusion, really belonged to the knower (the Self), then one would have to explain the special reason why it came about that some attributes of the body and the rest, which are knowable objects, really belonged to the Self, whereas others, such as old age and death, were falsely attributed to it through nescience.[21] We may infer, indeed, that the attributes of the body and the rest do *not* really belong to the Self, on the ground that they are falsely attributed to it, like old age and death, and also because they are subject to being avoided or attained. This being so, we may hold that transmigratory experience in the form of agency and enjoyerhood belongs to the realm of the knowable and is superimposed on the Knower through nescience. Hence transmigratory experience in no way affects the Knower, any more than impurities, falsely attributed to the ether of the sky by simple souls, really affect that ether. And therefore one should not attribute even a whiff of transmigratory experience to the

Lord, the Holy One, even though He is the 'Knower of the Body' (kṣetrajña) in all bodies. For we do not find in the world any advantage or disadvantage accruing from an attribute that has been falsely superimposed through nescience.

And as for the further statement about the example not agreeing with the case to be illustrated, that was wrong. You ask why? Because the only common point affirmed between the example and the case to be illustrated was superimposition through nescience. And that was in fact present in both. And it has been shown that your own view that superimposition through nescience cannot take place in the case of the Self (but only in the case of two previously known objects) does not hold good in every case, on account of the examples of old age and death (which have to be admitted to be superimpositions on your own premise that the soul is changeless and immortal).

If you say that the Knower of the Body [lit. Field] is the one who experiences transmigration because He is of the nature of nescience, that also is wrong. Nescience is of the nature of darkness. For it is a dark cognition (pratyaya) in the sense that its nature is to veil and cover over, whether by apprehending its object wrongly, or by setting up doubts about it, or simply as non-apprehension. This we know because wherever there is the light of discrimination there is no nescience, and because the three forms of nescience, beginning with non-apprehension,[22] are only found in the presence of 'dark' defects, like the timira eye disease, which cast a veil over one's vision.

Perhaps you will say that on this showing nescience will still be an attribute of the Knower. But such a view would be wrong. For it is in the *instrument* of cognition such as the eye that we find defects such as being afflicted with timira (and not in the Knower Himself). And then there is your view that nescience is an attribute of the Knower and that the very possession of this attribute is what constitutes the 'being subject to transmigratory experience' of the Knower of the Body. To this must be added your remark that the statement 'The Lord alone is the Knower of the Body and He is not subject to transmigration' is wrong. All this is unacceptable. For just as we find the defect causing wrong apprehension and the like in the instrument of cognition, the eye, and do not find either the wrong apprehension itself, or its cause, such as a defect like timira, in the Knower (so in the case of *any* example of nescience, it afflicts the instrument of cognition and not the ultimate Knower).

When timira has been removed from an eye through the treatment of that eye, it is not afterwards found to affect the Knower (although it is only the instrument that has been treated and not Him). And from this we conclude that the defect was not an attribute of the Knower. And in the same way, wherever there are cases of non-apprehension, wrong apprehension or doubt, the causes of such phenomena must always lie in some instrument of cognition and not in the Knower of the Body. Such phenomena cannot be attributes of the Knower for the further reason that they are themselves known as objects like the light of a lamp, which illumines objects but itself requires to be known by a separate knower. And whatever is known as an object is known by something different from itself, from the mere fact of being known as an object.

And another reason why such phenomena cannot be regarded as attributes of the Knower is that no school of philosophers admits the presence of nescience and other such defects after separation from all the instruments of cognition has been achieved through final enlightenment. If they were really attributes of the Self, the Knower of the Body, as heat is of fire, then they would never be separated from it. And because the Self is changeless, omnipresent and formless like the ether, it cannot be either joined to or disjoined from anything. Wherefore the Knower of the Body must ever be the Lord. And this has been confirmed by the Lord Himself (Gītā XIII.31), in the words, 'Because (the supreme Self is) beginningless and without qualities'.

But would it not follow from all this that there would be no such thing as transmigratory experience or anyone undergoing it, so that the doctrine would have such defects as making the Veda useless? One cannot say so, as our position is really accepted by all disputants (in that they all regard the Self as free from nescience in liberation and should see that this implies that it is always free from it). You cannot ordain that only one school of philosophers need explain away a defect that applies to the doctrines of all schools. Do you ask in what sense it applies to all of them? Well, all philosophers who accept an eternal Self (or soul) at all, deny that the Self (or soul) when released has any commerce with transmigratory experience or with the sense of being the one afflicted with it. And it is not generally agreed that their doctrines have the effect of making the Vedas useless. And again, we are quite prepared to admit that the Vedas *are* useless when the 'Knowers of the Body'[23] have realized their identity with the

Lord. They are useful during the state of nescience. In the case of all the dualistic philosophers, too, the Vedas and Smṛti are significant only in the state of bondage, not in the state of liberation. On this head there is no difference.

Objection: All we Dualists accept the two states of bondage and liberation as perfectly real. For us, therefore, the Veda and Smṛti can have significance, since bondage and liberation are states to be transcended and acquired respectively, and to (the achievement of) which *means* (such as the Veda) apply. But for the Non-Dualists (Advaitins) the Veda and Smṛti can have no significance, since duality is for them produced by nescience and not ultimately real. It follows that there can be no real state of bondage for the Self (on the theory of the Non-Dualist) and therefore that the Veda can have no subject to treat of.

Answer: No. For (it is indeed true that) the Self cannot have different states. We can show this, whether it be supposed to have them simultaneously or successively. Two different and contradictory states, such as being still and moving, cannot obtain in one and the same thing at the same time. Therefore bondage and liberation cannot both obtain in the Self simultaneously, since they are contradictory. Let us suppose, then, that the two states occur successively. If they arose uncaused, the impossibility of liberation would follow.[24] And if they arose caused by another, they would not be independently existent and so would not be real. And this would contradict the (Dualist's) premises. Moreover, if bondage and liberation be taken to be two states following on one another successively, then the state of bondage must be taken as occurring first and as being beginningless and yet as having an end, and that contradicts known laws.[25] And the state of liberation would then be accepted as having a beginning but no end, and that is also contradictory to known laws. Nor is it possible to show how anything which passes from one state to another could possibly be changeless and eternal.

Therefore if one wishes to avoid investing the Self with the defects of changeability and non-eternality, one must not assume any distinction of two real states, bondage and liberation. Defects such as rendering the Veda useless would then attach to the theories of the Dualists also, and they could not avoid them. It is not, then, incumbent on the Advaitin to explain away this defect in his system, since it is common to those of his opponents also. Nor do we admit that the Veda is useless (on our view), for, as is well-known, it has its scope among ignorant men. For it is only the ignorant who identify the Self with cause and effect, which are not-self. The enlightened, on the other hand, see the Self as other than cause and effect. They cannot identify themselves with cause and effect with the feeling 'I (am that)'. Even an extremely stupid person or a raving lunatic would not identify water and fire or light and darkness, what to say of a man of discrimination? So the injunctions and prohibitions of the Veda do not apply to those who see themselves as different from cause and effect. When Viṣṇumitra, standing by, hears an order to do something phrased 'Devadatta, you do this', he does not apply the command to himself, though he might have done so if (the command had not been associated with a different name and) he had no clear idea to whom it was addressed. Similar reasoning applies to the case of cause and effect (with which only the ignorant can identify themselves)....

Objection: Those who see the Self as beyond cause and effect will not engage in action (or renunciation of action) as a result of such texts as 'One who desires heaven should perform sacrifices'[26] or 'He should not eat the flesh of an animal killed with a poisoned arrow', and neither will those who see the Self as the body alone. So the Veda will be useless for lack of anybody to act upon it at all.

Answer: No, for experience shows that engagement in ritual and abstention from it are both applicable (in their respective spheres). The knower of the Absolute (brahma-vit), who perceives the identity of the Lord and the Knower of the Body, will not engage in ritualistic action. And the one who disbelieves in the existence of a Self (independent of the body) will not engage in action (as enjoined by the Veda) because he does not believe there is any world beyond this one. But all of us know that there exist persons who have no concrete intuition of the Self as it really is and yet who infer the existence of a Self according to their lights on account of the impossibility of explaining the injunctions and prohibitions of the Veda on any other basis, who feel thirst for the fruits of deeds and who engage in Vedic ritual in a spirit of faith. So the Veda is not useless.

Objection: The Veda is useless because people see that men of spiritual discrimination do not engage in the (mainly ritualistic) actions it inculcates, and then they imitate them in this abstention.

Answer: No, for it is rare to find a man of spiritual discrimination. Amongst a great multitude of living beings there will hardly be one who achieves spiritual discrimination, as we see today. Nor do the deluded follow the practice of the discriminative ones, as they are prompted to action by attachment and other defects. And we observe that they go in for evil practices like sorcery (which are just the opposite of the practice of the wise). And to engage in action is natural. It has been said, 'One's nature acts'.[27] Therefore transmigratory experience, the realm of appearance, is mere nescience. Wrong knowledge cannot introduce any defects into the reality in regard to which it arises. The water of the mirage cannot dampen the desert soil and turn it into mud, and neither can nescience affect the Knower of the Body in any way.

Very well: but how do you explain how even the wise have such feelings as 'I am such and such' and 'Verily, this is mine' just like those subject to transmigration? Listen. The 'wisdom' of such 'wise' souls consists in identifying the Self with the body. If they were really identified with the changeless Knower of the Body they would not feel any desire for action and enjoyment in the conviction it was theirs personally. For enjoyment and action are nothing but change.

Thus the ignorant one (avidvān) desires fruits and so engages in action. For the enlightened one, on the other hand, who feels identity with the actionless Self, action of any kind is unthinkable, as he has no desire for fruits. When the activity of his whole psycho-physical organism ceases, people speak loosely of his 'withdrawal from action' (nivṛtti).[28]

And here is another example of the sort of 'wisdom' that is advanced by some. The Knower of the Body, they say, is the Lord alone. The body is different from him and the object of his knowledge. But I am the one subject to transmigratory experience and the one who enjoys pleasures and suffers pain. Bringing transmigratory experience to an end is a task that I have to achieve. I shall achieve it by acquiring knowledge of the (difference between the) body and the Knower of the Body and by meditation (dhyāna) and by *becoming* established in the nature of the Lord, the Knower of the Body, after having acquired direct knowledge of Him first. And he who thinks thus thinks that the one who has this kind of 'enlightenment' and gives it to others is not himself the Knower of the Body (but the transmigrating soul). And the miserable 'sage' who holds such a view thinks he is bringing out the real meaning of transmigratory experience and of liberation from it and also the true meaning of the Veda as a whole. But in fact he is a 'slayer of the Self', confused himself and leading others into confusion. Because he is bereft of the true tradition for interpreting the Veda, he contradicts what it does teach and fancies all kinds of meanings that it does not teach. One who does not know the true tradition for interpreting the Veda is therefore to be ignored as an ignoramus, be he learned in all the sciences.

Objection: The mere fact that the Knower of the Body (the Lord) is associated with nescience at all constitutes His subjection to transmigratory experience. Moreover, the pain, etc., that he experiences arising from this is directly perceived.

Answer: No, for whatever is known as an object belongs to the side of the body-mind complex (kṣetra). Defects arising from it cannot pertain to the subject, the Knower of the Body. Whatever non-existent defect you falsely attribute to the Knower of the Body belongs to the realm of the knowable object and is an attribute of the body-mind complex, not of the Knower of the Body. Nor can the Knower of the Body be affected by it, as there can be no intermingling between the subject and the object. For if there were any intermingling, the object would no longer be an object. And even if association with nescience and being the one who suffers *were* attributes of the Self, how could they be directly known? And how could they be attributes of the Knower of the Body? When once it has been established that all the body-mind complex is knowable as an object and that the Knower of the Body is pure knower, it then becomes contradictory to say that nescience and being-in-pain are attributes of the Knower of the Body and are (at the same time) directly perceived. It is just babble based on pure ignorance.

Our opponent will here ask, 'Well then, to whom does nescience pertain?' We reply, 'It pertains to him who is seen to be ignorant'. 'Who is it who is seen to be ignorant?' To this our reply is that the question 'Who is it who is seen to be ignorant?' is meaningless. You ask why? If you see nescience at all, then by that very fact you see the one who has nescience. And if you see the one who has it, it does not make sense to ask 'Who has it?' If you see the person who has some cows, it does not make sense to ask 'Whose are these cows?'

Objection: The example you cite is not a fair parallel. If the cows and their owner are directly perceived, the relationship between them is also directly perceived, so that the question 'Whose are these cows?' is senseless. But one does not directly perceive nescience and the one who has it in the same way, so that in their case the question need not be meaningless.

Answer: If the relation between nescience and the one who

had it were known but not directly known, how would that affect your case?

Objection: Because nescience is the cause of evil, it would have to be got rid of.

Answer: Whoever *has* nescience, let him get rid of it.

Objection: Well, it is I who have it, is it not?[29]

Answer: In that case, you know both nescience and the one who has it, namely yourself.

Objection: I do, but not directly.

Answer: If you knew them only through inference, how could you know the connection? You cannot perceive the relation between yourself as subject and nescience as a known object while you are actually having knowledge of nescience as an object, for nescience, in the case of a knower, can only be the object of his knowledge.[30] Nor could there be anyone who knew the relation between the knower and nescience, or any separate cognition of it, for this would lead to infinite regress. If another knower were assumed to know the relation between the knower and his object, then another knower would have to be assumed to know the new knower and so on, so that infinite regress would be unavoidable. Or, to take the other side of the matter, if nescience or anything else were the known object, it would remain the known object only. And the knower would remain the knower only and could not become the known object. And if all this be so, the true knower, the Knower of the Body, is in no way affected by nescience and is not the one who undergoes suffering.

Objection: Well, there is a defect attaching to the Knower of the Body, the fact, namely, that He knows the body-mind complex which is associated with defects.

Answer: No, for the 'action' of knowing is here only loosely attributed to that which is of the very nature of Consciousness (and therefore actionless). It is as when we loosely attribute the 'action' of heating to fire when in fact heat is its very nature.[31]

❖

4. And another reason against the Self's being in any way affected by nescience is the fact that nescience is knowable as an object. The one who is aware of his own error-of-nescience as (an object and therefore) something separate from himself like a pot, is not himself the one afflicted by the error. Nor is it right to say that the Self is shown to be afflicted by errors of nescience because we have the experience 'I do not know, I am confused'. For this experience, too, is distinctly perceived. And the notions 'He perceives it clearly' and 'He is in error about it' are contradictory. You say that a person may have the experience 'I do not know, I am confused', and that the ignorance and confused state of such a person[32] are experienced by him and thus the objects of an act. How, then, since they are objects, can ignorance and confusion be characteristics of the subject, the agent of this act of experiencing? And even supposing (for argument) that they were characteristics of the knowing subject, how could they then be the object of the subject, in which case the latter would require to reach out to and encompass them (as if from the outside)?[33] For the object of an action, it is admitted by all, is encompassed by the action

of the agent. But that which encompasses something is necessarily different from what it encompasses; the latter cannot encompass itself. This being so, how could 'ignorance' and 'being confused' be characteristics of Consciousness? And when one who has a distinct perception of ignorance (ajñāna) perceives ignorance as an object of his act of knowing, he does not perceive it as having the characteristics of the perceiver, in the way that he sees the body, for instance, with characteristics like thinness[34] and a particular complexion.[35]

2. Nescience as Non-comprehension and False Comprehension

For Śaṅkara, nescience is a circular process with two main phases. If non-comprehension or non-discrimination of the Real is taken as the first phase, then positive misconception or 'superimposition' is the second. Viewed from the waking standpoint, itself a standpoint implying superimposition, each phase appears to condition the other in a cyclic process to which no beginning can be assigned. The second phase, that of superimposition, consists in the projection of the phenomenal world, a not-self, the latter giving rise to the painful experience of birth, growth, decay and death in the world. The second phase of nescience, when reflected on from the waking standpoint, has to be interpreted as itself having two stages, an 'unmanifest' or 'seed' stage and a 'manifest' or 'fruit' stage. Neither of these stages has any reality whatsoever from the standpoint of the highest truth. Both are illusions, superimpositions, unconscious projections, imaginative constructions. Yet they are *objective* illusions. They stand over against the Self, which, as pure Consciousness, is totally different in nature from them and unaffected by them. But the case with the first phase of nescience is different. It is the prior *condition* for the appearance of an experiencer, experience and objects of experience. That which is an *a priori* condition for the appearance of objects cannot itself be an object. It may be called the seed of experience, but in this context Śaṅkara warns us against taking the seed metaphor too literally and regarding this phase of nescience as in any sense a 'thing'. 'The seed', he says, 'is simply non-apprehension of the real'.[36]

In Śaṅkara's commentary on Gauḍapāda's Kārikās, many passages suggest that the objects of waking experience have no existence 'outside the mind', since this is the view propounded in the Buddhist texts of which Gauḍapāda made such extensive use. Even outside Śaṅkara's commentary on Gauḍapāda's Kārikās we occasionally find him using similar language. For example, he can say, 'The object exists in the mind',[37] 'The whole world is but a modification of the mind (antaḥkaraṇa)',[38] 'Even the objects of waking experience are brought into being by the ideas of the mind (mānasa-pratyaya)'.[39] At another place[40] the opponent is made to ask how pure Being could undergo any modification at all to form the objects of the world, seeing that the Upanishads say it is partless and modification presupposes parts. Śaṅkara replies, 'Modifications and forms can very well arise from parts of pure Being that have been imagined by the mind (buddhi-kalpitebhyaḥ sad-avayavebhyo), just as forms like "snake" arise from parts mentally imagined in a rope'. And it is in conformity with this language that Śaṅkara speaks of every 'world' of Hindu cosmology as being set up by the network of psychic 'impressions' (vāsanā) arising from the former deeds of the living creatures who compose it.[41]

All this seems to reduce the subject and object of waking experience to mere modifications of mind or of consciousness. And we shall see that when attacking the Buddhists, Śaṅkara produced arguments to show that such a view was quite untenable. But we need not agree with Stcherbatsky[42] when he says that Śaṅkara criticized the Buddhists with arguments that he did not himself believe in. What Śaṅkara above all else believed in was the realization of the infinitude of the Self through the upanishadic discipline. As the Buddhist schools prevalent in his own day only accepted perception and inference as their authority and did not accept the upanishadic discipline, they had to be met on their own ground with arguments derived from empirical experience. These arguments were for Śaṅkara an expression of the truth in the sense of being a preliminary part of the process of clearing away obstructions before the pupil could embark on the path. In the long run, Śaṅkara did not teach that the world existed either inside the mind or outside it, as he taught that it did not exist at all. But as the deliverances of perception and the other empirical means of knowledge could only be negated on the basis of personal spiritual experience,[43] the truth of any argument relating to empirical experience depended more on how far it was of practical aid to the student on his path to realization of the Absolute than on how far it corresponded with so-called empirical facts.

Once it is seen that Śaṅkara's main aim was to advance the student's chances of practical awakening to the true nature of his own Self, then it becomes intelligible that he should have used different lines of argument about the nature of the world for different spiritual purposes. For instance, the Buddhist philosophers of his day still had prestige, and it was his duty to protect his pupils from succumbing to their influence. For this purpose he attacked their subjective idealism with arguments based on their own criteria, perception and inference, alone. As he did not believe that one could apprehend the final truth through perception and inference alone, he was not greatly concerned if his arguments in this field seemed to affirm, provisionally, the existence of a common-sense world of permanent objects. On the other hand, it was also practically useful for the spiritual path to point out how the objects and even the instruments of perception apparently belonging to the subject in dream-experience are momentary (dṛṣṭa-naṣṭa-svarūpa) mental creations, and how on awakening from dream they are seen to have had no real existence at all. For this provides a sound analogy for explaining how, when the great awakening has come through the upanishadic texts, it will be seen that neither the individual experiencer, as such, nor his world of objects had any real existence. Śaṅkara uses dream-experience and erroneous cognition in the waking state to explain the great awakening from all nescience and duality called liberation. But if he sometimes spoke even of the ordinary objects of waking experience as mental, this does not mean that he thought that subjective idealism was a philosophical position that could be sustained on the basis of perception and inference. However, he saw no great harm in occasionally describing the objects of the world as purely mental, since this brought out the analogy with dream-experience and error and so helped to explain how, on awakening to a new standpoint, it would be known that they had never existed.

TEXTS ON NESCIENCE AS NON-COMPREHENSION AND FALSE COMPREHENSION

1. It is as in the world, when a rope has not been properly recognized for what it is in the twilight, and it is falsely imagined in various ways with the thought 'Is it a snake? Is it a trickle of water? Is it a stick?' and the cause (nimitta) is non-determination of the true nature of the rope.[44] For if the rope had already been determined in its true nature, there would not have been any imaginations such as snake, etc. Nobody falls into the grip of erroneous convictions about the fingers of his own hand! This is the example (given by the Teacher Gauḍapāda in the Kārikā under comment). And what it illustrates is this. The Self is not determined as pure Consciousness and non-dual Being, different from all the evils involved in the world, with its empirical characteristics beginning with cause and effect. And as a result the Self is imagined as the infinite variety of creatures such as the individual souls and the Cosmic Vital Principle (prāṇa), etc. This is the final purport of all the Upanishads.[45]

❖

2. The Absolute, within and without, is the 'Unborn', since there can be nothing to be a cause of its birth. For birth, as we have said, has its cause (nimitta) in nescience, like a rope-snake. And that nescience is extinguished through awakening to the reality of the Self. Hence the 'Unborn' is the 'Unsleeping'. Sleep (in this cosmic sense) is the beginningless illusion (māyā) of the nature of ignorance (avidyā-lakṣaṇa). The enlightened one has been awoken from his dreams by his

own Self, of the very nature of non-duality. Therefore the Absolute is the 'Dreamless'. For its name and form arise through not-being-awake (aprabodha) to its own true nature. They are destroyed like a rope-snake when there is an awakening (to the Self). Hence the Absolute (brahman) cannot be designated by any name, nor can it assume any form. Hence it is 'nameless and formless' (as the Kārikā says). And there are such Vedic passages as, 'From which words fall back, etc.'[46]

❖

3. Having got rid of ignorance (ajñāna), the root of false imagination and the pre-condition of transmigration, one should know one's own Self (ātman), the Absolute (brahman), the free (mukta), the eternally fearless. One should give up the triad consisting of waking, dream and their seed called sleep, composed of darkness, reasoning that because each of them excludes the others they are unreal and do not exist.[47]

❖

4. Cancellation (apavāda) occurs when, after a false notion about any object has previously been formed, a correct notion about it arises later which abolishes the earlier one. For example, the notion that the complex of the body and its organs is the Self is *abolished* by the correct notion of the Self based on 'That thou art' that arises later. Or (to take a worldly example) there is the fact that one's false sense of direction is actually *abolished* when one ascertains the correct one.[48]

3. The Self and the Not-Self: Non-Discrimination and Mutual Superimposition

The erroneous cognition that sets up the objects of the world is, when evaluated from the waking standpoint, a beginningless and endless self-perpetuating mechanism. Human fancy is endless. When one error is corrected, others supervene. So how can the upanishadic texts remove error once and for all? The answer is that there is one superimposition that is the root cause of all the others. If empirical cognition is by its very nature superimposition, there is one fundamental superimposition which makes all other superimposition possible, the superimposition, namely, that confuses the Self with the not-self and brings the empirical experiencer himself into existence. If once the clear distinction between the Self and the not-self can be effected, then the individual experiencer is seen not to exist as such, and the ground for future superimposition and the consequent evils of birth and death is removed. Nescience (avidyā) has been replaced by knowledge (vidyā) and the goal of the upanishadic discipline achieved.

In his famous introduction to his Brahma Sūtra commentary, later called the 'Adhyāsa Bhāṣya' or 'Section on Superimposition', Śaṅkara states his fundamental position. Self and not-self are contradictories that mutually exclude one another, like darkness and light. If they are identified, it can only be through error. Empirical experience is impossible without body, senses and mind, without the erroneous identification of the 'I' with the 'not-I', without the feeling of 'I am this' and 'This is mine'.

This illusion on which all empirical experience is based is a case of superimposition, defined as 'the notion that one thing is another thing'. Here a theoretical difficulty arises. In ordinary erroneous cognition in the world, we superimpose the idea of some previously known object onto some imperfectly perceived object standing in front of us. But as the Self is not an object, how can it become involved in superimposition? Śaṅkara replies, borrowing the language of the Mīmāṃsakas, that it is not altogether a non-object, being the object of the ego-notion (aham-pratyaya). If you were to complain that the question has not been answered, as the ego-notion is itself a superimposition onto the Self, his reply would be that the essential conditions for a superimposition onto the Self are already present. The Self is self-evident to all, and yet imperfectly perceived in the state of ignorance. It therefore corresponds with the imperfectly perceived object standing in front of the observer. There is no universal rule that superimpositions are only made onto imperfectly perceived objects standing in front of one, as children and simple souls superimpose blue colour and curved shape onto the infinite ether of the sky, though it is agreed that the latter is 'subtle' and not subject to perception.

At another place Śaṅkara analyses the special and peculiar nature of the superimposition of the Self and the not-self with the help of some rather subtle reasoning. It is true, he says, that the body, etc., and the Self are already familiar as objects, if the latter be taken as the object of the ego-notion. So far, then, we can admit that they can be mutually superimposed. Still, one does not superimpose the idea of previously known objects onto the Self in quite the same sense as one superimposes, say, the idea of a man onto a post in the dark in the course of ordinary waking experience. For when one superimposes the notion of the body, for instance, on the Self, and feels 'I am the body', it is not the case that the body and the Self have already been known separately as distinct objects in the form 'This is the body' and 'This is the Self'. On the other hand 'man' and 'post' have already been the object of separate cognitions. Thus the original superimposition that makes empirical experience possible by identifying the Self with the not-self to form the empirical experiencer is different in kind from superimpositions that occur *within* empirical experience in the form of erroneous cognitions. And a mere particular act of intellectual discrimination suffices to dispel the latter, but something more, namely the whole Vedantic discipline, is required to abolish the fundamental superimposition that brings empirical experience about.

Further difficulties are also raised and answered. To superimpose is to superimpose the erroneous notion of one thing onto another thing. But the superimposition of Self and not-self that brings the empirical experiencer into being is a *mutual* superimposition of the substance and attributes of each onto the other. The Self appears saddled with the attributes of the body and the mind, and feels 'I am tall' and 'I am sad'. The body and mind appear as equipped with the Being and Consciousness that pertain properly only to the Self. If, therefore, the Self is superimposed onto the not-self, will not this mean that the Self is a mere erroneous idea? Alternatively, if the body and mind and their attributes are superimposed onto the Self, it will imply that *they* are unreal, and will not this contradict perception and all ordinary experience? And is it not the truth that Self and not-self are both real and come into contact to give rise to worldly experience, like a pillar coming into contact with a beam in the formation of a house?

These objections have to be refuted, as the notion that the Self and the not-self are distinct and both real contradicts the Upanishads and reason alike. The view that the Self is joined with the not-self like a pillar with a beam is wrong because it would make the Self the object of the action of another and so would imply that it existed for the sake of another. But the upanishadic texts show that the Self is eternal and that it is that for the sake of which everything else that is dear is held dear.[49] However, from the fact that the Self is not really 'joined to' but only 'superimposed on' the body, the 'nihilistic' conclusion that the body has no real Self does not follow. For we have the example of objects existing in space. Space is agreed to be imperceptible and not a gross sense-object standing in any form of real contact with another sense-object. Yet it does not follow that no object occupies space or that space is unreal.

Nor can the doctrine that the body is superimposed on the Self be said to be contradicted by perception and ordinary experience. For perception and ordinary experience themselves imply that the body *is* illusory and superimposed on the Self. For they present us with the two identified, and this identity must either be an identity wrought by the real connection of two separate things or else a mere appearance arising through error and mutual superimposition. But they never present the body and the Self as a real connection or soldering of two things known otherwise to be separate in themselves 'like plums standing in a dish'. We can assert a real connection between the plums and the dish in which they stand, and identify them as forming one whole consisting of connected parts, namely a dish of plums. For the plums and the dish are also available to perception at other times as separate independent entities. But the body is never available to perception as an independent entity separate from the Self in this way. So the Advaitin's thesis, that the body and the Self are only connected through mutual superimposition and that the Self is real while the body is not, must stand.

At another place Śaṅkara uses the last point anew to strengthen his argument. It is because the Self and the not-self are not given in empirical experience as separate independent entities that their true nature is never known, and this is why each can serve as the ground for the superimposition of the other, even as the imperfectly perceived rope stands as ground for the superimposition of the idea of snake. From this point of view it can be said that it is *non-discrimination* of the Self and the not-self that is the original conditioning factor in empirical experience, and hence that the discrimination of the Self from the not-self is the goal of the Advaita discipline.

Every doctrine that aims, like Śaṅkara's, at transcendence of all plurality, is perforce practical and pragmatic in character. Its details are not ultimately and absolutely true. They are true only from the nescience-standpoint in which the student is placed. No theory of nescience is anything more than an extension of nescience, a dream within a dream. One is the victim of non-discrimination of the Self from the not-self in the course of each act of superimposition that constitutes empirical experience. And one is equally the victim of superimposition every time one attempts to give a causal explanation of it. Causal explanations have their pragmatic value in so far as they protect the student against the attractions of non-upanishadic world-views or misconceived interpretations of the Upanishads. But in the end any theory of nescience is itself nescience, and nescience is not rationally explicable. Śaṅkara's pupil Sureśvara says, 'This ignorance is without cause and violates all rules and reasons. It no more brooks investigation than darkness the light of the sun'.[50] And Śaṅkara also believed that empirical experience was not, *au fond*, rationally explicable. At one point he says, 'From the collocation of an object, light, the visual faculty, the mind in its lower and higher aspects and the Self there arises an inexplicable cognition in the mind, of the nature of nescience (ajñāna-lakṣaṇa). One should (learn to) discriminate one's own Self from this (inexplicable cognition) and know the supreme reality in its pure form, the Witness, present in all beings, everywhere the same, beyond all fear or danger'.[51]

TEXTS ON THE SELF AND THE NOT-SELF

1. When it is clear that the object and the subject, which pertain to the notion 'thou' and 'I' respectively, and which are contradictory in nature like darkness and light, cannot each be of the nature of the other, it is evidently even more incorrect to identify their attributes. Whence it follows that the superimposition of the object and its attributes, pertaining to the notion 'thou', onto the subject, which pertains to the notion 'I' and is of the nature of pure Consciousness, must be erroneous. And the opposite superimposition of the subject and its

attributes onto the object must be erroneous too. And yet, though these two principles are utterly distinct in nature, there is a failure to distinguish one from the other, and each, together with its attributes, is superimposed on and identified with the other. And from that there results this natural worldly experience, based on wrong knowledge (mithyā-jñāna) and involving a synthesis of the real with the false, which expresses itself as 'I am this' and 'This is mine'.

You will say, 'Well, but what is this thing you call superimposition?' We reply: It is the false appearance in one place of what has previously been seen at another place, of the nature of a memory. Some say that superimposition is the transference to one thing of attributes that belong to another. Some affirm that superimposition is invariably caused by some failure to discriminate differences. Others again say that a superimposition is nothing more than the wrong notion resulting from imagining contradictory attributes in a substratum (where they do not in fact belong). But in all these views the common point is that one thing appears with the attributes of another. And worldly experience agrees with this. For nacre appears as silver (in the well-known silver-illusion) and the one moon (in the case of the timira eye-disease) appears to be accompanied by a second moon.

But how can there be a superimposition of the object and its attributes onto the inmost Self, which is not an object? For a person normally superimposes one object onto another object standing in front of him, whereas you say that the inmost Self does not pertain to the sphere of the 'Thou' and is not an object. To this we reply that it is not altogether a non-object, for it is the object of the ego-notion (aham-pratyaya). And it is known to all as the inmost Self because it is immediately evident. Nor is there any universal rule that an object can only be superimposed onto another object that is standing in front of the perceiver. Simple-minded persons, for example, superimpose a curved surface and impurities (such as smoke, clouds, etc.) onto the pure (and colourless) ether of the sky, though the ether is imperceptible (and thus not apprehended as standing in front). So there is nothing contradictory in the idea of the superimposition of the not-self onto the inmost Self.

This very superimposition, thus defined, the wise call 'nescience' (avidyā). And ascertainment of the ultimately real principle through discrimination between the confused elements (in this mutual superimposition of the Self and the not-self) they call 'knowledge' (vidyā). And all this being so, that onto which a superimposition is made is not connected even in the slightest with the qualities or defects of the superimposed appearance.

All commerce between the attested means of knowledge (perception, inference, etc.) and their objects, whether in the Vedic or secular sphere, proceeds on the basis of this same mutual superimposition of the Self and not-self called nescience, as does all Vedic tradition, whether concerned with injunctions and prohibitions or with liberation.

But in what sense do we mean that perception and the other means of knowledge together with Vedic tradition belong to those in the realm of nescience? What we say here is this. Without self-identification with the body and senses expressed in feelings of 'I' and 'mine' there can be no empirical knower and so the processes of empirical knowledge cannot begin. Nor can the senses operate without a seat (the body). Nor does anyone act with his body without superimposing on it the sense of self. Nor can the relationless Self be a knower without all these preliminary conditions. And there can be no active application of the means of knowledge (perception, inference, etc.) without an agent engaged in the act of knowing. This is what we mean when we say that perception and the other means of knowledge, together with the traditional sciences, belong to the realm of those afflicted with nescience...

Thus one first superimposes the ego-notion onto the inmost Self, the Witness of all. And then, having done that, one proceeds contrariwise and superimposes that inmost Self, the Witness of all, onto the inner organ (mind) and other (elements of the finite personality). This 'natural' (i.e. uncaused) beginningless and endless superimposition, which is of the nature of false supposition and is the origin of agency and enjoyment, is directly familiar to everybody. And the entire upanishadic teaching is begun to communicate knowledge of the sole reality of the one Self and thus to put an end to this superimposition, the cause of all evil.[52]

❖

2. A certain Brahmacārin,[53] tired of empirical experience (saṃsāra) in the form of (repeated) birth and death and desirous of liberation from it, approached with due formality a knower of the Absolute, one established in the Absolute, and, waiting till he was seated at ease, asked him: Holy Sir, how can I achieve liberation, I who am visited with experiences of the body, sense-organs and sense-objects? I experience pain when awake, pain again in dreams, and then, after repeatedly

enjoying respite through periods of dreamless sleep, again experience pain in waking and dream. Is this my true nature? Or is it that this experience comes adventitiously, while my real nature is other? If this is my real nature, I have no hope of liberation, for one cannot escape one's own nature. So let me think of it as adventitious. Then liberation will be possible if I can remove the cause of this adventitious experience.

The Teacher said to him: Listen, my child, it is not your nature but adventitious.

Thus addressed, the pupil replied: What is the cause of this adventitious experience? What will put it to an end? What is my true nature? Tell me, that I may put a stop to the cause and thus be free from the adventitious experience and realize my true nature, like a sick man who puts an end to his illness.

The Teacher replied: Nescience (avidyā) is the cause. Knowledge (vidyā) is what puts an end to it. When nescience is at an end you will be free from its effect, transmigratory experience in the form of (repeated) birth and death, and you will no longer experience the pain of the waking and dream states.

The pupil said: What is this nescience? What is it ignorance *of*? And what is that knowledge that puts an end to nescience and through which I can realize my true nature?

The Teacher said: You take that which is the supreme Self and not subject to transmigration as other than what it is, thinking 'I am the one in transmigration'. What is not an agent, you take as an agent. What is not an experiencer, you take as an experiencer. What really and truly exists (i.e. the Self in its true nature as infinitude), you take as non-existent. That is nescience.

The pupil replied: Though I exist, I am not the supreme Self. Transmigratory experience in the form of agency and enjoyment is my very nature, for I have direct experience (anubhava) of it through perception and other means of knowledge. This cannot be caused by nescience, as nescience cannot obscure (and so act upon) that which is its own true Self. Nescience indeed, is the superimposition of one thing *(which one already knows)* onto another *(which one already knows)*, as, for example, when one superimposes silver, which one already knows, onto nacre, which one already knows; or when one superimposes (the figure of) a man, which one already knows, onto a post, which one already knows; or when one superimposes (the figure of) a post, which one already knows, onto a man. But one does not superimpose that with which one is not already familiar onto that with which one is familiar, nor that with which one is familiar onto that with which one is (altogether) unfamiliar. Therefore, one does not superimpose the not-self onto the Self, because the Self (being, precisely, what the Upanishads set out to teach) is not something with which one is initially familiar. Nor does one superimpose the Self onto the not-self, again because the Self is not initially familiar.

The Teacher replies to him and says: No, for the rule you cite admits of exceptions. You cannot, my dear one, establish that people superimpose only that with which they are already familiar onto that with which they are already familiar. For we find examples of superimposition of the Self. They assume the form of superimposition of the attributes of the body onto the

Self, which is the object of the ego-notion, in such expressions as 'I am fair', ' I am dark', and also the form of superimposition of the Self, the object of the ego-notion, onto the not-self, in such expressions as 'This (body) am I'.

The pupil says: But the Self must, in that case, be already familiar as the object of the ego-notion, while the body is familiar as 'this'. That being so, we have the mutual superimposition of the Self and the body as two things that are previously familiar, like post and man or nacre and silver. What then was it that you had particularly in mind, Holy Sir, when you said that it was not permissible to limit superimposition to superimposition of the already familiar onto the already familiar?

The Teacher replies: Listen. It is true that the body and the Self are already familiar. But they are not already familiar to everyone as objects of distinct ideas, like post and man. In what way, then, are they familiar? Always as objects of inextricably mixed ideas. No one has the apprehension 'This is the body' and 'This is the Self' in such a form that 'Self' and 'body' constitute perfectly separate ideas. Thus people are confused about the Self and the not-self and we hear 'The Self is such and such' and 'No, it is such and such'. This was the particular circumstance I had in mind when I said, 'You cannot limit (the range of superimposition) thus (to superimposition of the already familiar onto the already familiar only)'.

Objection: Whatever is superimposed through nescience is non-existent where it is seen. For example, there is no actual silver in the nacre, no man in the post, no snake in the rope, no concave surface or impurities in the ether of the sky, etc. Now, it would follow in the same way that, since the Self and the body are constantly and continuously confused, they are mutually superimposed on one another and each is ever non-existent in the other. And hence, just as there is ever complete non-existence of silver and the rest in nacre and the rest onto which they are superimposed, and of nacre and the rest in silver and the rest, so it would follow that the Self and the body were things mutually superimposed on one another through nescience and were nothing more (as, according to the opponent, one is never aware of the Self without the body or the body without the Self). And from this it would follow that they were both unreal. And this conclusion is unwelcome, since it is the thesis of the Buddhist Nihilists (who abhor the Veda). Or if, on the other hand, (the theory of mutual superimposition was dropped and) it was just held that the body was superimposed on the Self through nescience, then the Self would be real and the body unreal. But that conclusion would also be unwelcome; as it would contradict perception (and other sources of valid cognition which show that the body is real). Therefore, the Self and the body are not mutually superimposed through nescience. What then is their relation? They must be in constant conjunction, like the upright pillar and horizontal beam (in a house).

Answer: No, for it would then follow that both were non-eternal and existed for the sake of another. Because brought together, they would exist for the sake of another (i.e. for the sake of the one who brought them together), and then (because they would not have independent existence) they would be non-eternal, just like the pillar and horizontal beam, etc. And moreover, that Self which is supposed by the opponent to be connected with the body, would, from the mere fact of its being brought into connection with something, be a thing that only existed for the sake of another (i.e. the one who used it for his own designs). This is (absurd and is) enough to show that the Self cannot be brought into connection with anything, and must be transcendent, 'other' and eternal.

Objection: The Self, then, since it is not brought into real connection with anything, is falsely superimposed onto the body with a sense of identity, and has therefore the defects of non-existence and non-eternality, etc. Thus we have to say 'The body has no Self', and (again) we fall into the position of the Nihilists.

Answer: No, for the Self is taken as being beyond all connection by its very nature, like the ether of space. If it were maintained, 'It is the Self and beyond all (physical) connection' then it would not follow that the body and everything else would have no Self. You cannot say that it follows from the proposition 'The ether of space does not enter into any (physical) connection with anything' that nothing occupies (lit. 'has') space. So the doctrine does not involve the fault of falling into the position of the Nihilists.

As for the contention that if the body were non-existent in the Self there would result contradiction with perception and other sources of valid cognition, that also was wrong. For perception and the other sources of valid empirical cognition do not reveal the body as existent in the Self. The body is not apprehended by them as standing in the Self like a plum in a dish, or curds in whey or oil in seeds or a picture on a wall. So there is no contradiction with perception or other sources of valid empirical cognition.

How, then, can there be any superimposition of the body onto the Self, when the latter is not perceived through the organs of perception or known through other sources of valid empirical cognition? Or how can there be superimposition of the Self onto the body (in the same circumstances)?

There is nothing wrong here, for the Self is familiar to us by nature.[54] One cannot establish a definite rule that superimposition occurs only on that which is occasionally evident and not on that which is constantly evident.[55] For we find that concave surface and impurities are superimposed (by simple people) onto the ether of the sky (although it is agreed that the latter is never an object of perception at all).[56]

❖

3. But what is meant by speaking of conjunction between the body and the Knower of the Body? Evidently there cannot subsist between the body and the Knower of the Body that variety of relation, called conjunction, which subsists between a rope and a pot (at a well) and results from the mutual conjunction of the parts of the objects in question, since the Knower of the Body is partless like the ether. Nor can there be inherence,[57] since the Knower of the Body and the body are not accepted as standing to one another as (material) cause and effect.

To this we reply: The conjunction (mentioned in the Gītā verse under comment) between the Knower of the Body and the body, which are respectively subject and object and of utterly distinct nature, is in fact (no real conjunction at all but) a (mere mutual) superimposition of their attributes, conditioned by a failure to discriminate from one another these two utterly distinct entities. It is comparable to the process whereby 'conjunction' with a snake is superimposed on a rope or where silver is superimposed on nacre through failure to discriminate the two.

This 'conjunction' of the Knower of the Body and the body is essentially superimposition, and may be spoken of as wrong knowledge (mithyā-jñāna). It is, however, possible to separate out the Knower of the Body like the inner stem of a piece of muñja grass from its outer stalk and know it as we have defined it, through a discriminative knowledge of the Knower of the Body acquired in the manner already described. It is then possible to be aware of the Absolute (brahman), that which we are here to know, void of all particular adjuncts, as expressed in the formula 'It is not called Being or Non-being'.[58] Whoever does this acquires the clear conviction that (in ordinary waking experience) the non-existent is appearing as if existent, just as in the case of elephants conjured forth by magic (māyā)[59] or dream-visions or cloud-palaces. And, in the case of one in whom this clear vision has arisen, wrong knowledge disappears, because it is in contradiction with right knowledge and because its origin has been removed.[60]

4. The Standpoint of Nescience and the Standpoint of Knowledge

Śaṅkara's doctrine of the distinction between two standpoints, the standpoint of nescience and the standpoint of ultimate truth, holds good, like any other doctrine or distinction, only from the standpoint of nescience. But the student to whom the texts of the Upanishads are addressed himself occupies that standpoint, or he could not even hear them.[61] And his purpose in hearing them is to awaken to a new standpoint, the standpoint of knowledge. The distinction between the two standpoints is implicit in the upanishadic texts themselves. For instance, Yājñavalkya says in the Bṛhad-āraṇyaka Upanishad 'Where there is the *appearance* of something else over against the Self, there a Self who is one entity can (appear to) see an (object which is) other... But when all has become one's own Self, then what could he see and with what?'[62] This upanishadic text itself shows that the distinction between a 'standpoint of nescience' and a 'standpoint of ultimate truth' rests not only, or even principally, on the need to harmonize the upanishadic texts denying plurality with those that imply it, but on the actual experience of enlightened men who have attained to discrimination of the Self from the not-self. Śaṅkara admits that the enlightened man enjoys empirical experience, implying plurality, just like the ignorant man. But he maintains that he is never deluded into believing it is real.

Śaṅkara's distinction between the standpoint of nescience and the standpoint of knowledge is not the same as that between different grades of reality (prātibhāsika, vyāvahārika, pāramārthika) set up by his later followers. *Anything* experienced in the state of nescience is a superimposition on the Absolute and has no reality *whatever* except *as* the Absolute. This holds equally true of waking experience, dream and sense-illusion. For there can be no perception without a perceiver, and the perceiver himself, as we have seen,[63] is the result of an erroneous mutual superimposition of the Self and the not-self. This implies, incidentally, that the highest part of the upanishadic message is such that it cannot be known through the mere authority of revelation. It demands to be realized in actual experience. One cannot claim to know that one is immortal Spirit and distinct from the body on the mere authority of the upanishadic texts, since all acceptance of authority depends in the end on falsely identifying oneself with the perishable body, senses and mind in order to apprehend the authoritative statement.[64] However, until the final enlightenment comes, one has to accept the deliverances of perception, inference and Vedic revelation in the spheres to which they respectively belong. There is no attempt in Śaṅkara, like that we find in his contemporary, Maṇḍana Miśra, and even his pupil, Sureśvara, to argue away the reality of the world by negative dialectic. 'This our ordinary experience of the world', he says, 'solidly established as it is through perception and other means of knowledge, cannot be argued away by mere dialectic without rising to the direct apprehension of a higher principle. For when no exceptions can be shown, established rules hold'.[65]

We have seen that when Śaṅkara compared waking experience with dream-experience, what interested him about dream-experience, in this context, was not the fact that it was mental but the fact that it was subject to cancellation through awakening to a new standpoint. But within the dream-standpoint, dream-perception and dream-inference hold. Similarly, before enlightenment, every cognition is valid in its own sphere.[66] Knowledge that comes through the recognized means of valid cognition is determined by the form of its object.[67] It is quite different from mere subjective imagination, where the objects are purely mental and can be modified or suppressed consciously at the will of the thinker.

On such a view, as long as we are in the realm of nescience, as long as we feel ourselves to be individual agents and experiencers, we are in the realm where the recognized means of knowledge bear on external objects. This is a realm of plurality, the order and harmony in which is explicable only through appeal to the principle of an Inner Ruler, a divine guiding force, superintending the unfoldment of the seeds of future experience left by the deeds of living creatures. But what in the state of nescience we think of as 'the Lord' (īśvara) or the 'Inner Ruler' (antaryāmin) is in fact only the Absolute as it appears to the individual afflicted with nescience, who does not realize that the Absolute is nothing other than his own true Self. From the standpoint of enlightenment and final truth, the 'Lord' loses His quality of 'Lordship'. He just stands forth as the Self in its true nature. And the upanishadic texts which negate all finite qualities of the Self in its true form do not conflict with those that attribute finite characteristics to it or speak of it as 'the Lord'. For the one small group of texts is speaking from the standpoint of knowledge, while the larger group is speaking from the standpoint of nescience.

TEXTS ON THE STANDPOINT OF NESCIENCE AND THE STANDPOINT OF KNOWLEDGE

1. Thus false empirical experience based on distinction occurs both in the case of those for whom reality other than the Absolute exists and those for whom it does not. But when those who speak from the standpoint of the ultimate truth are actually engaged in investigating the world of empirical experience in the light of the Upanishads to see whether it truly exists or not, they lay it down once and for all that the Absolute alone exists, one without a second, and that it is void of subject-object experience altogether.

Hence there is no contradiction in our position. For when we are engaged in laying down the nature of the supreme Reality we do not affirm the existence of any other reality apart from it, since this would be to contradict the texts 'One only without a second' and 'Having nothing else inside and nothing else outside'.[68] Nor do we say anything to contradict the fact that, at the time of experience of name and form, those bereft of discrimination of the Self from the not-self have experience of action, its factors and results. Hence all human experience, whether based on the upanishadic wisdom or merely on the natural powers, has to be regarded as occurring from one of two particular standpoints, either that of ignorance (ajñāna) or that of enlightenment (jñāna). So there is no question of any contradiction in our position. No philosopher can deny that some experience is true absolutely and some from the standpoint of empirical experience only.[69]

❖

2. But (asks an objector) does not the state of not-being-the-Absolute and not-being-all occur without nescience? No, we reply. For it is taught that these states are removable through knowledge of the Absolute, and this would be impossible unless they arose through nescience. Knowledge of the Absolute is never found to obliterate any real quality of anything or to create a new one. But it is invariably found to remove nescience. So here also the idea is that it is the notion of not-being-the-Absolute and not-being-all that is to be removed by knowledge of the Absolute. But knowledge of the Absolute cannot make or destroy anything real. So it is useless to contradict the Veda or impute to it theories that it does not contain (by speaking, for instance, of liberation as a change of state).

But is not ignorance in regard to the Absolute logically impossible? No, for the Vedas enjoin knowledge of the Absolute. When a piece of nacre is lying before one's eyes, no one spells out the fact that it is a piece of nacre and says, 'This is nacre and not silver' unless someone has erroneously taken it for silver. Similarly, if superimpositions were not being made onto the Absolute through nescience, the Veda would not lay down that it had to be seen as a unity, in such passages as 'All this is pure Being, all this is the Absolute alone, all this is the Self only, there is no second thing that is not the Absolute'.[70]

Well, you will reply, we are not saying that there are no superimpositions onto the Absolute of characteristics that it does not possess, like the superimpositions of silver onto nacre. What we are saying is that the Absolute is not the author of that nescience which causes the superimposition onto it of characteristics that it does not possess.

We (Advaitins) reply that we agree that the Absolute is neither the author of nescience nor itself in the grip of nescience. And yet we do not admit the existence of any conscious being other than the Absolute which could be either the author or the victim of nescience...

You will say that, if the Absolute is neither the author nor the victim of nescience, then the Veda must be useless. But we accept this. Once the knowledge of the Absolute has been attained, it *is* useless. You will say that on our theory even knowledge of the Absolute is useless (as there can be no nescience and no one to be afflicted by nescience). But we reply that you are wrong, for knowledge of the Absolute is actually *found* to remove ignorance of it. You will say that removal of ignorance is in fact impossible if only unity exists. But we reply that you are wrong, for your statement contradicts what is actually found to be the case, namely the practical fact of the removal of ignorance through knowledge of unity. He who says that what is actually experienced is impossible, contradicts experience, and no philosopher accepts that one can contradict experience. What is experienced *cannot* be impossible, from the mere fact of having been experienced. And if you say that the experience itself was impossible, the same reasoning applies.[71]

❖

3. Here you might raise an objection and say that if the undifferentiated unity of the Absolute be accepted, then this would come into conflict with perception and inference and other means of knowledge, as it would rob them of any field of operation and degrade them into mere erroneous cognition like taking a post for a man. That part of the Veda, too, which consists in injunctions and prohibitions, since it presupposes distinctions, would be contradicted if all the distinctions were denied. Nor is this all. Even the revealed teachings concerning liberation, since they pre-suppose distinctions in the form of Teacher, pupil, teaching and so on, would be contradicted if distinctions did not exist. And how could the sole existence and reality of the undifferentiated Self, proclaimed by the texts dealing with liberation, be a truth if the texts themselves (being distinctions within that Self) were but falsity and illusion?

But we reply that there is nothing wrong in our position here. Before the rise of clear knowledge that man's Self is the Absolute, all practical experience can be defended as real, just as dream-experience is real before waking. Before he is aware of the unity and sole reality of the Self, no one entertains the notion that such transient modifications (vikāra) as perception and other means of knowledge, together with the objects of such means of knowledge and the cognitions arising from them, are illusory. Every living creature which lacks the knowledge of its natural identity with the Absolute identifies itself with the various modes apparently assumed by the Absolute and accepts them as 'me' and 'mine'. Hence all secular experience and Vedic teaching can stand before the awakening to the knowledge that one's Self is the Absolute. The case is like that of an ordinary man (dreaming) in sleep. Before awakening, he sees objects of various grades and degrees of value and takes this knowledge for authentic perception, without, at the time, having the remotest suspicion that such perception is a mere appearance of perception. In just the same way, one takes waking perception for genuine perception before enlightenment (although it, too, is false because based on the false identification of the Self with the not-self).[72]

❖

4. Thus the Lord conforms to the external adjuncts (upādhi) consisting of name and form[73] set up by nescience in the same sense that space conforms to the different external adjuncts such as the clay pot and the coconut vessel (in which it is apparently enclosed). And within the realm of human experience, He rules over the conscious beings called individual souls (jīva), who are in truth nothing but Himself, but who assume the limitations of body, mind and sense-organs in the same sense that space assumes the limitations of the pots in which it is apparently enclosed. But the body, mind and sense-organs are wrought of name and form which are set up by nescience. Hence the 'Lordship' of the Lord, as well as his omniscience and omnipotence, exist only in relation to external adjuncts which are of the nature of nescience. From the standpoint of ultimate truth there can be no talk of any opposition between a Lord and his subjects or of omniscience or

other attributes in the Self, in which all external adjuncts are by nature effaced through knowledge....

The author of the Brahma Sūtras, too, when he says in the present Sūtra (that the individual soul is) 'non-different from the Absolute', is speaking from the standpoint of final truth. But when he is speaking from the standpoint of ordinary empirical experience, he says 'Let it be as in the world'[74] and speaks of the Absolute as comparable to the great ocean (assuming modification through its waves). And here (i.e. in the earlier Sūtra just quoted) he does not refute this conception (of modification) but resorts to the doctrine that the world, as manifold effect, is a (real) transformation of the Absolute. For such a view will be needed (later) in dealing with meditation on the Absolute as associated with qualities.[75]

❖

5. Teaching is given by the Veda in accordance with what appears to be the case to men. The Veda does not first come before the new-born infant and teach it either duality or non-duality and then proceed afterwards to instruct the grown man either in ritual or in knowledge of the Absolute, whichever would be appropriate to the instructions he had received as an infant. Nor does duality need any teaching, as it is evident to the whole animal race from birth. Initially, no one would dream of thinking that duality was unreal. Hence the Veda has no need to begin by teaching duality before going on to establish its own validity.

Now, everyone accepts authority somewhere, even those who fall under the sway of unorthodox thinkers. So the Veda first conforms to the natural duality set up by nescience and teaches rituals to the one who is afflicted with natural nescience and has desire and aversion and other such defects. Such rituals lead to the attainment of a variety of human goals which present themselves initially to view. But afterwards, to one who has seen the faults inherent in the very nature of action, its factors and results, and who is longing for its opposite, establishment in the state of pure indifference, it teaches knowledge of the Absolute, which means knowledge that the Absolute is one's own Self, as this is the means to establishment in the state of pure indifference.

This being so, when a person has attained this state of indifference by this means, he ceases to have any interest in the question of whether the Vedic texts have authority or not, and for him the Veda ceases to be a body of revealed texts on account of this indifference. It is thus clear that the various parts of the Veda cannot conflict, since they serve the interests of different sorts of people. For distinctions pertaining to duality, such as those between pupil, doctrine and instruction, etc., cease when non-duality is known.[76]

NOTES TO CHAPTER II

References to Extracts are in bold type

1 ayam prapañco mithyaiva satyam brahmāham advayam / atra pramāṇam vedantā guravo 'nubhavas tathā, *Yoga Vāsiṣṭha* III.xxi.35.

2 G.K. I.15.

3 Vyāsa on Y.S. II.5, Vātsyāyana on N. Sū. IV.ii.35, Śabara on P.M. Sūtra I.i.2 and I.i.5.

4 Bṛhad.Bh. I.v.2, IV.iii.20, trans. Mādhavānanda, 146 and 457f.

5 B.S.Bh. II.iv.20.

6 See *Viveka Cūḍāmaṇi*, verses 108, 146, 198; *Ātmabodha*, 14; *Aparokṣānubhūti*, 94 etc.

7 Hacker, *Texte* I., 109ff., Cammann, 58ff. and 66ff.

8 B.S.Bh. II.i.14, II.i.27. Hacker, *Eigentümlichkeiten*, 262ff.

9 Hacker cites B.S.Bh. I.i.11, II.iii.40, II.iii.41: *Eigentümlichkeiten*, 250. Cp. Ānandagiri's ṭīkā on avidyādi-doṣa at Chānd.Bh. III.xiv.2, Ā.Ś.S. Ed. 158, which explains it as referring to Patañjali's kleśas.

10 Hacker, *Eigentümlichkeiten*, 250-3, gives exact references for this and the remaining examples cited.

11 Bh.G.Bh. XIII.2, trans. Shastri, 325f.

12 B.S.Bh. IV.i.3.

13 Bh.G.Bh. XIII.2, trans. Shastri, 332.

14 Self-interested actions leave impressions which issue in future worldly experiences in births to come. Cp. Bh.G.Bh. XVIII.67, introduction, trans. Shastri, 511.

15 Bṛhad. II.iv.14.

16 **Bṛhad. Bh. IV.iii.20.**

17 Action depends on vision of difference, and vision of difference on nescience. Yet nescience depends for its continuation on desire and action. Nescience is ignorance of the Self *plus* the action of superimposition. In dreamless sleep the seeds of nescience are present but nescience itself is not, as we shall see in Chapter IX, section 2, Extract 5. **Bh.G.Bh. XVIII.67 (introduction).**

18 Kaṭha I.ii.4.

19 M.Bh. XII. 201.17.

20 Pleasure, pain and delusion refer to the three guṇas, to be described in connection with Māyā in Chapter V.

21 It was common ground amongst all Hindu philosophers except the materialists that the Self was immortal.

22 Nescience is merely analysed into non-apprehension, wrong apprehension and doubt. See also Bṛhad. Bh. III.iii.1, trans. Mādhavānanda, 313f. These are not caused by any cosmic nescience. Cosmic nescience is itself a mere notion that belongs to the realm of wrong apprehension.

23 There is an ambiguity about the term 'Knower of the Body' (kṣetrajña) both in Śaṅkara's own texts and in those on which he commented. Fundamentally it refers to the non-dual Witness, identical in all bodies. But by an easy transition it can pass over to mean the knower in the body conceived as an individual, and the term can then be used loosely in the plural, as here.

24 Because ignorance, known to be existent and yet not requiring a cause, could spring up at any time without rhyme or reason, even after liberation. For the Advaitin, the one sure thing about nescience is that, once cancelled, it can never be revived. Once the rope is known there is the unalterable conviction 'There never was a snake'.

25 The law that whatever is beginningless is also endless and whatever has an end must also have a beginning.

26 See Ā.Ś.S. III.iv.8-13, Vol.I., 295f.

27 Bh.G. V.14.

28 Withdrawal here is not a deliberate policy chosen as a means to an end as, for instance, in the case of the monk who deliberately withdraws from the world to increase his chances of success on the spiritual path. Ānandagiri.

29 On all this argument, consult D. Ingalls in P.E.W., April 1953, 69ff.

30 And so standing over against the knower as his object, but not related to him or belonging to him.

31 Bh.G.Bh. XIII.2.

32 Reading tad-darśinaś ca with the Ā.S.S. Ed., 665, for the tad-darśanaś ca of Bhāgavat's text, which appears questionable here and at the places mentioned in the following two notes.

33 Reading vyāpyete with the Ā.S.S. Ed. *ibid.*

34 Reading kārśya with the Ā.S.S. Ed. *ibid.*

35 Bṛhad.Bh. IV.iv.6.

36 tattva-apratibodha-mātram eva hi bījam, G.K.Bh. I.11.

37 U.S. (verse) VII.5.

38 sarvam hy antaḥ-karaṇa-vikāra eva jagat, manasy eva suṣupte pralaya-darśanāt, Muṇḍ. Bh. II.i.4. Sac draws attention to the parallel with G.K.Bh. III.31.

39 Chānd. Bh. VIII.v.4, ed. Bhāgavat, 311, line 6.

40 Chānd. Bh. VI.ii.2, Ā.S.S. Ed., 304f.; Bhāgavat's Ed., 249; Jhā's Translation, Vol.II, 95.

41 Bṛhad.Bh. I.v.2, trans. Mādhavānanda, 146.

42 Stcherbatsky, *Nirvāṇa*, 63, Note 1. For Śaṅkara's arguments against Buddhist epistemological idealism, see Chapter XI, section 5, Extracts 5-8, below.

43 See B.S.Bh. II.ii.31 *ad fin*, trans. Gambhīrānanda, 426 and II.i.14, 330.

44 Ignorance of the rope is the prior condition (nimitta) and not the material cause (upādāna-kāraṇa) of the snake. Cp. Sac, *Sugamā*, 40.

45 G.K.Bh. II.17.

46 Taitt. II.4. **G.K.Bh. III.36.**

47 U.S. (verse) XVI. 17 and 18.

48 B.S.Bh. III.iii.9.

49 Bṛhad. II.iv.5.

50 Sureśvara, N. Sid. III.66.

51 U.S. (verse) XV.35 and 36.

52 B.S.Bh. I.i.1 introduction.

53 The ideal candidate for Advaita Vedanta teaching is a student (Brahmacārin) who has completed the period of study when he commits one or more of the Vedas to heart living a disciplined, celibate life in the house of the Brahmin who teaches him the Vedic texts. He is then ripe for enquiry into the meaning of the texts, which is more easily carried out as a student or monk than as a married householder. See Chapter XII, section 3, Extracts 20-25, below.

54 I.e. immediately, and not mediately through any operation, such as recourse to perception or the other sources of valid empirical cognition.

55 Reading nitya-siddhau. But D.V. Gokhale's reading 'nityā-siddhau' is worth noting.

56 U.S. (prose) paras 45-61.

57 Śaṅkara has in mind two technical terms of the Vaiśeṣikas, saṃyoga (conjunction) and samavāya (inherence). Two things that can exist independently may come into conjunction and be later disjoined. But inherence is an inseparable relation, such as that of the property of heat in fire or of an effect (such as a pot) in its material cause (clay).

58 Bh.G. XIII.12.

59 The reference is to the mass-hypnotist, familiar from the literature of the time, who brought forth illusory apparitions in the minds of his audience.

60 Bh.G.Bh. XIII.26.

61 Cp. above, section 3, Extract 1, *ad fin* (p 97).

62 Bṛhad. II.iv.14, quoted by Śaṅkara in this context at B.S.Bh. I.iii.12, Gambhīrānanda, 126.

63 Previous section, *passim*.

64 Sac, V.V.S., 10.

65 B.S.Bh. II.ii.31, Gambhīrānanda, 426.

66 Chānd. Bh. VIII.v.4 (trans. Jhā, Vol.II, 251ff) and B.S.Bh. II.i.14, Gambhīrānanda, 330.

67 B.S.Bh. I.i.4, Gambhīrānanda, 34.

68 Chānd. VI.ii.1, Bṛhad. II.v.19, III.viii.8.

69 Bṛhad.Bh. III.v.1.

70 Cp. Chānd. VI.ii.1, Muṇḍ. II.ii.11, Chānd. VII.xxv.2, Bṛhad. IV.iv.19 (Mādhavānanda).

71 **Bṛhad. Bh. I.iv.10.**

72 **B.S.Bh. II.i.14.**

73 On the notion of external adjunct, see Vol.II, Chapter V, section 1, introductory note, below. On the notion of name and form, see Vol.II, Chapter VI, section 2, below.

74 B.S. II.i.13.

75 **B.S.Bh. II.i.14.**

76 **Bṛhad. Bh. V.i.1.**

CHAPTER III

KNOWLEDGE OF THE ABSOLUTE

1. The Absolute is already known in a general way

Śaṅkara regarded the highest texts of the Upanishads, through which the truth is finally conveyed, as negative in character. The spoken word can give no idea of the Absolute, and would bring it down into the world of objects if it could. If this be the case, however, one might wonder how the texts could awaken the student to a true knowledge of his own nature and thus put an end to his experience of duality and suffering for ever. For the snake-illusion is only dispelled when one comes to a clear knowledge of the rope. But Śaṅkara replies that there is really no difficulty here, as we have *a priori* familiarity with the existence of our own Self.[1] All the distinctions of duality are superimpositions onto the Self. And, as we have seen,[2] there is no rule that superimpositions can occur only onto that which is known as an object. They can occur provided that the ground onto which superimposition is made is not known clearly. Onto a rope perceived vaguely as 'this dark wavy something' we superimpose the image of a snake.

The case with the Self is similar. We have the constant feeling 'I am', and onto this constant but vague and general notion we superimpose a variety of mutually contradictory determinate ideas. We feel 'I am happy, sad, confused, clear, young, old, etc.' To all these experiences the notion of 'I' is common, as the rope in its vaguely perceived form as 'this' is the common ground of successive erroneous notions when one supposes it in turn to be a snake, a stream of water and a stick. As the 'I' that is misconceived in all our empirical experiences is already familiar, there is no need for the revealed texts to acquaint us with it positively. No one needs to apply to the various means of knowledge such as perception, inference or revelation in order to know the Self, as it is by nature self-evident. In fact, one cannot know the Self in these ways. For whatever is known through the various means of knowledge is an object of one's knowledge, and one's own Self can never be an object of one's own knowledge. And if it were claimed that the purpose of the Vedic texts was to teach the existence of the Self, this would in fact make them technically inauthoritative. For those Vedic passages which merely restate what is already known from other sources are technically not classed as authoritative means of knowledge.[3] The purpose of the metaphysical texts in the Upanishads, therefore, is not to acquaint one with one's own Self, but only to remove the false notions such as 'happy, sad, confused, etc.' that we superimpose onto it. One has to make positive efforts for liberation. But these efforts are only made towards removing the obstacles to a recognition of the true nature of one's own Self.

But although the Self is immediately evident to all, we still need the texts of the Upanishads, allied to rational enquiry into their meaning conducted under the guidance of a Teacher, if we are to awaken to its true nature. Nevertheless, the Self is permanent and constant and has the character of a self-affirming essence. As such, it is not itself subject to negation.

TEXTS ON THE ABSOLUTE AS ALREADY KNOWN IN A GENERAL WAY

1. It follows, then, that there can be no injunction to acquire knowledge of the Self. All that requires to be effected is the cessation of the superimposition of name and form and other items of not-self onto the Self. There is no question of having to acquire knowledge (vijñāna) of the Self as consciousness, for the latter is already known under the forms of all objects projected through nescience. That is why the Vijñāna Vāda Buddhists came to the conclusion that nothing except cognitions exists, and were persuaded that the latter did not require the application of the empirical means of knowledge to be known, as they were already self-luminous. Therefore, all that has to be effected is the cessation of superimposition onto the Absolute. No positive efforts towards knowledge of the Absolute have to be made as one is (in a sense) familiar with it already. In the case of those who cannot practise discrimination, knowledge of the true nature of the Self is obscured by the particular manifestations of name and form that are imagined through nescience. Hence it comes about that that which is in closest proximity to them, which is their own Self, which is very well known and perfectly familiar, appears as if it were unfamiliar and hard to know and as if it were another. But in the case of those who have withdrawn their minds from preoccupation with external objects and who have received illumination from the Teacher and the Self, nothing else is such a joy as the Absolute, nothing so firmly in their grasp, nothing so well known and close....

Some persons, however, believing themselves to be very wise, say that the intellect cannot attain to the Self because the latter is formless, so that perfection in knowledge is difficult to attain. True indeed, it is difficult to attain for those who have no Teacher and belong to no tradition, who have not heard the upanishadic texts in the traditionally prescribed way, whose minds are deeply attached to external objects and who have not pursued the right path with diligence. But for those who are the contrary of all this and have all these qualifications, the (opposite) idea of the reality of the dualism of the empirical perceiver and his object of perception is even more difficult to attain, since they are aware of nothing else except the Self as pure (homogeneous) Consciousness.

It follows, therefore, that it is only the cessation in the mind of all notion of distinction based on external forms that can lead to true knowledge of the Self. For the Self is never at any time (completely) unknown to anyone, neither is it susceptible either to acceptance or rejection. Indeed, if the Self were entirely unknown, there could not be a motive for any of our actions (and hence we would not commit them, which is absurd). Nor can we conceive of them as being performed for the sake of the body or any other non-conscious being. And neither happiness nor misery exist for their own sakes, while all practical activity leads ultimately to experience for a Self. Therefore, just as (on account of its immediate proximity) no special means of knowledge are required in order to take note of one's own body, so none are required in order to take note of the Self, which is the inmost principle of all.

Hence it stands proved that, for those who can practise discrimination, establishment in knowledge of the Self is an already accomplished fact. Even those (the Pūrva Mīmāṃsakas of Kumārila's school) who try to maintain that knowledge is formless and not itself immediately known, have to admit (according to their own theory) that knowledge, just like happiness and other attributes of the mind, is evident to immediate inspection, for awareness of an object can only occur through knowledge. Further, it is (logically) impossible to seek for knowledge of knowledge. If knowledge were initially unknown, like the object of knowledge, then we should have to seek knowledge of knowledge, just as we seek knowledge of an object. In the case of an object of knowledge, like a pot, the knower seeks to encompass the object with his knowledge.[4] If this were also the case with knowledge, the knower would seek to encompass every cognition with another cognition. But (this would lead to infinite regress and) we do not find that this is so. Knowledge, therefore, is immediately evident, as also is the knower. Hence no effort has to be made to gain knowledge of the Self. It is to put an end to false identification of the Self with the not-self that efforts have to be made. The path of knowledge, therefore, is something perfectly within our grasp.[5]

❖

2. *Objection:* Teaching for enlightenment through the text 'That thou art' does not stand to reason, and neither does such a text as 'Verily, he came to know the Self'.[6] For the Self is ever of the nature of consciousness. We do not find that the sun, for instance, is ever illumined by anything else. So teaching for enlightenment as to the Self is useless.

Answer: This view is wrong, for teaching is given in order to remove people's superimpositions. People superimpose transient properties such as intellect (mind, body,) etc. onto the Self of all, even though it is eternal consciousness, through failure to discriminate the true Self. Teaching for enlightenment as to the true nature of the Self as consciousness is given in order to remove these superimpositions.

Moreover, enlightenment and unenlightenment in regard to the Self are intelligible, since they are introduced by external factors, just as when water (though naturally cool) is made hot through the application of heat, or as (contradictories like) day and night are brought about by the external conditioning factor, the sun. Burning and light are constant in fire and the sun respectively. But in ordinary empirical experience they are taken to be transient when conditioned according to their presence or absence relative to some other thing, as when we say 'Fire *will* burn (when lit here in the kitchen)' and 'The sun *will* shine (here when it rises over the horizon in the morning)'. And it is in this way that superimposition onto the Self of happiness, pain, bondage, liberation and the like occurs in the course of worldly experience. The texts 'That thou art' and 'Verily, he came to know the Self' relate to such superimpositions, and their only purpose is to remove them.[7]

❖

3. And the existence of the Absolute is evident because it is the Self of all. Everyone is aware of the existence of his own Self. No one thinks 'I am not'. If the experience of one's own Self were not evident, everyone would have the feeling 'I do not exist'. And the Self (ātman) is the Absolute (brahman).

Nor would it be correct to object that, if the Absolute were really evident as one's own Self, it would already be known and in that case there would be no point in investigating it through the discipline of the Vedanta. For there is disagreement about its *nature*. The materialists, and uneducated people generally, think that the Self is simply the body endowed with consciousness. Others (another school of materialists) think it is the sense-organs, which they take to be themselves conscious. Others (a school of Buddhists) think it is the mind. Some (another school of Buddhists) think it is but a mere series of momentary flashes of consciousness. Others (another school of Buddhists) think it is the Void. Others (Pūrva Mīmāṃsakas) say that it is the transmigrating entity, the agent and experiencer, who exists separate from the body. Others (the Sāṅkhyas) say it is the enjoyer only and not an agent. Others (theistic teachers) affirm (in opposition to the Sāṅkhyas) that there exists over and above the individual souls a God (Īśvara) who is omniscient and omnipotent. Others (Vedantins) say that God is the Self of the experiencer. Thus there are many different conflicting views about the nature of the Self, and their supporters all resort to various arguments and pseudo-arguments and quotation of texts, not always according to their true meaning. Anyone who just picks up whatever he hears on this subject and accepts it without a properly conducted enquiry will fail to achieve the highest end of life and will court destruction.[8]

❖

4. By 'not knowable through the instruments of empirical knowledge' (aprameya) the text means that the Self is not subject to determination through perception or inference or other such means. You cannot say that the Self is determined

through the means of knowledge called revelation (āgama), having indeed been already known through perception and inference and other empirical means of knowledge earlier. For the Self is self-evident. Only when the Self is already self-established and self-evident as the one applying instruments of cognition can there be anyone desiring knowledge, and only when there is someone desiring knowledge can investigation through instruments of cognition proceed. One cannot proceed to investigate objects through instruments of cognition until one has first established 'Here am I, such and such'. In fact, there is no one who is unaware of his own Self.

When it is said that the Veda is 'The final instrument of cognition' (antyam pramāṇam), it means that it is an instrument of cognition only in the sense of putting an end to the erroneous superimposition onto the Self of properties that do not belong to it, not an 'instrument of cognition' in the (more usual) sense of 'that which makes a previously unknown thing known'.[9]

❖

5. But is it not a fact (asks an objector) that the Self is divided into parts by the ether and the other elements? No, we reply, for there is the text 'The ether arose from the Self'. (Taittirīya Upanishad II.1) Indeed, if the Self were a modification (and so an effect) of something else, then, because the Veda mentions no other being higher than it, all effects, beginning with the ether, would be without a Self, as the Self would itself be an effect. And this would amount to the doctrine of the Void. But denial of the Self is impossible, from the very fact of its being one's Self.

The Self is not anything that accrues to anyone adventitiously. It is self-evident (and self-established). It does not require to be known through any of the empirical means of knowledge to establish itself. On the contrary it *uses* perception and the other empirical means of knowledge to establish the existence of objects as yet unknown. No one admits that the objects of the world, beginning with (the first emanation from the Absolute, namely) the element ether, can establish their own existence independently without being known through one or other of the means of knowledge. But the Self is the support of the whole play of the empirical means of knowledge with their objects, and must already stand established before it could begin.

Such an entity cannot be denied. A thing which supervenes adventitiously can be negated, but a thing which exists in its own essential nature (svarūpa) cannot. And the Self is the essential nature of him who denies. Fire cannot deny its own heat (because heat is its essential nature).

Moreover, we have the feeling 'It is I alone who know the objects about me at this moment, and it was that same I who knew past objects and objects which came even before them, and who will know future objects and objects coming even later than them'. Thus, while the objects change in past, present and future, the knower does not change, for its very nature is to exist eternally in the present. Even when the body turns to ashes, the Self is not destroyed, for its very nature is to exist in the present, and a departure from this nature would be inconceivable. And from the very fact of its existence being uncontradictable, it follows that the Self is not an effect.[10]

2. The Absolute is not known as an object

The preceding section has shown that, although the Self is in one sense self-evident, its true nature is obscured for unreflective immediate perception. It is in accordance with our ordinary natural experience to conceive the Self differently at different times, for example as tired, happy or sad according to the states of the body or mind, whereas the Self also affirms itself, in contradiction to these successive changing states, as ever identical. Two other means of knowledge, however, apart from immediate unreflective perception, are open to man in his search for the true Self. They are revealed teaching (śruti, āgama) and critical reflection (vicāra). But the question to be raised in the present section is, can *any* means of knowledge reveal the Self, since to do so is to make the Self an object for a knowing subject. You cannot know anything as an object until you are separate from it and it is standing over against you as an object ready to be known. Vedic revelation and critical reflection, therefore, as applied to the Self, are primarily negative in character. They do not yield determinate knowledge of the Self as if it were an object: their function, rather, is to negate that which impedes the self-manifestation of the Self in its true form as infinite consciousness.

The Self is not, in its true nature, immediately accessible to the natural faculties and can only be known through Vedic revelation,[11] while the latter is fundamentally negative in character. We come to the Veda and expect it to convey knowledge of the Self to us through the medium of words. It is as if we were to ask 'Who is Devadatta?' and were to receive the answer, 'The man with the spotted cows'. Such an answer would keep our attention away from all but Devadatta's immediate possessions. But ultimately we could not know Devadatta himself until our attention had been withdrawn even from the cows. As Devadatta can only be known shorn of his cows, so the

Self can only be known shorn of all knowable characteristics communicable through words, though such characteristics can be used, as was the case with Devadatta's cows, as a means to focus attention onto the object of enquiry. So Śaṅkara says, 'Whatever in our conception of the Self is open to objective determination as a 'this' is other than the Self and a mere adjunct, external to it. When all the external characters have been eliminated, then one becomes directly aware of the true Self as the knower, as in the case of the man with the spotted cows'.[12] The following Extracts illustrate and develop these points.

TEXTS ON THE ABSOLUTE AS NOT KNOWN AS AN OBJECT

1. But is it not a contradiction to say that the Self is unknowable (aprameya) and yet known (jñāyate)? For 'It is known' means 'It is measured and determined by a means of knowledge (pramāṇa)', while to say that it is unknowable is a flat contradiction of this.

We reply that there is nothing wrong here, as it is only intended to say that the Self is not subject to determination by any means of knowledge other than the Veda as traditionally interpreted (āgama). Other entities are subject to determination by the empirical means of knowledge such as perception and inference conducted in a secular manner and independently of Vedic revelation. But the metaphysical principle (tattva) is not subject to determination by the empirical means of knowledge conducted in this way. The Veda denies that any activity on the part of an active knower or any empirical means of knowledge could apply to the Self, in such passages as 'When all has become one's own Self, through what could one see what?'[13] And this denial is itself the Veda's peculiar mode of conveying knowledge of the Self. The Veda does not employ language in the form of direct statement for this purpose. So the nature of the Self is not taught directly even by the Veda, though the latter does employ direct statement when revealing the existence of heaven, Mount Meru and other realities lying beyond the reach of our natural faculties. For the Self would be the Self of the expounder. And an exposition by an expounder is only possible when he has an object to expound. And that is only possible if he and the matter he has to expound are different.

Furthermore, knowledge of the Self only means ceasing to identify it with what it is not. One does not have to perform any special intuition to realize that one is the Self, as one is already identical with the Self by nature. Everyone is constantly aware of himself as the Self, but this awareness seems (through nescience) to apply where it has no right to apply. That is why the Veda does not give any positive teaching about the nature of the Self, but merely recommends one to cease from the false application of the notion of Selfhood to the realm of the not-self (such as the body, senses and mind). When the notion of Selfhood is no longer applied to the not-self and one has the feeling that one's own Self alone truly exists, then it is said (figuratively) that the Self is 'known'. In itself, however, it is not an object of cognition, since it is not an object that can be measured or determined by any means of knowledge standing outside itself. Hence it is 'known' (in one sense) and 'unknowable' (in another sense), without there being the slightest contradiction.[14]

2. If the metaphysical teachings of the Veda are purely negative in purport, will not this result in nihilism? No. For negation means negation of erroneous and illusory notions, and an illusory notion can only come into manifestation on the basis of a real substratum (āspada), as the illusory notion of a snake, for instance, arises on the substratum of a rope. But is it not a fact that the Advaitin regards the rope also, in the end, as a mere illusion, so that the accusation of nihilism still stands? No. For whenever an illusion is corrected, the ground on which it stands emerges as real from the very fact of being that which (in contrast to the illusion) is not imagined. Nor can you say that the ground (the Self) on which all illusions ultimately rest is itself an illusion like the rope-snake. For it is not imagined at all, and is therefore to be taken as (eternally) real, just as the rope-element in the snake-illusion was (from the empirical standpoint) real even before it was known that there was no snake. Moreover, it is admitted that the one who imagines the illusion must himself exist before the rise of the illusion, and must hence be real.

But how can the Veda put an end to knowledge of duality if it does not reveal the real positively? Well, it can. For duality is a mere superimposition on the Self, like the illusory snake superimposed on the rope. This is clear from the fact that mutually contradictory notions are successively superimposed onto one and the same Self in the form of such feelings as 'I am happy, sad, deluded, born, subject to death, old, engaged in perception, manifest, unmanifest, an agent, an experiencer of the fruits of my actions, possessed of something, dispossessed of something, worn out, decrepit and so on', as well as the notions 'I' and 'mine'. But amidst all these various conflicting notions, the notion of the Self is constant and identical, just as the rope is the constant identical factor amidst successive illusory notions like 'It is a snake', 'It is a stream of water', etc.

This being so, the true nature of the Self under investigation is already given, and the Veda does not have to establish it. The function of the Veda (as an organ of revelation) is to establish what cannot be established otherwise.[15] If it merely confirmed what was already established elsewhere, it could not be an authoritative means of knowledge. The function of the Veda, therefore, is to negate all these notions such as 'I am happy' and the rest by teaching that the only reason why the Self is not realized in its true nature is the presence of these very illusory (superimposed) notions, and that beatitude consists in realizing the true nature of the Self (through the mere rejection of false notions). This it does by engendering the contradictory notion 'I am not happy' in regard to any such notion as 'I am happy', with the help of such (negative) texts as 'Not thus, not thus' and 'Not gross, not subtle', etc.[16] But none of these contradictory notions like 'I am not happy' constantly pervades all the successive apparent states of the Self as the Self itself does. If they did, the superimposition of positive forms like 'I am happy' that contradict them could never arise, any more than the notion of coldness can arise in relation to fire, which is constantly associated with the idea of heat. Hence all such characteristics as 'I am happy' and the rest are mere superimpositions on a Self which has no empirical characteristics. This shows that the statements in the Veda implying that the Self is not happy, etc., have only the force of negating imaginary characteristics like 'happy': they do not positively ascribe such characteristics as 'unhappy' to it. One who knew the right tradition for interpreting the Veda (i.e. Draviḍācārya) left the maxim, 'The validity of the Veda stems from the fact that its function is to negate'.[17]

❖

3. It should not be objected that if the Absolute were not an object it could not be revealed by the Vedic texts. For the purpose of the Veda is to negate distinctions that have been imagined through nescience. It does not purport to expound the Absolute as an object knowable as a 'this'. On the contrary, in revealing the Absolute as a non-object and as the inmost Self, it abolishes all distinctions, including those between subject, object and act of knowledge. And there are texts explaining this in the Veda itself, such as 'It is known by him who does not know it, and he who thinks he knows it does not know it. It is not known by those who "know" it and it is known by those who do not know it', and 'One cannot see the seer of seeing' and 'One cannot know the knower of knowing'.[18]

❖

4. If (says an objector) the Absolute were an object of the activity of the organs of cognition such as the mind and the senses, it would be known determinately as 'This is that'. If on the other hand, the mind and the senses were at rest, then the Absolute would not be known at all for lack of anything to know it with, and it would verily not exist. For it is agreed in the world that what comes within the range of the organs of knowledge exists and that what does not do so does not exist. Therefore, yoga is useless.[19] Or else we might put it that where there is no experience there is no object of experience, in this case experience of the Absolute.

In face of this we reply that the Absolute cannot be apprehended through speech, through the mind, through the eye or through any of the sense-organs. Yet it definitely exists as, even though it is bereft of particular characteristics, it must exist as the ground of the universe. For everything which is an effect dissolves into some existent principle. All this world consists of a hierarchy of more and more subtle and comprehensive effects which stand as the material causes of whatever is grosser. And knowledge of this hierarchy leads to the notion of Being as its support. For although the notion of anything lapses with the lapse of the thing, it does so leaving the notion of Being intact. And it is the mind which is the authoritative means of knowledge for determining being and non-being.[20] If there were no ground of the universe, it would be apprehended as non-existent because associated with non-existence. But this is not in fact the case. Everything is invariably apprehended in association with existence, just as clay pots are invariably apprehended in association with clay.

Hence the ground of the world, the Self, must be apprehended as 'Is'. Why? Well, consider the case of the sceptic. He dissociates himself from the one who affirms Being, from the one who is endued with faith and adheres to the revealed Vedic teaching. He denies that any ground of the world exists. He maintains that the world, as effect, will dissolve into non-being. How, the Upanishad asks, can one of such self-contradictory opinions apprehend the Absolute as it really is? It means that one cannot possibly do so.

Therefore the devilish sceptical doctrine has to be refuted. The Self has to be apprehended as Being, and as having the intellect, the body and the senses for its (mere) external adjuncts, and as that which remains as Being when the latter have been dissolved. But, as we know from the text 'A modification is a name initiated by speech, the truth is "there is only clay",'[21] no effect exists as other than its (material) cause. Hence, when the Self is without external adjuncts or modifications of any kind, it stands forth in its true nature, with no empirical characteristics (liṅga), beyond all ideas such as Being or non-being. And one should here understand the additional idea 'It is under this form that the Absolute must (ultimately) be apprehended'....

The Absolute is first known as Being when apprehended through the (provisional) notion of Being set up by its external adjuncts, and is afterwards known as (pure) Being in its capacity as the Self, void of external adjuncts. The text now adds that the real nature of the Self apprehended as Being in these two different ways manifests itself (finally) as of pure non-dual nature, neither known nor unknown, as indicated in such upanishadic texts as 'Not thus, not thus', 'Not gross, not subtle, not short', 'Invisible, bodiless, without a support'.[22] It is only to the one who has already apprehended it (positively) in the form of Being that the Self manifests in its true transcendent form.[23]

❖

5. *Objection:* 'Where one sees nothing else, hears nothing else, knows nothing else, that is the Infinite (bhūman)'... (Chāndogya Upanishad VII.xxiv.1). When this passage speaks of not seeing anything else in the Infinite, does it merely mean

to deny that one sees the things that one ordinarily sees and which are different from the Infinite? Or does it affirm positively that one does see the Self?

What is at issue here? Well, if (as the Advaitin holds) it only means that one sees nothing else, then the force of the statement is simply to affirm that the Infinite is totally different in nature from the duality of ordinary experience. But if it means that one actually sees the Infinite through negating all other particular vision, then this is as much as to accept that within the Infinite, which is one, there obtains the distinction between action, its factors and results (since the Infinite is affirmed to be the object of the *act* of seeing). And this would mean that there could be no end to transmigratory life, since the distinction between action, its factors and results constitutes transmigratory life (saṃsāra). Perhaps it will be said that if the Self has been realized to be One, the distinction between action, its factors and results would then no longer spell transmigratory life?[24] But to argue thus is not right, for if the Self is admitted to be One and without distinctions, then this would nullify any real distinction between action, its factors and results, which is nevertheless implied by any act of seeing.

Against the other view (i.e. against the Advaita view) that the force of the text is merely to deny that one sees the other things that one ordinarily sees and which are different from the Infinite, it could be objected that the words (in the text quoted at the head of the present Extract) 'where' and 'else' would be meaningless, as the true sense would be adequately conveyed by the mere words 'He does not see (anything)'. And the objection could be further supported by an argument from ordinary experience, in that when it is said of someone in an empty house that he does not see anyone else, this is not taken to mean that he does not see himself (i.e. his own body) or the columns or walls of the building, so that the same sort of rule would apply here (and the Self would still be an object of the act of seeing).

Answer: But this objection is wrong. For there can no longer be any such distinction as that into container and content after the teaching of absolute unity in the text 'That thou art' and after the declaration of the sixth Chapter (of the Chāndogya Upanishad) that pure Being, one only without a second, was the real. And one cannot see one's own Self, as is clear from such texts as 'In Him who is invisible and bodiless', 'He has no form standing within the field of vision' and 'Through what could one know the knower?'[25]

Nor does this circumstance render the use of the word 'where' in the text meaningless, as it is merely used in relation to distinctions set up by nescience. It is parallel with the case where we speak of pure Being as 'One only without a second' when considering it in relation to the notions 'real', 'oneness' and 'non-duality' even though (from the standpoint of the highest truth) there is no propriety in relating the Absolute with number at all. It is in this way that the text can specify 'where' in relation to the Infinite, even though the latter is One (and undifferentiated).

And the phrase 'does not see anything *else*' is also meaningful. Its purpose is first to recapitulate the 'seeing of other things' that is familiar in the state of nescience, and then to use that recapitulation to show that the Infinite is characterized by the absence of such seeing of other things. In short, experience of the transmigratory world does not take place in the Infinite. Hence, where in the realm of nescience a subject who is one sees an object which is another through an instrument of cognition which is a third, 'That is next to nothing'. That is to say, it exists only during the time of nescience. It is like that which is seen in a dream, which lasts only till one wakes up. Hence it follows that what is seen in the realm of nescience is mortal and destructible. And that which is of the opposite nature, the Infinite, is immortal.

Then Nārada asks Sanatkumāra, 'My lord, on what is the infinite based?' Sanatkumāra replies that if the questioner insisted on an answer to the question 'What is its base?', one would have to reply that its base was its own incomprehensible magnitude. But if the questioner was asking for the ultimate truth, then the answer would have to be that it is not even based on its own incomprehensible magnitude. The Infinite is not supported on anything whatever.[26]

❖

6. But why is it that the people of the world do not comprehend the principle of supreme reality just referred to? It is because it is naturally hidden by blind addiction to the unreal, that is, by the obstinate tendency to perceive duality. The real is obscured by the mere perception of duality, without anything else being needed. And we know that it manifests only with difficulty, as a knowledge of the real is rare.

The term 'Bhagavān' here means the divine non-dual Self.[27] Though this principle has often been taught by the Upanishads and presented in many different ways by the

Teachers who expound them, still no one (i.e. very few people) comes to know it. For there is the text, 'Wonderful is the Teacher of it, rare the one who comes to know it'.[28]

Even the subtle conceptions of trained philosophers only succeed in hiding the true nature of the divine Self with predications and negations, and the case with the thoughtless people of the world is naturally worse. To develop this theme, the Teacher proceeds as follows. One philosopher, he says, affirms that the Self exists. Another, the sceptic, denies that it exists. A third, the semi-sceptic, belonging to the naked sect of the Jainas, who tries to combine existence with non-existence, predicates both existence and non-existence of the Self. The absolute Nihilist, the exponent of the Void, says, 'It does not either exist or not exist'.

If the Self were affirmed to exist, such existence would be transient, as it would not be different in kind from the existence of an object like a pot.[29] If it were denied that the Self existed, such non-existence would have to be eternal, because there are never any distinctions in non-existence.[30] To affirm (with the Jainas) existence and non-existence would be an illogical combination of both, as it would combine the transient with the eternal. And the last alternative would imply the (impossible) non-existence of anything.

Anyone who relies on any of these four modes of judgement, affirmative and negative, is a mere child in metaphysical matters. He fails to discriminate the true Self and attributes to it some nature that it does not possess, whether transient or eternal or both, or else he denies its existence outright. If even the trained philosopher is but a child when he is not awake to the Self, the case with the people at large, who are thoughtless by nature, is evidently far worse.

'It exists', 'It does not exist', 'It exists and does not exist' and 'It does not either exist or not exist' are the four modes of judgement that produce the conclusions found in the treatises of the loquacious philosophers; and the Self is covered over and concealed from such philosophers by the convictions generated by these four modes of judgement. Yet the truth is that these four modes of judgement do not touch the Self in any way. The sage who sees this Self, referred to in the Upanishads as 'the supreme Spirit known through the Upanishads',[31] sees all. He is omniscient and has penetrated to the final reality.[32]

3. The Path of Negation

The classical theologians of Western Christianity have recognized that the finite understanding has the option of several different paths in its approach to the Infinite, and these paths do bear a certain family resemblance to those pursued in Advaita Vedanta. The most profound knowledge of God is that which recognizes the utter inadequacy of all finite conceptions, and this can only be reached by the 'Via Negationis', the path of the negation of all the finite. But only a few courageous souls can face the aridity of this path from the outset, and for minds of a devotional cast the 'Via Eminentiae' may be more appropriate, the path in which laudable characteristics that fall within human comprehension are ascribed positively to the deity, but with the clear recognition that they are but imperfect indications of His nature, since He transcends finite comprehension. According to a third path, the 'Via Causalitatis', the mind fingers, as it were, the various causal principles that it can conceive as operating in the world, and attempts to mount through speculation of this kind to some conception of the deity as the first cause, and yet as that which lies beyond any causal principle that can be determinately conceived and from which all such principles proceed as effects. According to a fourth path, the deity is sought to be perceived as the light present within the human intellect, illuminating its knowledge of truth. According to a fifth path, the mind tries to mount up from things that are good and desirable for some particular end to that which is itself the supreme end, lying beyond all particular ends, and which is desirable for its own sake, the highest value and supreme good.

Something parallel to, though not identical with, these various paths can be found in Śaṅkara's texts. As we have already seen, he gives preference to the path of negation and regards it as indispensible for the final knowledge which confers liberation from ignorance and death. This preference will be reflected in the repeated references to the path of negation that will be found in the present source-book. Extracts specifically concerned with this teaching will be given in the present section, and then after some chapters treating of more positive phases of Śaṅkara's theology, the path of negation will re-appear in Volume II, Chapter VII, where it will serve to remind us how tentative, for Śaṅkara, all positive conceptions of the Absolute are. And the essentially negative character of Śaṅkara's teaching will again emerge at the core of his doctrine of the human soul to be given in Volume III, Chapter IX and also at frequent intervals in the culminating teachings on the practical path to be set out in Volume VI, Chapter XV.

The Extracts immediately to follow show us how Śaṅkara conceived the upanishadic wisdom as consisting essentially in negation. The Absolute cannot be denoted through speech, and negation is the fundamental process which leads to 'viveka' or discrimination of the true nature of the Self from that with which it is falsely overlaid, the highest goal of the Advaita discipline. It is clear from the illustration of the man trying to teach the idiot, which has been attributed to Draviḍa,[33] that the process Śaṅkara has in mind is not one of brute reiterated negation but of a gradually ascending series of successive affirmations. The texts of the Upanishads are not exclusively negative. They give many and varied positive accounts of the Absolute and of its relation to the world and the individual, which alternate with passages in which all empirically knowable qualities are denied. The various positive accounts of the Absolute are only approximations which have the function of bringing it down, so to speak, into the universe of discourse, so that the student can acquire *some* idea of it which can be corrected in the light of subsequent negations. If the opening passage of Chapter III of the second Book of the Bṛhadāraṇyaka Upanishad teaches that the five great elements that emanate from the Absolute are a reality, then the Absolute can initially be conceived as the cause from which they proceed.[34] But the purpose of the passage as a whole is not to teach that the Absolute is the cause of the world. The aim, rather, is to present the Absolute first in the *guise* of the cause of the world so as to give the student *some* idea of it. When some conception of the Absolute is once in his mind, then it can be purified by the later text 'Not thus, not thus',[35] which negates all empirically knowable characteristics of the Absolute, including that of being the cause of the world.

As we have already seen, Śaṅkara did not invent this method of interpreting the texts, but inherited it from earlier Teachers such as Gauḍapāda and Draviḍa.[36] It is known as the method of false attribution and subsequent denial (adhyāropa and apavāda).[37] And Śaṅkara explains that the Absolute cannot be expounded to the ignorant without the help of false attribution of qualities that it does not in fact possess.[38]

The technique of false attribution and subsequent denial has many applications.[39] For example, the Upanishads undoubtedly teach that the Absolute is devoid of all distinctions, all-pervading, the Self of all and ever asserting itself as one's own true Self. Yet there are passages in the Upanishads such as 'The knower of the Absolute reaches the Supreme'[40] which speak of the Absolute as though it were something that has to be 'reached' or 'attained'. Clearly the text is here accommodating its teachings to the ignorant perspective of the student. But its function, once more, is ultimately negative. Its force is not to teach that the Absolute has to be reached at all. It has the negative force of showing that, given the ignorant perspective of the student from which it is something that has to be 'reached', it cannot be 'reached' by anything except knowledge. And it shows also that the text 'He reaches spiritual sovereignty' that had just gone before[41] did not imply the kind of 'reaching' that involves motion.

Again, there are passages in the Upanishads saying that the Absolute 'has to be known', such as 'That eternal principle which rests in the Self has to be known'[42] and 'That whereby one hears what has never been heard before, thinks what has never been thought before, knows what has never been known before'.[43] On the basis of these texts one might think that the Absolute was an object that has to be known, like a house or a tree. But such texts have to be taken in conjunction with others, such as the one saying 'Other than the known'.[44] In the light of these other texts, it is seen that the force of the texts apparently implying that the Self had to be known is really the negative one of saying that there is nothing other than the Absolute which it is worth striving to know.

In some places, such as 'Through what could one know the knower?'[45] the Self is spoken of as a 'knower'. In the light of other statements[46] elsewhere, however, one has to interpret such a text not as a final affirmation that the Self is the agent in acts of cognition but simply as a denial that the Self is the object of an act of knowledge. Other passages[47] state that the Self is a mere Witness (sākṣin), and the force of these is not to affirm 'witnesshood' of the Self as an ultimately true fact, for in the end there is nothing else for it to witness. The purpose of such passages is to point to the inactivity of the Self and correct the idea that it could be the agent in an act of empirical cognition. Again, some passages like 'Those who have mastered the upanishadic wisdom'[48] appear to suggest that the Absolute can be known from the upanishadic texts in the same sort of way that an empirically knowable fact can be learned from a trusted friend. But the negative texts to which we have drawn attention make it plain that the real force of such a text is to show that the Self cannot be known through the secular means of knowledge such as perception and inference. Conversely, there are passages which have the external form of bare negation, such as 'That from which words fall back, together with the mind',[49] where the real purpose, as the context shows, is to affirm that the Absolute in its true nature *is* accessible to immediate experience when the latter has been purified of the natural superimpositions of nescience.

It is not the case that each statement about the Absolute has to be interpreted mechanically as effecting one specific negation only. It may have several purposes. For instance, when the Absolute is spoken of as 'what has to be known', this does not *merely* mean that nothing else should be the object of our ultimate quest. It also implies that through knowledge of the Absolute one achieves omniscience and destroys ignorance once and for all. And since all manifestation of duality rests on ignorance of the Self, we have to conclude also that when the Self is known there is no further room for the play of subject, object and act of empirical cognition. Thus, although the Self cannot in the end be anything that 'has to be known', nevertheless speaking of it as 'that which has to be known' is a means of negating a whole series of false ideas, such as the idea that we should seriously pursue the knowledge of anything else, the idea that when the Self is known there is anything further to know, the idea that nescience can reappear after knowledge, the idea that the world-appearance is anything real, the idea that the Self is an agent in any act of cognition after liberation, and so forth.

The general rule is: 'The supreme principle has no empirical characteristics. Wherever any empirical features are attributed to it in the holy texts, the ultimate purpose is the negation of some superimposed feature contradictory to the one affirmed, and not the affirmation of that character as a final fact'. For clear texts will always be found elsewhere negating any affirmed characteristic whatever.

In the chapters to come we shall constantly find Śaṅkara making what appear to be positive affirmations about the nature of the Absolute, the world and the soul. But they all have to be understood as part of a wider process, which is negative in character. Śaṅkara did not believe that all the ancient texts were concerned with conveying the metaphysical truth. Some were concerned with the physical performance of ritual, others with fanciful meditations to be performed in obedience to Vedic injunctions which were a mere extension of the ritual. But he did believe that all texts that were concerned with communicating the metaphysical truth were ultimately negative in intention, whether they were positive or negative in grammatical form. Their long-term purpose was to abolish all finite conceptions of the Self and allow it to shine in its true nature as infinite. There will be a return to this theme in Volume II, Chapter VII and Volume V, Chapter XIII.

TEXTS ON THE PATH OF NEGATION

1. But how can the mere phrase 'Not thus, not thus' be of service in communicating the true nature of the principle called 'the reality of the real'? It does so, we reply, by negating all particular external adjuncts (upādhi). The Absolute is that in which there is no particularity. There is no name, no form, no action, no distinction, no genus, no quality. It is through these determinations alone that speech proceeds, and not one of them belongs to the Absolute. So the latter cannot be taught by

sentences of the pattern 'This is so-and-so'. In such upanishadic phrases and words as 'The Absolute is Consciousness-Bliss', 'A mere mass of Consciousness',[50] 'Brahman', 'Ātman', the Absolute is artificially referred to with the help of superimposed name, form and action, and spoken of in exactly the way we refer to objects of perception, as when we say 'That white cow with horns is twitching'. But if the desire is to express the true nature of the Absolute, void of all external adjuncts and particularity, then it cannot be described by any positive means whatever. The only possible procedure then is to refer to it through a comprehensive denial of whatever positive characteristics have been attributed to it in previous teachings, and to say 'Not thus, not thus'.[51]

❖

2. Nor can the Absolute be properly referred to by any such terms as Being or non-being. For all words are used to convey a meaning, and, when heard by their hearers, convey the meaning the speaker had in mind. But communicable meaning is restricted, without exception, to genus, action, quality and relation. For example, in the case of the words 'cow' and 'horse', the meaning is conveyed on account of the presence of a genus. In the case of 'he cooks' or 'he reads' there is meaning because there is an action. In the case of the words 'white' or 'black', there is meaning on account of the presence of a quality. In the case of phrases like 'a man of wealth' or 'possessed of cows', there is meaning on account of the presence of a relation (here, that of possession).

But the Absolute does not belong to any genus, so it cannot be expressed by a noun such as 'Being' or 'non-being'.

Being without qualities, it cannot be described by any adjective denoting quality. And being actionless, it cannot be expressed by any verb denoting activity. For the Upanishad speaks of it as 'Without parts, without activity, at rest'.[52] Nor has it any relation with anything. For it is 'One', 'without a second', 'not an object' and 'the Self'. Hence it cannot be expressed by any word. And the upanishadic texts themselves confirm this when they say 'That from which words fall back'.[53]

❖

3. One cannot adopt either of any pair of alternative possibilities about the true essence of all which lies beyond all speech and conception, and say either that it is or that it is not, either that it is one or that it is many, either that it has qualities or that it is qualitiless, either that it has knowledge or that it does not have knowledge, either that it acts or that it does not act, either that it produces results or that it does not produce them, either that it contains the seeds of future actions or that it does not contain them, either that it is happy or that it is not happy, either that it is central or that it is not central, either that it is a void or that it is not a void, either that it is different from me or that I am different from it. Whoever wishes to characterize the nature of the Self in this way is like one wishing to roll up the sky like a piece of leather and climb up on it as if it were a step. He is like one hoping to find the tracks of fish in the water or of birds in the sky. For we have such upanishadic texts as 'Not thus, not thus' and 'That from which words fall back' and the phrase from the Ṛg Veda, 'Who indeed knows?'[54]

How then is knowledge of the Self acquired? In this connection they recount a little story. A certain idiot, it runs, was told by some people, on the occasion of some prank that he had committed, 'You ought to be ashamed of yourself, you're not even a man'. Being an idiot, he began to have doubts whether he really was a man, and, wishing to reassure himself on the point, went up to someone else and asked him, 'Sir, what am I?' The newcomer saw that he was only an idiot and promised to explain the matter by degrees. He took him through all the classes of living beings from plants upwards, showed him that he was none of them, and then remarked finally, 'So you are not anything that is not a man'. Then he said no more. The idiot replied, 'Sir, you were going to explain the matter to me, but you have suddenly gone silent. Why do you not explain it as promised?'

The question, 'How, then, is knowledge of the Self acquired?' is on a par with the last reply of the idiot. He who cannot understand that he is a man when told 'You are not anything that is not a man' will not be able to understand that he is a man when told 'You are a man' either. Hence the correct method for acquiring enlightenment is that taught in the Veda, and not any other. Everything has to be done in its own proper way. Straw and other combustibles can be burnt by fire but not by anything else. In communicating the true nature of the Self, the Veda proceeds in the same way as the one who showed the idiot that he was not a 'not-man'. It says 'Not thus, not thus' and then says no more.[55]

❖

4. And here you might raise the following objection. Since the Self is included in the subjects touched on by the Vedic hymns, you might say, how is it that Nārada can be a 'knower

of the Vedic hymns' and yet not a 'knower of the Self'? The objection is unjustified, however, because the distinction into name and named implies a modification, and the Self is not a modification (so that it cannot be named or described in the hymns).

Well, you may say, is not the Self designated by the name Ātman? No, it is not. For we have such texts as 'That from which words fall back' and 'Where he sees no other'.[56] Well then, you will say, in a passage like 'The Self (ātman), verily, is below',[57] the words beginning with Ātman denote the Self. But this is no objection against our position. When the word Ātman is used, on the plane where distinctions and differences hold good, to denote the inmost Self (pratyag-ātman) considered as possessed of a body, its function is to deny that the body or any other empirically knowable factor is the Self and to designate what is left as real, even though it cannot be expressed in words. Take the case of an army which one sees and which includes the king, even though the latter, in the midst of it, is hidden behind a barricade of parasols, flags and banners. It would still be quite normal practice to say 'That is the king you can see'. If the question were then asked, 'Which *exactly* is the king?', some idea of the king could still be had, even though he remained separate and invisible, through the negation of all the rest that was visible. It is in just this (negative) way that the word Ātman denotes the Self.[58]

❖

5. The Upanishad first denies all particulars of the Self in the text 'And so there is the teaching, "Not thus, not thus".'[59] Then, perceiving that if the Self is taught thus (merely in negations)

it is scarcely intelligible, the text proceeds to a series of other positive explanations, resorting to various indirect means. And then, once more, it denies everything said (positively) about the Absolute in the course of the explanations. It negates everything that is knowable, everything that has an origin, everything that is the object of a mental cognition.

In other words, in its successive reiterations of the phrase 'Not thus, not thus'[60] the Upanishad shows that the Self is not a perceptible object. It openly declares that the Self is unknowable, lest the one who did not realize that the various symbols were only introduced as a means (upāya) to convey the symbolized (and were not anything real in themselves) should think that the Absolute was knowable in the same way as the symbol was (i.e. as an object). This is the meaning of Gauḍapāda's verse.

And then (after the negation has been completed), for the one who realizes that the symbol was used merely to convey the meaning to be symbolized, and that the nature of the symbolized was in no way affected by the use of the symbol, the unborn Self shines forth of its own accord as the metaphysical reality, present within and without.[61]

❖

6. It (the Absolute) is not called Being, says the text, and neither is it called non-being. But is it not out of place to turn round and say 'It is not called either Being or non-being' when there had previously been so much emphasis on the idea 'I shall now proclaim to you that which has to be known'? [62]

No, it is quite in order. For the whole purport of the Upanishads is to convey knowledge of the Absolute, and yet it is only conveyed by a negation of all particulars, as in such texts as 'Not thus, not thus' and 'Not gross, not subtle'.[63] For the Absolute can only be expressed in the form of a negation saying 'This is not that', since it is beyond the range of words.

Here you might argue against us as follows. That to which the phrase 'It is' cannot be applied does not exist. What cannot be referred to as 'It is' cannot be anything that 'is to be known'. To say 'That has to be known' and 'It cannot be referred to as "It is"' is a contradiction.

We reply that the Absolute (on our definition) certainly does not *not* exist, as we do not apply to it the formula 'It does not exist'.

Perhaps you will reply that all notions must either assert or deny existence. This being so, a thing that has to be known must either be expressed in an idea that asserts existence or else in an idea that denies it. But this is wrong. For the Absolute is beyond the reach of the senses, and hence no notion either asserting or denying its existence can be applied to it. It is only to an object like a pot which stands within the range of sense-perception that one may apply a notion implying existence or non-existence.

But this particular object of enquiry, the Absolute, since it is beyond the range of the senses, can only be known through the authority of revelation. One cannot apply to it, as one could to a pot, any notions that imply either existence or non-existence. So it cannot be said to be either Being or non-being. Nor was it contradictory to say that the Absolute was something which had to be known and yet was at the same time neither Being nor non-being. For we have the Vedic text, 'It is other than the known, but higher than the unknown'.[64]

❖

7. If the Absolute as 'that which has to be known' was not the meaning conveyed by the word Being, one might conclude that the Absolute did not exist. So the following verse (i.e. Gītā XIII.13) is introduced to remove this idea and show that it does exist as that which has for its external adjuncts the organs of all living beings.

The existence of the 'Knower of the Body' (i.e. the Self as the unattached Witness of the physical and mental experiences) is brought out through attributing to it adjuncts such as the psychic and physical organs of all living beings. It is called 'The Knower of the Body' in relation to the illusory adjunct, the body (lit. the 'Field' in which the results of acts performed in previous births are 'reaped'). And the body itself is subdivided (in the verse) in various ways into organs such as hands and feet.

The idea that the whole complex of particular characteristics resulting from distinctions in the adjunct called the body really belong to the Knower of the Body is in itself false. So it was said (in the previous verse, Gītā XIII.12, cp. previous Extract) that the Self had to be known through negating that idea, the formula used being 'It is not called either Being or non-being'.

(The Absolute is that which ultimately has to be known.)

So, in order to show that it exists, it is first spoken of in its false form set up by adjuncts, and fancifully referred to as if it had knowable qualities in the words 'with hands and feet everywhere'. For there is the saying of those who know the tradition (sampradāya-vid) 'That which cannot be expressed (in its true form directly) is expressed (indirectly) through false attribution and subsequent denial'.

Hands and feet and other organs, which are known to all as they form parts of all bodies, and which derive their power to fulfil their functions from that Absolute which has ultimately to be known, are said figuratively to 'belong' to what has ultimately to be known because they are signs (liṅga) pointing to its existence. And the other characteristics attributed to the Absolute here are to be understood in the same way.[65]

❖

8. It has been explained how the Vital Energies (prāṇa) are called 'the real' (satyam). Their secret names (upaniṣat) have been explained in connection with those of the Absolute (brahman). With a view to explaining the nature of the five Vital Energies and the sense in which they are 'the real', this new section is begun to lay down the nature of the five great elements as 'reality' (satya) in both their causal and conditioned forms. But the ultimate aim is to show the true nature of the Absolute by negating these particular attributes through the formula 'Not thus, not thus', (occurring at the end of the passage, Bṛhadāraṇyaka Upanishad II.iii.6).

From this point of view, the Absolute may be considered to have two forms. It stands connected with the bodies and organs arising from the five elements. Hence it is 'the gross *and* the subtle'.[66] Its nature is both mortal and immortal. In so far as it consists of impressions (vāsanā) arising from activity amongst the elements, it is omniscient and omnipotent and open to conception by the mind. Being here of the nature of action, its factors and results, it is the basis of all activity and experience. But it is this very same Absolute which, as void of all particular external adjuncts, as the content of right knowledge, as unborn, deathless, immortal and beyond danger, as beyond the range of speech and mind on account of its non-duality, is taught negatively through the formula 'Not thus, not thus'. These, verily,[67] are the two forms which are negated when the Absolute is taught through the formula 'Not thus, not thus'.[68]

❖

9. The Vedic passage which begins 'Verily there are only two forms of the Absolute, the gross and the subtle'[69] divides the five great elements into two classes (the visible ones, earth, water and fire, and the invisible ones, wind and ether). Then it proceeds to speak of the forms of the 'essence' (rasa) of the subtle called Puruṣa, such as 'dyed with turmeric', etc. Finally it says, 'And so there is the teaching "Not thus, not thus". And it is called "Not thus" because there is nothing beyond this'.

Here we enquire into what it is that is being negated. For in the present passage no definite assertion of the form 'So and so is such and such' has been made which could be the direct object of the negation. That *something* expressed by the word 'thus' is being denied is clear from the use of the word 'not' in the phrase 'not thus'. The word 'thus' is normally used of that which has just gone before, as in 'Thus spoke the Teacher'.

Here the context shows that what have just gone before are the two forms assumed by the Absolute (brahman) when associated with the world-appearance, and also the Absolute itself, as that which has these two forms (gross and subtle).

Here a doubt may confront us. Does this negation negate both the forms and also that which has the forms (*viz.* the Absolute as it is in itself) or only one of these alternatives? If only one alternative, is it that it negates the Absolute and leaves the forms standing, or does it negate the forms and leave the Absolute standing?

And, seeing that both alternatives could be taken as forming the topic under discussion, we might at first suspect that the text negates both alternatives, especially as the words 'Not thus' are repeated, yielding two negations. One of the negations, we might think, negates the two forms (gross and subtle), and the other negates that which has the two forms, the Absolute. Or again, one might take the view that it is the Absolute itself, that which has the two forms, which is being negated, since the Absolute is beyond speech and mind, so that its existence is unprovable and subject to negation, whereas the world-appearance is not subject to negation as it is within the range of perception and other empirical means of knowledge....

Here we interpose with our own view and say: At all events negation of both alternatives cannot be right, as that would entail the doctrine of the Void. For that which is not real can only be negated on the basis of (the affirmation of) something which is real, as in the case of the rope-snake, etc.[70] And the whole process is conceivable only if some positive existent remains over after the negation. But if (as in the present context) both (the two forms of the Absolute and the Absolute itself) were negated, what other existent would be left over? If nothing else is to remain over existent after a negation, it turns out that what is sought to be negated cannot be negated and is therefore real....

The Absolute is referred to in this passage in the genitive case as that which *has* the two forms to be negated, not as the direct object of the negation itself. And after the description of its two forms, there would naturally follow a desire to know the nature of that which has the two forms, and this is answered by the formula 'And so there is the teaching "Not thus, not thus".'[71] And this is seen to be the way of communicating the true nature of the Absolute through negating its imaginary forms. For the entire world of effects resting in the Absolute is negated by the text 'Not thus, not thus'....But the Absolute itself cannot be negated as it is the presupposition of all imagination....

The Veda does not mention these two forms of the Absolute (as associated with its gross and subtle adjuncts) in order to affirm their existence. On the contrary, it takes up these two imagined forms of the Absolute, generally believed to exist, with a view to negating them and affirming the (sole) existence of the Absolute in its pure and true form. The negations, being two in number ('Not thus, not thus'), negate the two forms of the Absolute serially, the gross and the subtle, as they, also, are two in number. Or else the first negation negates the great elements and the second their subtle impressions. Or else in the expression 'Not thus, not thus' the (repeated) term 'thus' (iti) covers all possibilities, so that the meaning of the phrase as a whole is, 'Whatever the Absolute is thought of as being, that it is not'. For if it were only a specific negation that were being made, the question would remain over, 'Well, if the Absolute is not *that*, then what else is it?' But if there is a negation covering all possibilities, then, since all objects have been negated collectively, it follows that the Absolute must be that which is not an object, i.e. the inmost Self, and all further enquiry is silenced. So the conclusion would be that the text negates the whole world-appearance that has been imagined in the Absolute and leaves the Absolute over as the final remainder. And the text confirms this because it proceeds, after the negation, to affirm positively 'There is something else higher than this'. For if a total negation had been intended, implying the non-existence of anything, then how could the text have gone on to speak of 'something else higher than this'? [72]

❖

10. If the Lord were not-self, one could never have the conviction 'I am He'.[73] But if the Lord be taken as the Self, then the conviction 'I am He' extirpates all other notions. If the negations such as 'not gross'[74] and the like applied to something other than the Self, they would apply to something unknowable, and mention of them would have been useless. But if they are taken as applying to the Self, they are significant, as they negate all notions of (i.e. all identification with) the not-Self. Therefore the texts like 'Not gross' must be accepted as being for the sake of negating false super-impositions that have been made on the Self. If they were for the sake of negating anything anywhere else, they would be a mere (useless) description of vacuity. And again, if the ultimate

subject of the teaching of the Upanishads were anything other than the inmost Self of the enquirer, then texts such as 'Without Vital Energy, without mind, pure'[75] would be useless.[76]

❖

11. Because the Self cannot be negated, it is that which remains after the practice of saying 'Not thus, not thus' to all else. It is directly apprehended through the practice of saying 'I am not this, I am not this'. The ego-notion (on the contrary) arises from the notion that the Self is a 'this'. It falls within the sphere of the activity of speech. When once the notion that the Self is a 'this' has been negated, the ego-notion can never again be accepted as authentic, for it depends on the prior notion that the Self is a 'this'. A later idea cannot supersede an earlier idea (with the same referent) without contradicting and cancelling it (bādha). The one Witness is self-revealed. Because (as the light of Consciousness) it is the resultant awareness (phala) in all knowledge processes, it is itself never subject to contradiction and cancellation.[77]

❖

12. When the text says 'invisible' it means unknowable through any of the senses. For sight (dṛśi) is a general word for outer knowledge through the five sense-organs. The Self is not the object of the organs of action either.... It has no origin or support with which it is in constant (dependent) relation. It is colourless, in the sense either of having no attributes such as materiality, or else literally colourless, not white or any other colour. That which is here called colourless is the Indestructible Principle.[78]

The Indestructible Principle is without eyes and ears. The ear and the eye are the sense-organs whereby all living beings perceive name and form.... Texts such as 'He who is all-knowing and omniscient',[79] which declare that the Absolute has consciousness, suggest that it is equipped with eyes and ears and other sense-organs just like those in transmigratory life. This is negated in the present text by the words 'without eyes and ears'. And we have other texts of similar purport, such as 'He sees without eyes, He hears without ears'.[80]

Further, it is without hands and feet. That is, it is without any of the organs of action. Because it can neither act nor be acted upon, it is eternal and indestructible. And yet it encompasses all distinctions that go to make up the universe of living beings, from the creator-god Brahmā down to the meanest clump of grass. It is all-pervading like the ether. But it is more subtle than the ether, because it does not have sound or any of the other elements that portend grossness. For sound and the other attributes belong to ether, wind and the other elements, and make them progressively more gross in descending order.[81] Because these attributes are all absent in the Indestructible Principle, it is supremely subtle.

It is also not subject to diminution for this very reason. For that which has no body cannot increase or diminish according to whether its body increases or decreases, as an embodied thing can. Nor can it diminish through the diminution of its treasury, like a king. Neither can it diminish through the diminution of its qualities, first because it has no qualities and secondly because it is the Self of all.

Sages perceive this Indestructible Principle all around as

the Self of and the womb of all beings, as the earth is the womb of all terrestrial beings. The knowledge by which this principle is known is called the supreme knowledge (parā vidyā).[82]

4. Going Beyond the Mind

How is the Self finally known? According to Śaṅkara, the true nature of the Self must ever remain a mystery for the mind in its thinking capacity, for in this capacity it inhabits the realm of subject-object dualism, which the Self transcends. Subjective idealism, though implicit in some of Śaṅkara's texts, is not, as we have already seen, representative of his fundamental position. But the doctrine that it is possible to pass beyond identification with the mind and to go beyond subject-object experience is. This transcendence is not dependent on, or affected by, any of the transient states of the mind, such as the intense form of concentration attained in some forms of yogic practice (samādhi), or the dissolution of the mind in dreamless sleep.[83] The Self, the ultimate source of our being and knowledge, stands beyond the mind and illumines it with its light. The enlightened sage eventually passes beyond all cognition, even beyond the apprehension of the Self reflected in the mind as if in a mirror, and beyond the feeling 'I am a knower of the Absolute'.

It is not that the sage undergoes any change of nature on attaining enlightenment. It is simply that, when his ear has been attuned through the spiritual discipline provided by the Teacher, the supreme metaphysical texts of the Veda remind him of his own true nature and he refrains from seeking the Self externally. His position is like that of the villager who crossed a river with nine colleagues. Counting the members of his party, he became distressed because there were only nine, not ten. But a kindly bystander reminded him, saying 'Thou thyself art the tenth', and the villager was instantly aware of the situation. Similarly the Self is ever-present, ever in being, ever realized. It is like the necklace which one is wearing on one's own body but which one has forgotten and for which one is searching all over the house. It can only be found through knowledge, or rather through the removal of that ignorance which promotes the external search. The rejection of the not-self is effected through the administration of the key Vedic texts by a spiritually enlightened Teacher who follows the hallowed traditional methods.

TEXTS ON GOING BEYOND THE MIND

1. An illusory snake, imagined in a rope, turns out to be the reality when perceived in its true nature as the rope. Similarly, the mind turns out to be a reality when perceived in its true nature as the Self, of the nature of true knowledge. In dream, however, the mind oscillates as subject and object to produce an appearance of duality through illusion, like the false appearance of a snake arising in a rope. And in the waking state, also, it oscillates as subject and object to produce the appearance of subject and object in exactly the same way.

In the case of dream, there can be no doubt that the mind assumes a mere appearance of duality while remaining non-dual in its true nature as the Self, just as the erroneously imagined snake remains throughout real in its true nature as the rope. For in dream there are in reality neither the elements which are beheld as objects nor the eyes and other sense-organs which 'perceive' them. There is nothing but consciousness. And our argument is that it is exactly the same in waking experience too. There, too, the only reality is consciousness, so that from this point of view there is no difference between the states of waking and dream.

It has been affirmed that it is verily the mind that assumes the form of duality, itself (i.e. the mind) a mere imagination like a snake imagined in a rope. What is the proof of this? The sage Gauḍapāda replies that it is an inference based on the method of agreement and difference,[84] and proceeds to analyse it as follows.

The proposition to be proved is, 'This whole duality seen by the imagined mind is itself nothing but mind'. The reason advanced is that when the mind is present, duality is also present (agreement, anvaya), and when the mind is not present, duality is not present (difference, vyatireka). For duality is not perceived when the mind has reached the state known technically as 'no-mind', that is to say when its movements have been suppressed through the practice of discriminative insight and dispassion; nor is duality perceived when the mind is dissolved in dreamless sleep like the snake dissolved in the rope. From this we conclude that duality is unreal.

And how is this state called 'no-mind' to be achieved? The sage Gauḍapāda explains the matter as follows. Only the Self is real, in the same way that only the clay is real and not its effects (pots, etc.), as is shown by the Vedic text, 'A modification is a mere name, a mere activity of speech: the truth is, there is only clay'.[85] To become awake to this through the instruction of the Veda and the Teacher is to become awake to the reality of the Self. When this occurs, there is no more imagining and there is nothing more to imagine, just as there can be no more burning when there is no more fuel. When this has resulted, a person is in the state called that of 'no-mind'.

And because there is then nothing to perceive, his mind perceives nothing and is without that imaginary process called perception.

But you might ask here who it was that became awake to his own true nature as the unborn Self if all this world of duality were unreal. To this the sage Gauḍapāda replies as follows. The enlightened ones, he says, proclaim that the pure principle of knowledge, void of all representations, is identical with the Absolute, the highest reality, that which has to be known. No break is ever found in the knowing of the knower, any more than there is a break in the heat of fire. This is confirmed by such texts as 'The Absolute is Knowledge and Bliss' and 'The Absolute is Reality, Knowledge, the Infinite'.[86]

It is this knowledge which is said in the text to 'have the Absolute for its object'. That knowledge which 'has the Absolute for its object' is itself the Absolute, as non-different from the Absolute as heat is from fire. The Self knows itself as unborn through this unborn knowledge, which is its own nature. Like the sun, which is constant light by nature, the Absolute requires no other knowledge to illuminate it (so that it is not an 'object' of knowledge in the generally accepted sense). For it is a mass of pure, homogeneous light.[87]

❖

2. Whatever is seen anywhere, at any time, in any intellect, is seen by (the real 'I' ever present in) me. Therefore I am the Absolute, the supreme, omniscient and omnipresent. As I am the one Witness of the activities of my own mind, so am I the one Witness in the minds of others. I am subject neither to increase nor to diminution. Therefore I am the Supreme.

The Self is not subject to mutation, neither is it impure or material. Being the Witness of all minds everywhere, it is not of limited knowledge like the mind.

Just as the red hue and other qualities of a jewel stand illumined in sunlight, so do all things stand illumined in and by me as if by sunlight.

Objects exist in the mind, but only when the mind is in manifestation.[88] But the Witness ever remains as Witness. This proves that duality does not exist.[89]

Just as the mind first fails to see the Supreme through lack of discrimination, so, when discrimination supervenes, nothing exists apart from the Supreme, not even the mind itself.[90]

❖

3. Just as, when a person's body is standing in light he identifies himself with it and thinks it is manifesting on its own account,[91] so also does he identify himself with his mind, which in fact only reflects the light of the true knower, and thinks 'I am the knower'. The deluded soul in the world identifies himself with whatever he sees, and this is the cause of his not finding his own true Self. Just as the tenth person regarded himself as included within the nine he was counting, so the deluded people of the world identify themselves with the objects of experience. Were it not for this, they would be aware of their own Self in its true nature....

When the yogin has a mental cognition in which the Witness as pure Consciousness is reflected like a face in a mirror, he is apt to think he has seen the Self. But only he deserves to be called the best of yogins[92] who has risen beyond this as beyond all other false notions. But because the Veda says 'Thou art He who is the Knower of Knowing'[93], this must be the immediate experience (anubhava) of the highest yogin. And all other experience is false. How can there be either vision or absence of vision in Me, who am of the nature of eternal Consciousness? Therefore we do not admit the existence of any experience apart from that (i.e. eternal Consciousness).

Just as the Witness witnesses the heat arising from the sun and afflicting the body as an object located in the body, so does it witness the passions afflicting the mind as objects located in the mind. I am the Absolute, transcendent, ever free and unalloyed. I am the knower, homogeneous like the ether, without a second, the negation of the element of 'this'.[94] There can be no other 'knower of knowing' beyond Me. Therefore I am the supreme knower in all beings, ever free. He only is a knower of the Self who is aware of himself as unbroken light, void of agency, and who has lost the feeling 'I am the Absolute'.[95] The discriminative cognition of the mind 'I am the knower, not to be known as an object, eternally pure and free' is itself an object to the Witness and hence transient.... The notion that the Self is an agent is false as it arises from the false idea that the body is the Self. The true notion arises from the appropriate authority (the Vedic texts) and is 'I do nothing'.... As the ether pervades all from within, so do I pervade the ether from within, changeless, immovable, pure, beyond decay, liberated, eternal, without a second.[96]

❖

4. From the standpoint of the highest truth, the individual is

already the Absolute. But he identifies himself with the body and other finite external organs composed of the elements. His mind becomes engrossed in these, and resembles the mind of the villager, who, engrossed in counting the number of his confederates, failed to take note of his own self which would have completed the number, even though he was in no way separated from it. Like the mind of the villager, man takes his own true Self, the supreme reality, to be non-existent and on account of this ignorance he identifies himself with various external 'selves' such as the physical body (and the mind), and will not admit that he is anything different from the aggregate of them. In this way the Absolute remains 'unattained' through ignorance, even though it is one's own Self.

Such a one, then, fails through ignorance to attain to his own true nature, the Absolute, to his own true Self, to the one thing that would complete his enumerations. But when he is reminded of it by anyone, he 'attains' it through knowledge. And thus it is reasonable to speak of someone enlightened by the Veda as 'attaining' the Absolute by acquiring vision of it as his own Self through spiritual knowledge, even though he is already the Absolute and the Self of all.[97]

❖

5. Attainment of the Self is nothing other than knowledge of the Self. Attainment is not here, as it is in other contexts, attainment of something that one does not already possess, because there is here no difference between the attainer and that which he wishes to attain. If the Self wished to attain the not-self, then the Self would be the attainer and the not-self the object of his attainment. And that object of its attainment

would be something not already possessed, something which required action for its attainment or even production. It would have to be attained by some act brought about by the requisite instruments of action. Such an object of attainment, not yet possessed, would necessarily be impermanent. It would proceed from action, which in turn proceeds from desire, itself born of wrong knowledge. Its 'attainment' would be like the 'attainment' of a son in a dream.

But this Self is the opposite. As it is one's own Self, it never becomes separated from itself through the typical forms of activity such as production. Being eternally attained by nature, the only impediment to its possession is ignorance. One may be perceiving a piece of nacre and yet not perceive it on account of its appearing through error as a piece of silver. Here the only barrier to the possession of the nacre is wrong knowledge, and right knowledge is the only means for its attainment, because right knowledge has the quality of cancelling wrong knowledge, the obstacle to the attainment of the nacre. The same is the case with the Self. In non-attainment of the Self, the sole barrier is ignorance. Therefore attainment of the Self can never be anything other than removal of ignorance regarding it through right knowledge.[98]

❖

6. Because the Absolute is the hearer of hearing and the seer of seeing, etc., the eye cannot attain to the Absolute, for nothing can attain to its own self (i.e. act upon it as an object). Neither can speech attain to it. For we speak of speech 'attaining' some matter when words are pronounced through

speech and they reveal it. But the Absolute is the Self both of words and of the instrument (speech) through which words are pronounced. So speech cannot attain to it. Just as fire burns and illuminates but cannot illuminate itself, so speech cannot express the Absolute, its own Self. Neither can the mind. The mind can imagine or determine things other than itself, but it cannot imagine or determine its own true Self. And its Self is the Absolute.

Things are known determinately (vijñāna) through the sense-organs and the mind. But we cannot know the Absolute determinately as 'such and such' because the Absolute does not fall within their range. Hence, as the Upanishad proceeds to say, we do not know how the Absolute can be taught, that is, be taught to a pupil. That only which is an object of the instruments of cognition can be taught to another, and it is taught by indicating its genus, qualities or active properties.[99] Hence, because it is a difficult matter to communicate the Absolute to pupils by word of mouth, special efforts have to be made. That is what the text means when it says 'We do not know how it should be taught'.

The text, having first implied that there is no way of teaching the Absolute at all, now goes on to show that this is not in fact the case. It is true enough that the Absolute cannot be known through any of the empirical means of knowledge beginning with perception. But it can be communicated through a traditional method (āgama), and the text goes on to state that method in the words 'It is other than what is known and higher than the unknown'. That is to say, the 'Hearer of Hearing' under consideration is not an object of hearing, speech or the other faculties mentioned. It is other than what is known. Whatever is known comes completely within the purview of cognitive activity, becomes its object. As such, it is something known to someone somewhere. Whatever is (thus) manifest is called 'known'. The Absolute is other than that. Are we then to say that it is unknown? No, it is higher than the unknown, higher than that which is the opposite of what is known, higher, namely, than the principle called the Unmanifest, which is the seed of the manifest, of the nature of nescience.[100] That is to say, it has a different nature. For what is higher than something is quite evidently different from it.

Whatever is known is fragmentary, transient, of the nature of pain and to be rejected. Therefore, when the Absolute is said to be 'other than the known' it is implied that it is not to be rejected. And when it is said that it is 'above the unknown' (i.e. above the Unmanifest Principle) it is implied that it is not subject to being 'accepted'. An instrument of action (e.g. a tool) is 'accepted' (taken up) by someone other than that instrument for the sake of producing an effect that is something different again. And so the (ultimate) Knower does not have to resort to any means different from Himself to attain any goal different from Himself...

When the text proceeds with the words 'Thus have we heard', it implies that the meaning of the texts which affirm that the Absolute is the light of pure Consciousness, devoid of all particularity and the Self of all, has to be learned from the teachings of a Teacher (ācārya) who belongs to a traditional line, and not through independent reasoning, even though it be supported by culture, intelligence, wide learning, austerities, sacrifices or any other auxiliaries.[101]

7. Now the reasoning is being given to show why the Self is nameless and birthless and sleepless, etc., as explained in the previous verse.[102] Speech is the organ of all naming, and the Absolute is beyond speech. In fact the word 'speech' is used here metaphorically to stand for all forms of external physical activity. It is also beyond all thought. That is, it is without any mind (buddhi) or internal organ (antaḥ-karaṇa). For we have such texts as 'Without Vital Energy (prāṇa), without mind (manas), pure, the Spirit stands beyond even the Indestructible Principle'.[103]

Because the Self is Consciousness unassociated with objects, it is supremely peaceful. Being Consciousness-by-nature, the Self is eternal light. It is called one-pointed meditation (samādhi) because it can only be known in the high state of consciousness (prajñā) attained in one-pointed meditation (samādhi). Or else the term one-pointed meditation (samādhi) may here be interpreted as meaning 'That on which one-pointed meditation (samādhi) takes place'. It is not subject to change and is for this reason not subject to fear (or danger).

Because the Absolute (brahman) is of this nature, more follows. Neither acceptance nor rejection occur in it. For gain and loss can only occur where there is change or possibility of change. And there is no change in the Absolute. For nothing external to the Absolute exists to bring about change in the Absolute, and the Absolute is in itself constant and eternal and also without parts. A further implication is that where there is no thought, on account of there being no mind, there can be no acceptance or rejection.

Whenever true knowledge of the Self arises, then that

knowledge exists in the Self, like heat in fire, as it does not bear on any external object. Such knowledge is (the) unborn (Principle of pure Consciousness). It is homogeneous throughout.[104]

NOTES TO CHAPTER III

References to Extracts are in bold type

1 G.K.Bh. II.32.

2 Above, Chapter II, section 3, introduction, para 3.

3 G.K.Bh. II.32, trans. Gambhīrānanda, 259. The point will be established in more detail below, Vol.V, Chapter XIII, section 1.

4 See below, Vol.III, Chap.VIII, section 3, Extract 5.

5 Bh.G.Bh. XVIII.50.

6 Bṛhad. I.iv.10.

7 Kena (Vākya) Bh. I.3.

8 B.S.Bh. I.i.1.

9 Bh.G.Bh. II.18.

10 B.S.Bh. II.iii.7.

11 For details, see Vol.V, Chap.XIII, sections 1 and 2.

12 U.S. (verse) VI.5.

13 Bṛhad. II.iv.14.

14 Bṛhad. Bh. IV.iv.20.

15 Cp. Note 3 above.

16 Bṛhad. II.iii.6 and III.viii.8.

17 On Dravida, see above, 27ff. **G.K.Bh. II.32.**

18 Kena II.3 and Bṛhad. III.iv.2. **The Extract is from B.S.Bh. I.i.4.**

19 If yoga is conceived as the discipline leading to the direct intuitive knowledge of the Absolute and the latter does not exist, yoga is evidently useless. Opponents of the view that

yoga could lead to a knowledge of the Absolute were the Mīmāṃsakas. Any claim to supra-normal knowledge threatened the sovereign authority of the Veda, in their eyes the sole source for knowledge of matters beyond man's usual ken, and an authority to be accepted in passive acquiescence. Biardeau, *Connaissance*, 81.

20 Cp. the similar point that existence and non-existence depend on our notions, 206 below.

21 Chānd. VI.i.4.

22 Bṛhad. II.iii.6, Bṛhad. III.viii.8, Taitt. II.7.

23 Kaṭha Bh. II.iii.12-13.

24 On the ground that one could no longer be taken in by such an illusory distinction.

25 Taitt. II.7, Kaṭha II.iii.9, Bṛhad. II.iv.14.

26 Chānd. Bh. VII.xxiv.1.

27 Sac, M.R.V., 420, quotes V.P., VI.v.71, which says that the Absolute, though beyond speech, is figuratively referred to as 'bhagavān', the Lord.

28 Kaṭha I.ii.7.

29 Reading ghaṭādy-anitya-vastu-lakṣaṇatvāt with M.R.V., 417.

30 Śaṅkara reiterates this view a little more explicitly at Bh.G.Bh. XVIII.48, quoted towards the end of the section of Extracts refuting the Vaiśeṣikas to be given at Vol.IV, Chap.XI, section 4, Extract 8, below.

31 Bṛhad. III.ix.26.

32 G.K.Bh. IV.82-84.

33 Sac, Ś.Ś.P.B., Book.I, 22. English version, Vol.1, 29f.

34 Bṛhad. Bh.II.iii.1, introduction, trans. Mādhavānanda, 228.

35 Bṛhad. II.iii.6.

36 See above, Chap.I, section 6.

37 Bh.G.Bh. XIII.13, Extract 7 of present section. The word 'apavāda' is etymologically cognate with the English word 'apophatic'.

38 Praśna Bh. VI.2, trans. Gambhīrānanda, Vol.II, 483. We have already glanced at an earlier Buddhist text proclaiming the doctrine, Chap.I, 25.

39 Cp. Sac, Ś.Ś.P.B. Book II, 22f., English, Vol.II, 41ff.

40 Taitt. II.1.

41 Taitt. I.6.

42 Śvet. I.12.

43 Chānd. VI.i.3.

44 Kena I.4.

45 Bṛhad. II.iv.14.

46 Ait. Bh. II.i.1 (introduction), see the opening of Extract 3 of present section.

47 E.g. Śvet. VI.11.

48 Muṇḍ. III.ii.6.

49 Taitt. II.9.

50 Bṛhad. III.ix.28, Bṛhad. II.iv..12.

51 Bṛhad. II.iii.6. **Bṛhad. Bh. II.iii.6.**

52 Śvet. V1.19.

53 Bṛhad. II.iii.6, Taitt. II.4. **Bh.G.Bh. XIII.12.**

54 Bṛhad. II.iii.6, Taitt. II.4, R.V. III.54.5.

55 Ait. Bh. II.i.1 (introduction).

56 Taitt. II.4, Chānd. VII.xxiv.1.

57 Chānd. VII.xxv.2.

58 Words cannot communicate any image of the king. But they can direct the mind to the king, first by excluding anything that is not the army and then by excluding anything visible in the army. **Chānd. Bh. VII.i.3.**

59 Bṛhad. II.iii.6.

60 Bṛhad. II.iii.6, III.ix.26, IV.ii.4, IV.iv.22.

61 G.K.Bh. III.26.

62 Bh.G. XIII.12. The objector thinks that what is indefinable cannot be proclaimed.

63 Bṛhad. II.iii.6, etc., as in Note 54, also Bṛhad. III.viii.8.

64 Kena 1.4. **Bh.G.Bh. XIII.12.**

65 Bh.G.Bh. XIII.13.

66 These are the 'two forms' of the Absolute that will be negated in the last sentence of the Extract.

67 See previous Note.

68 Bṛhad. Bh. II.iii.1 (introduction).

69 Bṛhad. II.iii.1, cp. previous Extract.

70 In order to negate the rope-snake, one has to have positive knowledge of the rope.

71 Bṛhad. II.iii.6.

72 B.S.Bh. III.ii.22.

73 For the fundamental identity of the soul with the Lord, see Vol.III, Chap.VIII, section 4.

74 Bṛhad. III.viii.8.

75 Muṇḍ. II.i.2.

76 U.S. (verse) III.1-4.

77 U.S. (verse) II.1-3.

78 The word rūpa means both colour and form or shape.

79 Muṇḍ. I.i.9.

80 Śvet. III.19.

81 For the theory of the elements, see Chap.VI, section 3, below.

82 Muṇḍ. Bh. I.i.6.

83 Na cāyaṃ vyavahārābhāvo 'vasthā-viśeṣa-nibaddho, B.S.Bh. II.i.14.

84 In reasoning by the method of agreement and difference (anvaya and vyatireka), one reviews one's experience and notes what things have been observed in (anvaya) constant concomitance (e.g. smoke and fire) and what things are (vyatireka) either never observed in association or only occasionally so (e.g. smoke and water). From constant concomitance arise universal laws from which further deductions can be made.

85 Chānd. VI.i.4. Clay pots appear at first sight to have independent existence, but on reflection it is seen that they are nothing apart from the clay of which they are composed. They are only the clay, arbitrarily given a separate name for practical purposes. Similarly, the objects of the world are only Being, arbitrarily given names for practical purposes.

86 Bṛhad. III.ix.28.7 and Taitt. II.1.

87 G.K.Bh. III.29-33.

88 I.e. in waking and dream but not in dreamless sleep.

89 According to the principle enunciated at G.K. II.6, 'What does not exist before its beginning and after its end does not exist even between the beginning and end.'

90 U. S. (verse) VII.1-6.

91 I.e. the body could not be manifest without light from some external source, but in ordinary experience we do not reflect on this.

92 Reading śreṣṭho not preṣṭho.

93 An adaptation of Bṛhad. III.iv.2.

94 Cp. Extract 11 of preceding section (section 3) above.

95 Cp. Kena (Pada) Bh. II.1.

96 U.S. (verse) Chapter XII (with omissions).

97 Taitt. Bh. II.1.

98 Bṛhad. Bh. I.iv.7. *ad fin.*

99 Cp. above, section 3, Extract 2 *ad init*. The same idea is touched upon at Māṇḍ. Bh. 7 (introduction) trans. Gambhīrānanda, 204, and U.S. (verse) XVIII.28.

100 Sac explains in his ṭīkā to this passage that the Unmanifest is nowhere identified with nescience. Name and form in their unmanifest state constitute the world-seed and are themselves imagined through nescience, cp. B.S.Bh. II.i.14 (trans. Gambhīrānanda, 333f), Bṛhad. Bh. I.iv.7(trans. Mādhavānanda, 79). More detail on this topic will be found at Vol.II, Chap.VI, section 2, below.

101 Kena (Pada) Bh. I.3 and 4.

102 G.K.Bh. III.36.

103 Muṇḍ. II.i.2.

104 **G.K.Bh. III.37-38.** The reference in this Extract to 'samādhi' as a 'state' in which the Absolute is known goes back to the G.K., and is uncharacteristic of Śaṅkara's Vedantic teaching as a whole.

CHAPTER IV

THE ABSOLUTE AS BEING, CONSCIOUSNESS AND BLISS

1. The Definition of the Absolute as 'Reality, Knowledge, Infinity'

We have seen that, like his counterparts among Christian theologians, Śaṅkara admitted that there were several different lines of approach which the mind could take in its advance towards knowledge of the Absolute, before the final leap into the abyss of transcendence.[1] We have seen, also, that Śaṅkara's theology was basically a path of negation. For him, the full significance of the upanishadic texts could only be seen when they were viewed collectively as constituting an affirmation of the Self in various finite forms that had to be corrected and purified of all empirical elements through negation. The Extracts of the previous chapter emphasized chiefly the negative part of this process and showed that Śaṅkara's teaching is ultimately a doctrine of transcendence. But the path that ends with transcendence begins with affirmation, and the texts from Śaṅkara that are concerned with the initial affirmation can be divided into two groups, corresponding to a similar division to be found in the upanishadic texts on which he was commenting. In the present chapter we shall be concerned with Extracts that argue affirmatively that our experiences in this world imply a positive ground lying behind the world-appearance as its basis and support. In the chapter to follow (in Volume II) we shall find Extracts in which Śaṅkara uses arguments of a more teleological kind, which point out the need to assume a personal God as creator and controller of the phenomenal world in which we live.

Broadly speaking, the texts brought forward in the previous chapter were those dealing with the process of passing beyond metaphysical enquiry to direct mystical experience; those presented in the present chapter deal with the Absolute as an impersonal principle and an object of metaphysical enquiry; while those in the chapter to follow will deal with that same principle viewed in a more anthropomorphic guise. From the highest standpoint, the existence of the world and its objects is denied. But given the fact that we appear to live in a world of limitation, change and suffering, the Extracts of the present chapter argue that this very experience implies the existence of an impersonal ground that is not characterized by limitation, change or suffering. And those of the chapter to follow argue that, viewed from the standpoint of worldly experience in which we live, this same Being may be endowed with personality and regarded as a divine magician who projects and controls the universe, animating and presiding over it from within. The texts of the previous chapter were mainly concerned with direct experience (anubhava) of the Self. Those of the present chapter are mainly concerned with that process of metaphysical enquiry (vicāra) without which the supreme texts of the Upanishads, which lead to direct experience of the Self, cannot be understood. The group presented in the chapter to come also embraces 'vicāra' but covers a phase of it in which it merges with devotion (bhakti) to a deity conceived in personal form.

The passages quoted in the previous chapter revealed the setting in which Śaṅkara's theology, taken as a whole, must be viewed. His doctrine must not be taken as an 'ontology' in the Western sense, but rather as a practical path of mysticism in which all duality is eliminated from the student's experience step by step. This dynamic element in Śaṅkara's teaching is also illustrated in his treatment of the upanishadic text to be considered in this opening section of the present chapter, a text from the Taittirīya Upanishad in which the Absolute (brahman) is defined as 'Reality, Knowledge, Infinity' (satyam, jñānam, anantam). It is a text which lays down some of the guidelines which show where metaphysical enquiry has to run. Metaphysical enquiry seeks for 'Reality' as the self-existent principle that appears from the standpoint of nescience as the first cause. It seeks for 'Knowledge' as the inmost unchanging Witness present within the human mind and illumining it with its unchanging light while the passing images come and go. And it seeks for 'Infinity' as the principle of beatitude or bliss in which there is no division, duality, limitation or suffering. After the present section has given an account of Śaṅkara's treatment of the definition of the Absolute mentioned above, the following three sections of the present chapter will deal in turn with the search for the Absolute as first cause, as the self-luminous principle within the human personality, and as the principle of infinitude and bliss. It is true that the above-mentioned definition speaks only of infinitude and not of beatitude or bliss. And it is also true that the famous Advaitic definition of the Absolute as 'Being-Consciousness-Bliss' (sac-cid-ānanda) does not appear in Śaṅkara's certainly authentic works. But it is appropriate to deal with Śaṅkara's doctrine of the Absolute as Bliss here, as the Upanishads do also describe it as 'Consciousness-Bliss' (vijñānam-ānandam),[2] and the formula 'Reality-Knowledge-Bliss' is already found in Śaṅkara's direct pupil Sureśvara.[3]

As we shall see in the Extract immediately to follow, Śaṅkara accepts the traditional Indian view that the function of definition is to mention the characteristics that mark off the objects or object denoted by the term from all else.[4] On this view, and in some contrast with traditional Western logic, definition is more concerned with the extension of the term, with delimiting the range of objects to which it applies, than with its comprehension, with bringing out the essential attributes that it connotes. The defining characteristic is not chosen to distinguish the class of objects or the object denoted by the term from others *and* to relate it to them, but *solely* to distinguish it. We have definition solely by the difference, not by the genus and specific difference. The defining mark of the class 'cow' is 'having a dewlap', and the definition need in no way bring out the fact that the cow is an animal and a mammal and a ruminant and so forth. On such a view, when the class or universal is granted objective existence, as it is in Hindu philosophy, the definition of a universal term and of the class of objects for which it stands amounts to the same thing. And it follows further that definition is not confined, as it is in traditional Western logic, to concepts and universal terms; as definition does not imply the mention of essential attributes, it can very well apply to an individual within a class, merely by mentioning sufficient delimiting characteristics to mark that individual off from its fellows within the class.

Thus Śaṅkara cites the phrase 'The large fragrant blue lotus' as marking out an individual from other members of its class. He then introduces an opponent who points out that definitions in this case only apply to individuals that exist within classes and have separate characteristics not possessed by all the individuals within the class. The phrase 'blue lotuses' then marks off a certain group of lotuses from those of other colours. But the Absolute is unique, so the mention of particular characteristics will not mark it off from others of its class.

This objection is merely introduced to show that, in the case of a unique entity like the Absolute, definition is achieved not by marking it off from others of its class but by marking it off from everything else whatever. And from this other points arise. When we mark a particular individual off from others of its class by mentioning the particular characteristics which it has but they do not have, we 'characterize' it. We treat it as a substance having such and such attributes which we can enumerate. But the phrase 'Reality, Knowledge, Infinity' is not a 'characterization' (viśeṣaṇa) of the Absolute but merely a 'definition' (lakṣaṇa) of it. Where there is characterization, the empirical characteristics attributed to the individual characterized must belong to it *as attributes*. But where there is only definition, it is enough if the characteristics merely serve to debar the mind from thinking of anything other than the unique entity being defined. They may indicate the whole nature (svarūpa) of the unique entity negatively, by debarring the mind from all else, without characterizing it positively as a substance possessed of such and such attributes. They may thus 'define' it, in the Indian sense of the term, while leaving it transcendent. Śaṅkara admits that the words 'Reality, Knowledge Infinity' do, formally speaking, attribute characteristics to the Absolute. But he claims that the purpose of the phrase is not to attribute empirically knowable attributes to the Absolute, but only to mark if off from anything that has empirically knowable characteristics.[5]

Śaṅkara then proceeds to analyse the definition. When he remarks initially that the terms 'Reality', 'Knowledge' and 'Infinity' do not qualify each other but only the Absolute, that is a grammatical point made in his capacity as commentator. The words do qualify each other's meaning, as we shall see. But what Śaṅkara means here is that of the string of four words in the nominative case in the Upanishad text 'satyam jñānam anantam brahma', Brahman (brahma) is the subject and the other three words constitute three separate predicates applied to it. In other words the phrase represents in contracted form three separate statements of the nature of the Absolute, 'The Absolute is Reality', 'The Absolute is Knowledge' and 'The Absolute is Infinity'. We are not being confronted with the statement that the Absolute has three separate characteristics, but with three separate statements of the nature of the Absolute. It has been claimed that in his exposition of this phrase, Śaṅkara passes beyond the normal Indian conception of definition, concerned solely with the extension of the term, and raises the question of its comprehension also.[6] He contrasts, by way of illustration, the definition of the ether through its accidental attribute of conveying sound with that through its essential attribute of 'giving things their extension in space'. But though, as we shall see, Śaṅkara regarded the definition of the Absolute at present under consideration as concerned with the nature (svarūpa) of the Absolute, no words have power to characterize it positively. To do this is beyond the power of words, as the Extracts of the previous chapter have well shown. Once again, their function in relation to the Absolute is no more than to debar the mind from all else.

A definition of the form 'X is Y' can be represented as a tautology or as a mere statement of the way in which the author proposes to use words. But Śaṅkara was only concerned with words in so far as they can be used to promote immediate experience (anubhava) of the Absolute. The prime instrument for this being the texts of the Veda, he interprets definitions of the Absolute found there with this end in view. And he seeks for the meaning of the terms used in the definition from sources outside the definition. He asks what the definition must mean according to the context in which it is found, if the words are considered according to their meanings as settled by previous tradition and the usage of the elders. He starts by asking what is normally meant by the term 'reality'. When a thing is known to have a certain form and that form never fails to accompany the thing, then we have reality. When on the other hand, a thing is first found to have one form and then later ascertained to have another form, then we have unreality. The criterion of reality is non-alteration in past, present or future. All modifications are unreal. In interpreting the statements in the Upanishads about reality, we cannot afford to pay attention to the arguments of the secular school of philosophers called the logicians, but must go back to the upanishadic texts themselves. Chāndogya Upanishad VI.i.4 says that a modification is a mere name introduced by speech, the truth being that all modifications of clay are in fact only clay. When confronted with toy carts and oxen formed from clay, we call some of the toys carts and some oxen. But there are no carts and no oxen: there is only the one substance clay. We also speak of carts and oxen in the ordinary world. But the truth is that there are no carts or oxen, there is only the one principle, Being. All the various modifications of Being have a beginning and an end, but Being itself undergoes neither birth nor destruction. Hence the purpose of the present Taittirīya Upanishad text in 'characterizing' the Absolute as 'Reality' is the negative one of excluding all its apparent modifications.

However, if the matter were suffered to remain there, we would be left with the Absolute constituting the material cause of the world of effects or modifications, as clay is the material cause of the various objects into which it is moulded. A material cause, however, as ordinarily understood, is a mere factor (kāraka) in a causal process and a non-conscious (acid-rūpa) substance (vastu). So the Taittirīya adds further 'characterizations' and first calls it 'Knowledge' and then 'Infinity'. Although each of these three words, if properly understood, indicates the whole nature of the Absolute, and they are therefore synonymous, nevertheless they qualify one another (niyama-niyāmaka-bhāva) *in respect of the meanings they convey to us*. If the Absolute is 'Knowledge', then it cannot be a material cause in the same sense as the material causes we observe in the world, which are invariably objects of our knowledge and therefore not themselves knowledge. Similarly, if the Absolute is 'Reality' and 'Infinity' it cannot be 'knowledge' in the sense of a particular act of cognition or any factor of such an act, such as the knowing subject conceived as agent in the act of knowing. That which is infinite cannot undergo any sub-division,[7] whereas an act of knowing implies a distinction between a subject and an object. The Self cannot know itself as an object, as this would contradict the texts of the Veda which say that it has no internal distinctions or parts. Again, it is unintelligible that the Self should be able to know itself as an object. For if it were at any moment the object of knowledge it could not at the same time be the subject.[8] And if anyone were to claim that the Absolute were already known as an object and familiar to all in its true nature, that also would contradict the Vedic teaching in the sense of making it useless, since the ultimate purpose of the Veda is to reveal the hitherto unrecognized true nature of the Self.

When, therefore, the Absolute is characterized as 'Knowledge' while also being called 'Reality' and 'Infinity', such knowledge must not be understood as the subject-object activity of knowing (vijñāna) familiar to us in our everyday life, but as the non-active ('witnessing') Consciousness that lies behind empirical knowing as its light and support, and which is identical with Being (bhāva). For Śaṅkara, the fact that Being and Knowledge were in their true nature identical followed from the presence in the Upanishads of such texts as 'A mere mass of Consciousness' and 'He is to be known only as "He is".'[9] In the definition of the Absolute under discussion,[10] each of the three terms so conditions the meaning of the others that, while retaining their power to indicate the Absolute indirectly, they lose their power to characterize it positively in any way that would limit it. In this connection, Śaṅkara draws a certain distinction between the word 'Infinity' on the one hand and the terms 'Reality' and 'Knowledge' on the other. The former merely negates finitude, while the latter do, formally speaking, 'characterize' the Absolute positively, though it later turns out that they too, while affirming the existence of the Absolute, can 'characterize' it only in the sense of debarring the mind from their own contradictories.[11] Śaṅkara does, in the course of the Extract to follow, say that the terms 'Reality' and 'Knowledge' both 'are' and 'are not' characterizations (viśeṣaṇa) of the Absolute. They are characterizations in the sense of identifying it with that which asserts itself in our own experience as Being and Knowledge, which is not known as an object yet cannot be denied. But the principle of absolute Being and Knowledge cannot itself be 'characterized' but only 'indicated' by words.[12]

Thus the three terms 'Reality, Knowledge, Infinity' must each be taken as defining characterization. They are not mere empty negations, or they would reduce the Absolute to a meaningless non-entity like the son of a barren woman. Standing in immediate contiguity, however, they affect one another. They each negate that part of the meaning of the other that is contradictory to themselves. They show, taken together, that the Absolute stands beyond the meaning of each term as it is ordinarily understood in everyday life. Each of them, however, when taken as modified by contiguity with the others, *still refers* to the Absolute and indicates its nature negatively by marking it off from what it is not. It is that which is not unreal, not non-conscious and not finite, and that is the most we can say about it. For it is 'avākyārtha':[13] it cannot be contained within the meaning of a sentence. It can be indicated by a definition, but cannot be characterized as a substance having this or that particular quality, as we characterize a lotus by calling it 'fragrant' or 'blue'. Hence the Taittirīya Upanishad in the passage following the present definition proceeds to say that the Absolute is that 'from which words fall back, together with the mind' and to speak of it as inexplicable (anirukta) from the standpoint of ordinary thought.

Since the terms 'Reality', 'Knowledge' and 'Infinity' are each by themselves 'indications' (lakṣaṇa) of the total nature of the Absolute, they are in one sense synonyms. But they are significant because each negates different misconceptions.[14] The idea behind the definition is: If the enquirer can withdraw from all false imaginations, which are unreal, non-conscious and finite, he will come finally to rest in the Self. But it is not a mere intellectual operation. The discipline and guidance of the Teacher will normally be needed.

TEXTS ON THE ABSOLUTE AS 'REALITY, KNOWLEDGE, INFINITY'

1. The text 'The Absolute is Reality, Knowledge, Infinity' is a definition of the Absolute. The three words 'Reality, Knowledge, Infinity' convey the characteristics of the Absolute, the latter being that which is defined by the possession of these characteristics. It must be understood that in the phrase 'The Absolute is Reality, Knowledge, Infinity' it is the Absolute that is being defined, because the Absolute is being presented as the primary thing that one has to know. Therefore the reason why the words 'Reality, Knowledge,

Infinity' are set in the same grammatical case as the word for the Absolute, and in apposition with it, is that they represent the characteristics by which it is to be defined. As characterized by these three characteristics beginning with 'Reality', the Absolute is determined as distinct from all other definable entities. This, indeed, is the way in which one has knowledge. One knows that which is determined as distinct from other things, as, for example, one speaks in worldly usage of 'the large, fragrant, blue lotus'.

Objection: A thing is distinguishable from others if it is distinguished as lacking some of their characteristics, as when we specify a lotus by calling it either 'blue' (and so *not* red) or 'red' (and so *not* blue). An adjective is meaningful when there are various substances of the same class, each having its own peculiarities. But it is not so meaningful in the case of a unique entity, where the question of possessing different peculiarities (from other members of its class) does not arise. We can only say, for instance, 'That is the one sun' (not 'That is the bright sun in distinction from the dull sun'). And we can speak of the unique Absolute only in the same way. For there are no other Absolutes from which it can be distinguished, as the blue lotus (can be distinguished from lotuses of other colours).

Answer: No, there is nothing wrong here, as the adjectives are used to define the Absolute (from all else). Why? Because the adjectives are being used primarily not to characterize the Absolute positively but simply to mark it off from all else.

What then is the difference between a definition and its object on the one hand and a characterization and its object on the other? Characterizations serve to distinguish what they characterize from other members of its own class. But a definition marks its object off from everything, as when we say 'The ether is that which provides space'. And, as we have already said, the present text (though in grammatical form a characterization) is intended as a definition.

The words 'Reality', 'Knowledge' and 'Infinity' do not explain each other mutually, as they explain something that is different (from any of them). What they explain is the object of the definition, the Absolute. So each of these three words is (grammatically speaking only) a characterization of the Absolute and each is an independent characterization of it. The Absolute is Reality. The Absolute is Knowledge. The Absolute is Infinity.

We have said 'Reality'. When a thing is determined as being of a particular form and that form never fails, that is its real form. When a thing is determined as being of a particular form and that form fails, it is said to be an unreal (false) form (anṛtam rūpam). Thus a modification is something false....

This, however, would suggest that the Absolute was the material cause (of the universe). A material cause is a factor in action, and, as a substance (vastu), would be non-conscious like clay. So to prevent this last supposition the text says 'The Absolute is Knowledge'. And because it is used along with the terms 'Reality' and 'Infinity' as a characterization (viśeṣaṇa) of the Absolute, it follows that the term 'Knowledge' is here used (not in the sense of an act but) in the sense of a state (bhāva-sādhana). It is not that the Absolute is the agent in an act of knowing.

If the term 'Knowledge' here referred to the knower in an

act of cognition, the terms 'Reality' and 'Infinity' would be out of place. For if the Absolute were the agent in an act of cognition, it would be subject to modification, and how then could it be real or infinite? Only that can be called infinite which undergoes no subdivision from any cause. If the Absolute were an agent in an act of cognition, this would imply its subdivision into known and knowledge (as well) and so it could not be infinite. And there is that other Vedic text 'Where one knows nothing else, that is the Infinite; but where one knows something else, that is the finite'.[15]

Objection: In the passage 'Where one knows nothing else, etc.' the force of the denial of particular knowledge is (not to deny that knowledge is to be taken as an act of cognition but) to affirm 'One has knowledge of one's own Self'.

Answer: No, for that text is only concerned with stating the marks which define the Infinite. The whole passage beginning 'Where one does not see anything else' is such a text. Appealing to the generally acknowledged principle that, (in the act of seeing) one (an agent) sees (an object which is) another, that definition conveys the nature of the Infinite by saying 'That is the Infinite in which that situation does not occur'. Since the force of the text is simply to deny the familiar experience of 'seeing another', it does not have the purpose of affirming that there can be any action (such as cognition) bearing on one's own Self. Moreover there cannot be determinate knowledge (vijñāna) in regard to one's own Self, as it admits of no distinctions. And if the Self were knowable, there could be no knower, for it would be exhausted in its function as object.

If you say that it is the one Self that is both the subject and object of knowledge, that is wrong. For it cannot have more than one rôle at a time. What is partless cannot be subject and object at the same time. And if the Self were an object of ordinary empirical knowledge, like a pot, the teaching of the special means to know it would be useless. For it does not make sense to teach a special means to knowledge of something that is already familiar, like a pot.

And for similar reasons, if the Absolute were knower (or agent in any act of knowledge), it could not be infinite. And if the Absolute had such determinate characteristics as agency in the act of knowing, it could not be pure Being...

Therefore, when the word 'Knowledge' is used along with 'Reality' and 'Infinity' in the definition of the Absolute, that word means 'knowledge' (not in the sense of an act but) in the sense of a state (bhāva-sādhana). And another reason for saying 'The Absolute is Knowledge' is to deny that agency or any other of the factors of action pertain to it, so that it cannot be (a mere) non-conscious (object) like clay. But when you say 'The Absolute is Knowledge' this does at first suggest finitude, as ordinary empirical knowledge in the world is seen to be finite. So to negate this idea the text says, '(The Real is) Infinity'.

Objection: The terms 'Reality', 'Knowledge' and 'Infinity' are concerned merely to negate (contradictory) characteristics such as falsity, non-consciousness and finitude. Therefore, (as there are no positive characteristics,) we cannot affirm the existence of the Absolute as that which bears them, like a lotus (affirmed to bear the attributes blue colour and fragrance, etc.). So the phrase 'The Absolute is Reality, Knowledge, Infinity' points to the Void, like the verse which says, 'This son of a barren woman, having bathed in the waters of a mirage, is walking along with a top-knot of sky-flowers, holding a bow made from the horns of a hare'.

Answer: No, because the phrase is intended as a definition. We have already said that, though the terms 'Reality', 'Knowledge' and 'Infinity' are characterizations of the Absolute (in a purely grammatical sense), their main purpose is to serve as a definition. And if the object of the definition were the Void (i.e. non-entity), all mention of a definition would be useless. Since the text is clearly intended as a definition, we maintain that it cannot refer to the Void.

In their (purely grammatical) function of 'characterizing' the Absolute, the terms 'Reality', etc. do so without giving up their own meanings (even though it will turn out that those meanings can only give an indirect *indication* of the nature of the Absolute). If the terms had no meanings, they could not be used to mark the defined entity off from other things. But if they retain their meaningfulness, they can be used to mark the Absolute off from things having contradictory characteristics. Furthermore, the word '(the) Absolute (brahman)' (which also occurs in the definition) has its own meaning and is significant.[16]

In this connection, the term 'Infinity' characterizes the Absolute (merely) by negating finitude. But the terms 'Reality' and 'Knowledge' characterize the Absolute (even if inadequately) by investing it with their own positive meanings...

Objection: Well then, if the Absolute is the Self (ātman)

(as established through quotation of upanishadic texts) it will be the agent in knowing, for it is familiar to all that the Self is the knower.... So the notion 'The Absolute (brahman) is (mere) Knowledge' is wrong, seeing that it is the agent in the act of knowing. And it is also wrong because it would imply that the Self was not eternal. If you interpret 'Knowledge' as 'knowing' and so as an activity of the Absolute, this leaves the Absolute transient and subject to the control of another. For verbal roots (in grammar) signify (acts which proceed in) dependence on factors of action. And the word 'Knowledge' (jñāna) (used in the definition) is a verbal root. So knowledge must be something impermanent and dependent on another.

Answer: Not so. For knowledge in no way differs from the Absolute. It is only figuratively spoken of as arising adventitiously. Since the very *nature* of the Self is knowledge and it never departs from that nature, knowledge is eternal. True, appearances of objects such as sound and other elements manifest in the intellect (buddhi), a mere external adjunct (upādhi) of the Self, an adjunct which transforms itself into the shape of objects through the instrumentality of sense-organs such as the eye. These (cognitions), however, are objects for the Self as Consciousness as soon as they arise. They are semblances of the Self as Consciousness, and hence are called 'consciousness (vijñāna)' (*qua* cognitions). Being referred to (as 'cognitions') by a verbal noun (i.e. the word 'vijñāna'), they are imagined by persons lacking in discrimination to be transient properties of the Self.

But when the Absolute (brahman) is spoken of in the texts as 'vijñāna',[17] we have an affirmation that knowledge is of the very nature of the Absolute and inseparable from it, as light is inseparable from the sun or heat from fire. Such knowledge is not anything that depends on any external cause, as it is the eternal nature of the Absolute. Because the Absolute is itself the cause of space and time and all other conditioning factors of the objective realm, no object can be separated from it in space and time. And because it is supremely subtle, there cannot, either in the past, present or future, be anything separate from it, greater than it and unknown to it. It is in this sense that the Absolute is omniscient...

Thus the Absolute never abandons its status as knower (vijñātṛ) and is in no way dependent on the senses or other instruments (for its knowledge). And for these reasons it is evidently constant and eternal, even though of the nature of knowledge. So it is not what is signified by the word 'know' as a verb,[18] because it is not of the nature of an action. Likewise, it is not the agent in the act of knowing. And this shows that the Absolute cannot be literally designated by the word 'knowledge'. It is indirectly indicated and not directly designated by the word 'knowledge', a word that designates directly that which is a mere semblance of the Absolute, that is to say, knowledge considered as an attribute of the intellect. For the Absolute itself is void of any of those characteristics such as genus, etc., to which speech applies.[19]

Similar considerations apply to the use of the word 'Reality' (in the definition at present under analysis). For the Absolute is by nature void of all particular characteristics. In the phrase 'The Absolute is Reality', the word 'Reality', which in its direct meaning designates external reality as the genus Being, merely indicates the Absolute indirectly (as that which is not unreal). The Absolute is not open to direct designation by the word 'Reality'.

In this way the terms 'Reality', 'Knowledge' and 'Infinity', placed next to one another, condition each other mutually and negate their own direct meanings of the Absolute, while at the same time serving to indicate it indirectly. Thus it is shown that the Absolute is not open to direct verbal designation, in agreement with such texts as 'That from which words fall back together with the mind' and 'Unintelligible, without support'.[20] Nor is the Absolute the meaning of any phrase (of subject-predicate type) like 'The lotus (is) blue'.[21]

2. The Absolute as the Self-Existent Principle

Though Śaṅkara's theological method culminates in negation, it begins with provisional affirmation. The existence of the Absolute is first provisionally affirmed in some conditioned or limited form which will be intelligible to the student, and then the content of this provisional affirmation is later purified of all limiting factors by subsequent negations. The present and remaining sections of this chapter will deal with the three highest forms of the provisional affirmation of the Absolute, those of the Absolute as first cause, as self-luminous consciousness, and as Bliss.

If all distinctions are ultimately illusory then from the standpoint of the highest truth it is clearly inaccurate to speak of the Absolute as the cause of the world. But the enquirer is still by definition in the standpoint of ignorance or nescience, and for him distinctions hold and the world and its objects are real. He needs to be told that behind the changing objects of the world there lies a principle that is eternal and does not change, that from which the perishable objects come forth and into which they finally dissolve. The same Upanishad that, as we saw in the previous section, defined the Absolute according to its true nature as 'Reality, Knowledge and Infinity' also defined it as that from which the objects of the world came forth and to which they will return. Śaṅkara spoke of the latter as a 'preliminary' definition,[22] not made according to the true nature (svarūpa) of the thing to be defined. His followers were later to contrast the definition of the true essence (svarūpa-lakṣaṇa) with the definition through something external (taṭastha-lakṣaṇa). In the second kind of definition, the defining mark did not actually belong to the thing defined, as when we indicate a house as 'the one with the crow on the roof'. The definition of the Absolute as the cause of the world was of the second kind. The later distinction between the two kinds of definition was already present in germ in Śaṅkara, as he spoke of the definition of the Absolute as the cause of the world as 'preliminary', as one which would require modification and correction later. Thus the Extracts of the present section will speak of the Absolute as a cause, as a universal and as pure Being, but all these notions require to be negated in apprehension of the final truth.

Of the Extracts to follow, No. 1 gives the upanishadic authority for appealing to the cosmological argument for a self-existent first cause. No. 2 states the principle that all effects imply a material cause from which they proceed and into which they will dissolve back. Nos. 3 and 4 picture the world as a mounting hierarchy of causes, in which each succeeding cause in the series includes its predecessors as effects. No. 3 takes the series consisting of the elements. No. 4 takes the world as consisting of a hierarchy of universals, each later member of the series containing the rest, which turn out to be strictly nothing over and above it, so that the whole world, in its true nature, is nothing but Being, the supreme and all-inclusive universal. Nos. 5-8 develop the notion of Being. Being must be affirmed, as it is constantly affirmed in all our judgements, while the series of dependent effects implies a self-existent cause. Even though Being is the material cause of the world, it is not non-conscious. Nos. 9 and 10 remark that even though the world be conceived as an illusion, an illusion implies a reality behind it.

TEXTS ON THE ABSOLUTE AS THE SELF-EXISTENT PRINCIPLE

1. Bhṛgu said, 'What is the definition of the Absolute?' The answer he received (from Varuṇa) was as follows. That from which all beings from the highest god (brahmā) to the meanest tuft of grass proceed, that through which they maintain life and grow, and that to which they go when the time comes for their dissolution and with which they attain identity, that with which beings remain essentially identical even while being projected forth, maintained or withdrawn — that is the definition of the Absolute.[23]

❖

2. Fire, too, is an effect, as it comes into being and passes away. As fire, my dear one, is an effect, its cause is Being, one only without a second, the highest reality. That on which all this (world) is superimposed through nescience by an activity of speech, being the mere delusive object of a name, like the host of imaginary entities such as the snake superimposed on the (imperfectly perceived) rope... that is the ground of this world-appearance. Hence, my dear one, all these creatures, stationary and moving, have Being for their ground, Being for their original cause.

Not only is Being their original cause. Even now, during the time of their empirical existence, they have their basis in Being. For effects such as pots can have neither existence nor empirical reality without a basis in some material cause like clay. So the creatures have their basis in Being, because Being is their material cause, as clay is the material cause of pots. Being is also their support, in the sense that it is that into which they will eventually dissolve and which will remain over after their destruction.[24]

❖

3. In what sense, then, is 'that which has to be known' extremely subtle? This (element) earth is gross (perceptible) and is associated with sound, hardness to the touch, colour, taste and smell, and is an object of all the sense-organs.[25] The same applies to the body. But in the series earth, water, fire, air, ether, which arises when the distinguishing quality, such as odour in the case of earth, is removed from each grosser element in the series respectively, there is found a hierarchy in which each succeeding member of the series exceeds its predecessors in subtlety, extension, purity and permanence. What then to say of the absolute subtlety, infinite extension, perfect purity and eternity of that in which none of these distinguishing features are found, all of which latter are 'gross' because they represent a degeneration (vikāra).

When the text here speaks of that which has no sound, no feeling to the touch, no colour, taste or odour and which is imperishable, it is describing the imperishable Absolute. For whatever has sound and the other (gross and perceptible) characteristics is perishable...

And there is another reason why it (the Absolute) is eternal and constant. It is beginningless and has no cause. Whatever has a beginning is an effect and therefore non-eternal. It dissolves into its (material) cause like (the great elements such as) earth, etc.[26] But because the Absolute is the cause of all, it is not an effect. It has no material cause into which it can eventually dissolve... It is constant and eternal in the absolute sense, not with the relative permanence of the earth and the other great elements. One who arises to an awareness of the Absolute as his own Self and as being of the nature here described is liberated from the mouth of death, that is, from the realm of death in the form of nescience, desire and action.[27]

❖

4. 'As in the case where a lute is played'. Various examples are cited here to show that universals are many. For there are many different universals, some pertaining to conscious beings, some to non-conscious beings. What illustration can be given to show how they form a continuous hierarchy and all exist within one great universal, massed Consciousness?

The example given in the text is that of the various universals formed by the drum-sound, the conch-sound and the lute-sound, all existing within the wider universal sound-in-general.[28] In the same way, we should understand that the Absolute alone exists, even during the time that the universe is in manifestation, because the various universals are nothing over and above it.[29]

❖

5. And thus it is right to put up with heat and cold and other pairs of opposites without giving way to grief and delusion. For pairs of opposites, like heat and cold and their causes, are not found to be real when critically examined through (perception, inference and other) recognized means of knowledge.

For they are modifications, and every modification is subject to change. Every formed object, like a pot, is unreal because, when it is examined through the eye, nothing is found apart from the clay or other material cause. And similarly every other modification is unreal, because it is not found to be anything over and above the causal substance from which it is composed. Moreover, it is not apprehended at all before its production or after its destruction. Even the material cause itself, clay, together with its own material cause, are not found to be anything over and above the causal substances from which *they* are composed, and are hence unreal.

But will it not follow that if these are unreal everything is unreal? No, for we find everywhere two notions, the notion 'existent' and the notion 'non-existent'. That, the notion of which never changes, is existent. That, the notion of which is transient, is non-existent. The distinction between the existent and the non-existent depends on our notions. Everywhere we find two notions arise with reference to one substratum. We are not speaking of (specification through an additional qualifying notion, as in the case of) ideas like 'the lotus is blue'. We are speaking of (the succession of impressions having the form) 'The pot is existent', 'The cloth is existent', 'The elephant is existent' and so on. In these pairs of notions, the notions of 'pot', 'cloth' and 'elephant' are transient, as has already been pointed out. But the notion of 'existent' is not. Therefore the objects for which the notions 'pot', 'cloth', 'elephant', etc. stand are unreal, because these notions are transient. But that which is conveyed by the notion 'existent' is not unreal, because it never fails.

Perhaps you will object that when the pot is destroyed, the

notion 'existent' fails. But this is not so, as it is found to accompany whatever else one perceives, say a cloth. The notion of existence refers to the character only (and not to the thing characterized, which turns out to be transient). One cannot say that the notion 'pot' is (non-transient) like the notion 'existent', inasmuch as it is found in the perception of other pots. For the notion 'pot' is not found in other objects such as cloth.

Nor can one argue that the notion 'existent' too, is cancelled when the pot is destroyed. For there is nothing for it to characterize. The notion 'existent' occurs, as we have seen, as a character referring to something being characterized. Where there is no longer anything to be characterized there cannot be a character, and there is no longer anything for the notion 'existent' to apply to. But it is not the case that the notion 'existent' has nothing to apply to anywhere (merely because it ceases in the case of a no-longer-existent pot).

Perhaps you will say that it (was not right to speak of the union of two notions as character and characterized when the characterized (i.e. 'pot', 'cloth', 'elephant') does not really exist. But this objection is not right. For in the case of a mirage, for instance, we say 'This is water', and this is an example of the union of two notions as character and characterized where one of them (namely the water) does not really exist. Hence it follows that (as we stated originally) the body and the pairs of opposites (like heat and cold) together with their causes are unreal and do not exist. And similarly the real, the Self, is never found not to exist, because, as we explained, it never fails....

As for what is real, it is said (in the Gītā verse under discussion) that that exists eternally. The text calls the real indestructible, and uses the word 'but' to point the contrast with the unreal (just discussed). Know that that, the Absolute, called the real (sat), by which all this universe, together with the ether, is pervaded, like pots and other hollow entities being pervaded by the ether, is indestructible. Being indestructible, it undergoes neither increase nor diminution. Because it is partless, the Absolute, called the real, does not depart from its essential form, as the body and other entities of the empirical world do. And because the Absolute has no external possessions, it does not undergo loss of external possessions, as Devadatta would if he lost his wealth. No one can bring about the destruction of the Absolute. No one, not even the Lord Himself, could bring about his own destruction. For the true Self (of all) is the Absolute, and it would be a contradiction to suppose that it could act on itself.[30]

❖

6. This, however, might lead one to suppose that the Absolute (brahman) must be unreal. Why? Because whatever exists is perceived with its peculiar characteristics, as for example a pot, while what does not exist, such as the horn of a hare, is not perceived at all. And the Absolute is not perceived. Because it is not perceived with its particular characteristics, it follows that it does not exist.

But this reasoning is wrong, for the reason that the Absolute is the cause of the whole world, beginning with the ether. Hence it is not right to say that the Absolute does not exist: it is not right, because all this world is perceived as the effect of the Absolute. It is an admitted principle in the world that that from which something proceeds is real, such as the clay from which the pot proceeds or the seed which is the cause of the sprout. Hence the Absolute exists because it is the cause of the whole world beginning with the ether.

No effect is ever seen in the world to proceed from an unreal cause. If name and form and the rest, the world of effects, were unreal in the sense of having no real essence,[31] then they would not be perceived. But the fact is that they are perceived. Hence the Absolute exists. If the world proceeded from non-being (asat), it would invariably be perceived as associated with non-being.[32] But this is not the case. So it follows that the Absolute exists. This is confirmed by another Vedic text, which runs 'How could being proceed from non-being?'[33]

But if the Absolute is a (material) cause like clay or a seed, will it be non-conscious like them? No, for the Absolute forms desires.[34] It is not admitted in the world that a being who forms desires can be non-conscious. We have already declared that the Absolute is omniscient, hence the fact that He can form resolutions is explicable on our doctrine.

But if the Absolute can form desires would not that imply that He had unfulfilled desires like us? No, because He possesses sovereign independence. The 'desires' of the Absolute do not prompt Him to act in the way that desire and other passions get hold of other beings and prompt them to act (like puppets). The desires of the Absolute are His very Self and are of the nature of knowledge and truth; they are completely pure (devoid of the passionate element), and it is not that the

Absolute is prompted to act by them but rather that the Absolute prompts *them* to arise in accord with the merit and demerit of living beings. Hence the Absolute is possessed of sovereign independence in relation to His desires, and it is not correct to say that His desires are unfulfilled.

The same result follows from the fact that the Absolute does not depend on external instruments. The desires of beings other than the Absolute are not the very Self of those beings and hence depend for their rise on merit and demerit and other extraneous factors, as well as implying separate acts and instruments for their gratification. But the 'desires' of the Absolute do not imply instruments or secondary causes in this way. On the contrary, they are non-different from Him, their own Self.[35]

❖

7. That (supreme principle) Being 'took thought'. This alone is enough to show that the 'pradhāna' conjectured by the Sāṅkhyas cannot be the cause of the world.[36] For they assume the 'Pradhāna' to be non-conscious. But this principle 'Being' (mentioned in the Chāndogya Upanishad text under comment) is conscious, as it is capable of 'taking thought'.

How, then, did 'Being' take thought? It thought, 'Let Me increase and multiply'. (It was not a real multiplication but an apparent one,) as when clay 'multiplies' by assuming the form of various objects like pots or when a (misperceived) rope or the like assumes the form of a snake or the like, the latter being a mere imagination of the mind.

Does it follow that everything that is perceived is

non-being (asat), like a rope in so far as it appears (through erroneous perception) as a snake? No, that is not our position. For we hold that it is invariably real Being that is perceived, only it is perceived under the distinctions of duality and hence as different from what it really is. Thus we do not maintain that anything anywhere is non-being.

The rationalist philosophers (Vaiśeṣikas) believe in the existence of entities other than pure Being. Hence they speak of the non-existence (asattva) of these entities before their rise and after their final destruction. But we do not believe that any entity other than pure Being exists anywhere or at any time, whether a name or a named object. On the contrary, every name is (in truth) only Being, and it is Being to which other names are given through the notion that it is something else. It is parallel with the case of the snake-illusion, where it is in fact the rope that is called a snake under the impression that it is a snake. And it is parallel with the normal worldly practice of thinking of the lump of clay (taken up by the potter for use) and the clay pot (that he makes from it) as different from clay and calling them 'the lump' and 'the pot' respectively. But for those who discern the rope in its true nature, the name and notion of the snake cease, as do the name and notion of the pot and the rest in the case of those who distinctly perceive that their true nature is clay. And in much the same way the name and notion of all modifications of Being into other forms cease for those who discern the true nature of pure Being.[37]

❖

8. 'But Being cannot 'come into being', for that would be impossible'. So says the author of the Sūtras. The idea is this.

The coming into being of the ether or the wind is scarcely conceivable (by the human mind) and yet we know from Vedic revelation that they did come into being. So one might think that even the Absolute rose from some other source. And again, one learns from Vedic revelation that from entities like the ether, which are themselves but modifications, there arise further entities through further modification. And one might conclude from this that because the ether arose from the Absolute, the Absolute, in turn, was a modification of something else. To rebut this suspicion the author of the Sūtras says, '(No,) for that would be impossible'.

Verily, one should not suppose that the Absolute, which is of the nature of Being, could arise from anything else. Why not? Because such a thing is impossible. For the Absolute is pure Being. It could not arise from pure Being, for, since pure Being is in no way different from pure Being, there could not be any relation of 'original substance' and 'modification' between the two. And neither could pure Being arise from any particular being, for that would contradict known laws. Particulars like pots arise from universals like clay, not universals from particulars. Nor could pure Being arise from non-being, for the latter is non-existent, and we have the text 'How could Being arise from non-being?'[38] which negates the idea....

On the other hand, the fact that the ether and the wind have an origin is directly proclaimed. The fact that this is not so in the case of the Absolute marks a radical difference. Nor is the fact that we find modifications arising from things that are themselves modifications of other things an argument for saying that the Absolute is itself a modification of something else. For if we do not accept some original (self-existent) entity somewhere we fall into infinite regress. And the original entity that all accept is in fact none other than what our tradition calls the Absolute.[39]

❖

9. Here the Self might be dismissed as unreal on the ground of being ever unknowable. But this would be wrong, for its effect is knowable.

It is as in the case of a magician (mass-hypnotist). An illusory production or effect can arise through hypnotic illusion from a magician who is himself real. Just as, in this case, the perceived illusion forces us to infer an unperceived but real magician behind it, so the production of the world as a perceived effect forces us to infer the absolutely real Self as the ground of the world-illusion. Like the magic elephant and other productions of the mass-hypnotist, the production of the world is intelligible as proceeding from a real cause, not from an unreal one. But it must be remembered that the Self cannot undergo real production of any kind.

Alternatively, we might argue that it can undergo production 'through illusion (māyā)' but not in reality. Just as a real object like a rope can undergo 'production' (lit. birth) as a snake through illusion but not in reality, so can the Self, which is real though not perceived, undergo production through illusion as the world, the latter corresponding with the rope-snake. But the Self does not undergo any real process of production. As for the thinker who says that the Self, which is an unborn, absolutely real principle, undergoes real birth as the universe, his doctrine is self-contradictory, as that which is (by nature) unborn cannot undergo birth. So his doctrine (that something is really born) can only refer to birth from what has already been born. But the notion that all birth is birth from something already born implies infinite regress. So it stands proved that the Self is the one real principle, itself unborn.[40]

❖

10. Being void of all organs, the Absolute which has to be known is relationless (transcendent). Even so, it is, as the text says, 'The support of all'. Everything has Being for its support because every judgement we make is accompanied by the idea of being. Not even a mirage or other illusion can occur without a real base. Hence the Absolute is the support of all.[41]

3. The Absolute as the Self-Luminous Principle

It was shown in the last section that our experiences in the realm of nescience are inexplicable unless we assume that some self-existent principle underlies the system of effects that we call the world.[42] And it has on several occasions been pointed out that this principle must be a conscious one. Self-existent as Being, it is self-luminous as Consciousness, and the numbered Extracts to follow in the present section show Śaṅkara's meditations on this latter theme. No. 1 explains how the entire domain of the seen, mental and physical, is composite and objective and *per se* non-conscious (the mental phenomena are illumined by a mere *reflection* of the Consciousness of the Self, cp. Extract 7) and exists for the sake of another, namely the simple (non-composite) principle of Consciousness, the Self. No. 2 draws attention to the peculiar nature of the light of Consciousness. It is self-evident and self-established, since it persists unchanged throughout the experiences of waking, dream and dreamless sleep. It does not know itself as an object and does not need to as it is self-evident light. Though it is the light behind all knowledge, it is not the agent in any act of knowing. No. 3 shows how the existence of the pure Self can be established indirectly as it is implied by the constant awareness that accompanies all our cognitions. No. 4 explains that knowledge is the nature of the Self and not due to an act. No. 5, a long Extract, recapitulates the above points and shows that the knowledge of the Self is independent of the sense-organs, citing the example of men who lose their eyes but still continue to have dreams.[43] No. 6 also reviews the same points and remarks that they are fatal to the common-sense view, supported by the Vaiśeṣikas, that the Self is an agent in acts of perception. No. 7 shows how the luminosity of all luminous bodies is dependent on the light of Consciousness present within the observer. No. 8 remarks that the natural omniscience of the Self as Lord of the Universe can be viewed, from the standpoint of nescience, as a kind of constant activity, not dependent on organs.

TEXTS ON THE ABSOLUTE AS THE SELF-LUMINOUS PRINCIPLE

1. Thus the supreme Self created the world and its denizens and guardians, all dependent on food, just like a city with its citizens and garrison. Then He thought to Himself, just like a king would, 'How will this aggregate of body and organs be able to function if I am not present, seeing that by nature it (is a composite creation and therefore) exists for the sake of another (and is consequently non-conscious)?' If speech were nothing more than the activity of the vocal cords (without the presence of a speaker behind them) it would be meaningless and in fact could not occur, any more than there could be payment of taxes or recitation of eulogies to the king if the city had no king.

Let Me, therefore, who am the supreme Master and Controller and Witness of what is done and what is not done and of the results of deeds and omissions, behave as if I were the king of the city. If indeed the activity of the compounded aggregate could go forward without Me, Consciousness, for the sake of whom it exists, like a city and its citizens carrying on without their king, then who would I be? What would be My nature? Over what could I be Lord and Master?

If I do not enter into this aggregate of body and organs and observe the results of the activity of its organs such as speech and the rest, like a king coming into his city and taking careful note of what his officers have and have not been doing, then nobody will be able to know Me as existent and of such and such a nature. But if I do come into the body as the Witness of the operations of its organs, I shall be able to be known as the one who perceives the sounds made by these vocal organs as 'this' (i.e. as an object), and who is existent and of the nature of Consciousness and who is the one for whose sake this vocal and other activity proceeds on the part of the composite organs. For these composite organs must exist for the sake of another, just as the pillars and walls assembled to form a mansion must exist, along with their parts, to serve some non-composite being.[44]

❖

2. The pupil said: If, holy Sir, my true nature is free from all modifications, and the state of dreamless sleep is evidence of this fact, then how do dream and waking arise?

The Teacher replied: Well, do you experience waking and dream continuously?

The pupil answered: I experience them, but with breaks and not continuously.

The Teacher replied: Then they are adventitious and not your true Self. If they were your true Self, they would be self-established like pure Consciousness and would be continuous. Moreover, dream and waking cannot be your true nature for the further reason that they pass away like a worn out garment, while you remain. The essential element in anything (its real nature, svarūpa) cannot pass away while the thing remains. But dream and waking pass away, while pure Consciousness remains constant (throughout waking, dream and dreamless sleep). If your true nature as Consciousness were lost in dreamless sleep then it would stand destroyed or could be negated as non-existent. For what is adventitious (and so impermanent) and not the real property of a thing is found to be subject to destruction and non-existent, as for example clothes and wealth are subject to destruction, and advantages merely dreamed of or falsely imagined are (found to be) non-existent.

Well, but in this way, holy Sir, Consciousness itself in its real nature will be found to be something that supervenes adventitiously, for there is no experience of it in dreamless sleep as there is in waking and dream. Or else I shall have to say, 'I am not Consciousness in my true nature'.[45]

No, replied the Teacher. For if you look carefully you will see that this argument is fallacious. If you enjoy some superior power through which you enjoy Consciousness as something adventitious, then continue to do so by all means. But for my own part I could not establish the truth of this logically even if

I tried for a hundred years, and neither could anyone else, even if he were (as the theory would imply) actually non-conscious. For if Consciousness were adventitious, no one could prevent the logical consequence that it would have to be composite, and hence that it (was not self-existent but) existed for the sake of another, was multiple and subject to destruction. For, as we have already said, that which does not exist for its own sake (and is therefore composed by and for another) cannot establish itself as real. But no one can deny the independent self-existence of the Self as pure Consciousness because it establishes itself as real (i.e. manifests itself) by its own power and never fails.

But, replied the pupil, did I not cite an example of its failure when I said I experienced nothing in dreamless sleep?

No, replied the Teacher, because the statement was self-contradictory. You ask where the contradiction lay? When you are experiencing enough to say 'I am experiencing nothing', that is a self-contradictory statement.

But, holy Sir, I have never experienced anything in dreamless sleep, whether Consciousness or anything else.

And yet you *do* have experience in dreamless sleep, replied the Teacher, because you deny that you have experienced anything, while not denying the fact of experiencing. I told you before that that experience of yours was itself Consciousness. That which is present and enables you to make the denial 'I did not experience anything', that is your experience, your knowledge. Therefore, since the light of Consciousness never fails in waking, dream or dreamless sleep, it is self-established as eternal and constant and raised above all change, and it does not depend on being established by empirical means of proof.

The cognizer, though himself self-evident, requires to resort to an empirical means of cognition to determine the object of his knowledge, which is different from himself. But there is another different (and fundamentally superior) *constant* principle of determination that is needed to determine that which is not itself yet determinate (i.e. the not-self, which is non-conscious). This principle is eternal, changeless and of the nature of self-luminous light. It requires no additional means of knowledge to establish either itself or the (empirical) cognition or the cognizer, for it is their own true nature. Brilliance and heat in (red hot) iron and (warm) water depend on the action of something external, like fire or the sun, because brilliance and heat are not the nature of iron and water. But the light and heat of fire and the sun do not depend on any external agency, as they are the very nature of fire and the sun.

But is it not the case that right knowledge (pramā) is necessarily transient (in that it arises in regard to something that was not known before) and could not exist if it were not? Not so, for there is no distinction in the nature of awareness itself, whether (it appears to us as) eternal or transient. It is invariably of the nature of right knowledge. We do not experience any distinction of the form, 'When awareness is transient it constitutes right knowledge, when it is constant it does not'.

Perhaps you will say that there is such a distinction. It takes the form: 'When awareness is eternal and constant it does not depend on a knowing agent (pramātṛ), but where it is transient it depends on a knowing agent, as it depends on effort'.

But even if this were so, it would merely illustrate how the Self as (ultimate reality behind) the knowing agent does not require to be established by any external means of proof and is self-evident. And if you (try to suggest the argument is absurd and) say that (according to its terms) absence of dependence on a means of knowledge could equally imply absence of all awareness, since that, too, would be constant, we reply that this position is excluded, as it has already been shown that awareness verily exists in the case of the Self. If you say that the establishment of the Knower depends on a means of knowledge, then who would be the one seeking that means of knowledge? It must be admitted that the one who desires to know is himself the knowing subject. And his desire to know must bear on an *object* of cognition, not on himself, the knowing subject. If it were supposed to bear on himself as knowing subject, there would be infinite regress, for there would have to be another knowing subject to know the first knowing subject and another subject to know the new one and so on. Similar considerations apply when desire (in any form, including that of desire to know,) is supposed to bear on the knowing subject.

Another reason why the knower cannot be the object of any external means of cognition is that he is in no way separate from himself as knower. An object of right knowledge through an external means of knowledge is only possible if it is separated from the knower through the intervention of desire, memory, effort and the ensuing application of the aforesaid means of cognition. Knowledge of an object is never found without this condition. But the knower could in no way be conceived as separate from himself through the intervention of any of these factors. Memory, too, bears on the object of remembrance, not on the one remembering. Similarly, desire bears on the object of desire only, not on the one having the desire. If the one remembering or the one desirous (of something) were taken as the object of such memory or desire, the same infinite regress would inevitably arise as arose just now when we tried to make the knowing subject the object of his own desire to know.

Well then, you might say, if there cannot be any knowledge of the knowing subject, he must just remain unknown. But this is not right. True, the knowledge of the knowing subject is directed to the object of his cognition. If it bore on the knower himself, there would be infinite regress, as we have already shown. But we have also shown that the light of the Self, eternal and raised above all change, is ever established as present in the Self without dependence on any external factor, like the heat and light in fire and the sun. If Consciousness, as the Light of the Self, were not constantly present in the Self, then the Self could not exist for its own sake. It would then be composite, like the psycho-physical organism, and would exist for another and have imperfections, as we have already explained.

What imperfections do we mean? If Consciousness as the Light of the Self were not constantly in the Self, then it would depend on the intervention of memory and other factors and have gaps. This Consciousness as the Light in the Self would then be non-existent before it arose and non-existent again after it subsided. And it would be a composite entity like the eyes and other organs and exist for the sake of another. And if it were found to be *produced* in the Self (as in the theory of the Vaiśeṣikas), then the Self would not exist for its own sake. For it is the presence of the eternal Light in the Self that shows that the latter exists for its own sake, while it is the absence of this eternal Light in the not-self that shows that the latter exists for the sake of another. Thus it is proved that the Self is of the very nature of Consciousness as eternal Light, without dependence on any other thing.

You might remark that if all this were true, the (ultimate) knower would not be the one who enjoyed empirical cognition (as he would be above all change and activity). And you might ask in what sense he could then be regarded as the knower. To this we reply that there is no difference in the nature of right cognition (pramā), whether it be taken as eternal or transitory. Right knowledge is just awareness, and it makes no difference to its real nature (svabhāva) whether it be associated with memory and desire, and so transient, or whether it be considered as eternal and raised above all change. For in the case of such activities as standing, for instance, we do not think that the result is essentially different whether the activity is preceded by moving about, and so transient, or whether it is permanent: which is why we use the same term in either case and say 'The men are standing' and also 'The mountains stand'. In the same way, there is no contradiction in speaking of that which is eternal awareness by nature as 'knower' because the result (of both kinds of knowledge) is the same.

Here the pupil (takes up the argument and) says: Since the Self, being of the very nature of eternal awareness, is not subject to any kind of change, he could not be an agent, like a carpenter working with tools, unless he entered into intimate relation with the body and the senses. If that which is by nature unrelated with anything else were supposed to enjoy the use of the body and organs we would have infinite regress.

Carpenters and the like are ever intimately related with their bodies and organs, so that in their case there is no question of infinite regress when they enjoy the use of their tools.[46] But the case with the Self is different. Being by nature unrelated with anything else, it could not be an agent unless it acquired organs. But to acquire organs would imply (action and so) undergoing a change, and other organs would have to be supposed to exist to make it an agent capable of effecting this change, and further organs would have to be supposed to exist to supply the second set and so to infinity. So a knower who was an active agent in the process of knowing could not be conceived as an independent self-existent principle without infinite regress.

You cannot (to avoid the difficulties just mentioned) say (with the Pūrva Mīmāṃsakas) that action itself introduces action into the Self, because that which has not yet come into being (the original first act) has no nature of its own that it could function as a cause. Nor would it help to say that any other entity advances on the Self and causes it to act. For nothing other than the Self can be a self-established reality, nor could it be anything but an object for the Self (and so powerless to affect or alter the latter). What is other than the Self is non-conscious, and nothing of this kind can have self-established existence. All objects, from sound (the first to manifest of the great elements which compose the objective world) onwards, can be established only through an empirical cognition that culminates in awareness as its final result. If awareness belonged to anything other than the Self, that thing, too, would be nothing but the Self, non-composite and existing for its own sake and not for that of another. But neither the body nor the senses nor external objects can be held to exist for their own sake. For we find that their existence can only be established by a cognition culminating in awareness.

But is it not the case that no special act of cognition is required for awareness of the body (so that the latter is independently real)? Yes, that is true in the waking state. But at death or in dreamless sleep even the body can only be established through perception and other such acts of cognition (performed by other people). The sense-organs, too, (depend on acts of cognition to be known). For it is sound and the other great elements (such as wind, water, fire and earth which go to make up the objective world) which undergo modification to assume the form of the body and sense-organs.[47] And we have already said that 'establishment' (siddhi) means that awareness which is the 'product' (phala, lit. fruit) of the application of the empirical means of cognition. Awareness *per se*, however, is self-established, raised above all change and the pure essence of the Light of the Self.

Here an objector intervenes to claim that it is a contradiction to say that awareness is the product of the application of the empirical means of knowledge and proof and *at the same time* raised above all change and the pure essence of the Light of the Self. But the reply given is that it is not a contradiction. Why not? Awareness is in fact eternal and raised above all change. But it is referred to figuratively as the culminating point in empirical cognitions since they proceed for its sake.

And since the empirical cognitions arising from perception and the other means of knowledge are transitory, awareness (in their case) seems to be transitory too. Hence it is referred to figuratively as their 'product' (phala).

If this is so, revered Sir, proceeds the pupil, then awareness must indeed be eternal, raised above all change, the pure essence of the Light of the Self and self-established, since it will not depend on the application of any external means of knowledge to establish its own existence. And whatever is different from this, the non-conscious, will operate only in conjunction with other things and will exist for the sake of another. And the not-self will have its existence-for-another only as the content of awareness in cognitions promoted by pleasure, pain and delusion[48] and will exist in no other form.[49] That is, from the standpoint of ultimate truth it will not exist at all. In ordinary experience in the world we find that the erroneously perceived snake and mirage and so on have no existence apart from our awareness of them. Hence it is but reasonable to suppose that the duality apprehended in waking and dream has no existence apart from our awareness of it.

And thus it is, revered Sir, that from the standpoint of ultimate truth there is no break in awareness, which is the Light of the Self and hence eternal and raised above all change, one without a second. For it is invariably present amidst all the different cognitions, whereas none of them are invariably present with it. We say that the various cognitions of blue and yellow, etc., seen in a dream, do not exist from the standpoint of ultimate truth, because they pass away while awareness remains. But the various cognitions of blue and yellow beheld in waking, too, pass away while that same awareness remains.

Hence they, too, must be of illusory nature. And there is no other principle to be aware of this awareness. Therefore it cannot of its own accord either accept itself (perceive itself as something new) or reject itself as an illusion, since nothing apart from it exists.

It is indeed so, replied the Teacher. It is nescience (avidyā) which causes this flow of transmigratory experience in the form of waking and dream.[50] What puts an end to this nescience is spiritual knowledge (vidyā). Thus thou hast attained to the state beyond all fear. Never again wilt thou experience the pain of waking and dream. Thou art liberated from the pain of transmigratory experience.

'It is so! (OM)' replied the pupil.[51]

❖

3. To that worthy pupil the Teacher replied as follows. Hear the answer to your question about the nature of the Divine Being that prompts the mind and other organs to apprehend their objects, and about how He does so. 'The Hearer of hearing' says the text. 'Hearing' is the organ through which one hears. It means the sense-organ called the ear through which one hears sound. The 'Hearer' of that hearing is that Divine Being about whom you asked when you said, 'What Divine Being presides over seeing and hearing?'

You might perhaps say that I ought to have replied, 'So and so, being of such and such a nature, presides over hearing and other such functions, and that it was an irrelevant answer to say 'The Hearer of hearing'. But in truth there was nothing wrong with my reply, as the one who presides over seeing and hearing cannot be conceived in any other way. If the one who presided over hearing and the other functions were conceived as having His own particular brand of activity, different in nature from the activities over which He was presiding, like one mowing with a scythe, then my answer would have been irrelevant indeed. But the one who presides over hearing and the rest cannot be conceived as having His own separate mode of activity, like a mower. We infer His existence indirectly through the activities of the various organs, which are composite entities (and therefore exist for the sake of another) performing acts of perception, fancy and determination, the sign (for inferring the existence of the Lord within as the Witness for whose sake they perform their operations) being that they culminate in awareness as their final result. We conclude that there must be some being that uses, but does not enter into composition with, hearing and the other functions, since things that are composite exist for the sake of another (conscious being who devised them for an end), like a house. So my answer 'The Hearer of hearing' was relevant to the question.

But what, you might ask, is the meaning of the (tautologous) phrase 'The Hearer of hearing'? 'Hearing' surely does not need a second hearing, any more than light needs a second light. We reply that there is nothing wrong here. The meaning of the phrase is explicable as follows. The ear has the power to reveal its own special object (sound). But that power to reveal its own special object is only found because of the presence within all of Consciousness as the Light of the Self, and would not be found if the latter were not present. So to speak of 'The Hearer of hearing' and so on is but right....

The same is true in the case of the mind or inner organ. The inner organ would not be capable of carrying out its functions of fancy and determination unless it were lit from within by the Light of Consciousness.[52]

❖

4. As for your request that I should exhibit the Self to you like a pot, said Yājñavalkya, that I decline to do, as it is impossible. Why is it impossible? On account of its inherent nature. What is its inherent nature? It is the Seer of seeing and so forth. The Seer of seeing is the Self.

Seeing is of two kinds, that which passes for such in the world and that which is really such. That which passes for such in the world is a function of the inner organ (the mind) associated with the faculty of sight in the eye. It is an act and hence it has a beginning and an end. But the Seeing of the Self is the very nature of the Self as Seer, as heat and light are the very nature of fire, and hence it does not begin or end. Because it appears to be identical with that form of seeing which is an act and which is only its external adjunct (and so not part of its true nature), the seeing of the Self is spoken of as 'the Seer' (as if it were an agent in the act of seeing), and a distinction is set up between 'the Seer' and His 'seeing'.

That 'seeing' which passes for such in the world, and which is impregnated with colours through the operations of the faculty of sight, is something which has to be produced. As it appears to be identical with the eternal and changeless vision

(Consciousness) of the Self, it comes into being as a reflection of the latter, and is pervaded by it, and subsequently comes to an end. It is from this circumstance that the ultimate Seer (the Self), though always seeing, is loosely spoken of as sometimes seeing and sometimes not seeing. It is not that the seeing of the Seer in reality ever changes. Thus it will be said in the Fourth Chapter of the Upanishad 'He (only) *seems* to think, He (only) *seems* to move' and 'No break is found in the Seeing of the Seer'.[53]

This is the point that the present text, also, is conveying. You do not see the Seer who pervades the act of empirical seeing with His eternal vision. The act of empirical seeing, which reveals colour and is itself impregnated with colour, cannot penetrate to the Self, the inmost principle that pervades it. Hence you do not see that inmost Self, the Seer of seeing... Nor can you think that which pervades thinking, since thinking is a mere function of the mind... That is the inherent nature of the real. So it cannot be exhibited (as a distinct object) like a cow....

Perhaps you will say that if the Self were really beyond all modification, the Veda could not have referred to it by such terms as 'the Seer', 'the Hearer', 'the Thinker', 'the Knower' and so forth at all. But this objection is not right. For these expressions simply reproduce worldly speech usage as it is ordinarily employed. Because the other phrase 'You cannot see the Seer of seeing'[54] cannot be explained on any other basis, it is clear that the present phrases must mean just what we have said they mean.[55]

❖

5. An objector might (point to the different forms of the Self taught in the upanishadic texts and) ask how that Self can be known as one only without a second, beyond transmigratory experience. There is no problem, for instance, about knowledge of the individual soul (jīva). He is known as the hearer, the thinker, the one who sees, who commands, proclaims, understands and plumbs profound depths. Such an objector, it is true, could be told that if the true Self were taken in that way as the agent in the activities of hearing and the like, it would contradict such texts as 'The unthought Thinker, the unknown Knower' and 'You cannot think the Thinker of thinking, you cannot know the Knower of knowing'.[56] The objector might agree that there would be such an objection if the Self were taken to be known directly in the course of empirical experience, in the manner of mental experiences such as joy. Such direct knowledge is admittedly denied in texts like 'You cannot think the Thinker of thinking'. He is, however, known indirectly in that His existence is implied by the fact of hearing, etc. So the objector might consider that this view was not in contradiction with the Vedic texts.

Difficulties, however, arise. How can the Self be known even as that which is implied by the fact of hearing, etc.? For when the Self hears any sound, then, on account of the activity of hearing, there can be no activity of thinking or knowing, whether directed to the Self or elsewhere. And the same is true of the activity of thinking and of the activity of all the other faculties (i.e. each one excludes all the others whenever it is in play). And each of these faculties bears only on objects within its own sphere. The faculty of thinking, for instance, can only be exercised on objects of thought. You will say everything can be thought of by the mind. It is true, but nothing can be thought without a thinker. What follows if this is so? Well, the point is that the thinker, who can think of everything, can only be the thinker and never the thing thought, and there is no second thinker to think of the thinker.[57] If the thinker were supposed to be thought of by the Self, then we should have two separate principles, a Self by whom the Self was thought of and a Self that was the object of that thought. The Self, which must be one and undivided, would have to be conceived as cloven into two parts, consisting of thinker and object thought, like a bamboo split down the middle. Neither part could then fulfil the function assigned to it, any more than two lights could stand to one another as illuminator and illumined, both being identical (as light).

Nor has the thinker any time to think of the Self while thinking of objects of thought. Supposing for argument's sake that the thinker could think of the Self indirectly through a sign or symbol; even so, there would still be, just as before, two separate principles, the Self that was being thought of through a sign or symbol and the Self that was doing the thinking. So there would result the same fallacy that arose before, that of taking the Self, which is one and undivided, as consisting of two separate principles.

But if the Self cannot be directly perceived, and if it cannot be known through inference from signs either, you might ask how it was that the Vedic text could say 'He is my Self; this one should know'.[58] And how, too, could He be called 'the Hearer' and 'the Thinker'?

Here you might yourself reply that the Self has 'being the

Hearer' and so on as its intermittent qualities, while it is well known that it is not the Hearer by nature, and you might ask what the difficulty was in that. Well, there might not be any difficulties for you, but there would be for me. When He was the Hearer, He could not at the same time be the Thinker, and when He was the Thinker, He could not at the same time be the Hearer. On this assumption, from one point of view (the relative standpoint) He would be both the Hearer and the Thinker, and from another point of view (the absolute standpoint) He would be neither the Hearer nor the Thinker. And similar remarks would apply regarding (his rôle in relation to) the other cognitive faculties. This being so, you would be faced with the necessity of admitting that the Self might have, or equally plausibly might not have, the qualities of being the Hearer and so forth, and being locked in this doubt you cannot very well deny that you are in a difficulty. When Devadatta is moving about he is not a 'stander' but just a 'mover'. And when he is standing still he is not a 'mover' but just a 'stander'. Thus he is either a 'mover' or a 'stander' only at a particular time: he is not constantly and by his very nature either a mover or a stander. The difficulty with your view of the nature of the Self is just of this order (i.e. by attributing merely accidental characteristics to it, it fails to determine its essential nature).

The Vaiśeṣikas and others have a similar view. They say that it is only in particular circumstances that we can attribute hearing to the Self and call it the Hearer or the Thinker as the case may be. And they maintain that knowledge can only arise through sense-contact and that (although they may follow on one another very quickly) no two cognitions can be simultaneous. They illustrate their thesis that the mind cannot be engaged in more than one kind of cognition at any one instant by appeal to the argument mentioned in the upanishadic text, 'I did not see that, as my mind was elsewhere'.[59]

Well, you might ask, what harm would result to our (objector's) position if all this were so? We reply, 'Let it be so, if you wish. Only it cannot be the doctrine of the Veda'. It will not do to retort that the Veda speaks of the Self as the Hearer and the Thinker, as there are other texts in which it denies that the Self is either the Hearer or the Thinker. Nor will it help to accuse me of having myself admitted that the Self was a hearer and thinker at one time but not at another. For I do not maintain that doctrine at all. I stand by the doctrine that the Self is the *eternal and constant* Hearer, as expressed in such texts as 'No break is found in the Hearing of the Hearer'.[60]

Against this you might object that, if one accepts that the Self is the eternal and constant Hearer, one accepts by implication that there can be a plurality of simultaneous cognitions of different kinds, which is against our experience,[61] while denying any ignorance whatever; both of which positions are untenable.[62] But neither of these criticisms will stand. The Vedic texts affirm roundly that the Self is the Hearer of hearing and the Thinker of thinking and so forth. It is the seeing and so forth of the sense faculties such as sight that is transient and impermanent, since these faculties pertain to sense-organs which are material objects capable of entry into contact and disjunction. Such seeing and so forth is impermanent because it depends on contact with objects, just as the burning of a fire is impermanent because it depends on contact with combustibles like straw. But that which is eternal and changeless, purely spiritual in nature and not capable of entry into contact or disjunction, cannot have transient qualities like seeing, understood in the sense of sense-perception, which depends on the contact of the sense-organs with objects....

Thus there are two kinds of seeing, the transient seeing of the sense-faculty of vision operating through the eye, and the eternal and changeless seeing of the Self. Similarly, there are two kinds of hearing... thinking... and knowing... Even from the ordinary common-sense standpoint it is admitted that the seeing of the visual faculty is 'impermanent' in the sense that there are cases where it is first removed and then restored due to an attack of eye-disease and subsequent recovery from it; and it is also generally admitted that hearing and thinking and other cognitive faculties are 'impermanent' in this sense, while the seeing, hearing and thinking of the Self within are constant. For one who has lost his eye-sight will say, 'Today I saw my brother in a dream' and one who is well-known to be deaf will say, 'Today I heard the recitation of a Vedic verse in the course of my dream'. If the seeing of the Self arose purely from contact with the faculty of vision present in the eye (as the Vaiśeṣikas and others claim), it would be lost with the loss of the eye, and the one who had lost his eye could not see vivid colours in his dreams....

The eternal seeing of the Self apprehends the transient external seeing of the eye. The idea that because the external seeing comes and goes and is impermanent, the seeing of the Self which apprehends it is of like nature and impermanent too — this idea is nothing more than a common confusion. It is an illusion, like the illusion that your own sight is being whirled about when it becomes fixed on a torch or other brilliant object that is being whirled about at night.[63] And this is confirmed by the Vedic text 'He (only) *seems* to think, He (only) *seems* to move'.[64]

Therefore, since the seeing of the Self is eternal and constant, the question of whether it does or does not bring about several different cognitions simultaneously does not arise. But the erroneous notion of the people at large, and of the secular philosophers, that the seeing of the Self is intermittent, is intelligible as rising from the Self's illusory conjunction with the act of external seeing, which is intermittent. For the secular philosophers and the people at large do not have the benefit of a Teacher who knows how to communicate the texts of the Upanishads in the traditional way.[65]

❖

6. Perhaps, says the opponent, you will say that the Self is the Seer of seeing, the Hearer of hearing, the Thinker of thinking and the Knower of knowing. But such a way of speaking introduces no new qualification into the idea of 'seer' (that would render the expression anything more than tautology). Whether a 'seer' is 'seer' of seeing or 'seer' of a pot is immaterial; he is just the seer in either case. You have only introduced a distinction into the nature of the seen, not into that of the seer.

But here the Advaitin demurs. A distinction, he says, *has* been introduced into the nature of the seer. If the Seer of seeing is Himself the seeing, He *always* sees the seeing and the seeing is never not seen by the Seer. In this case the seeing of the Seer must be constant and eternal. If the seeing of the Seer were not constant, then the seeing would sometimes not be seen, as an object of empirical vision, like a pot, is sometimes seen and sometimes not seen. But the Seer of seeing never omits to see seeing in this way.

Is it then that the Seer has two seeings, one eternal and constant and not itself requiring to be seen like an object, and the other occasional and requiring to be seen like an object? Yes, it is. The occasional seeing is evident to us all, as we find, for instance, that some people are blind, others not. If (this kind of) seeing were eternal and constant, no one would be blind. But the seeing of the Seer *is* eternal and constant, for we have the Vedic text 'There is no break in the seeing of the Seer'.[66]

Inference, too, would point to the same conclusion. Even a blind man has vision of pots and other imaginary objects in dream. This is the seeing that is not destroyed when empirical vision is destroyed, and this is the seeing that belongs to the Seer. As Seer of seeing, it eternally and constantly beholds the impressions of dream and perceptions of waking with its constant and eternal vision, which is its very nature, called 'self-luminous light (svayaṃ-jyotiḥ)'. Seeing is thus its very nature, as heat is the very nature of fire. It is not, as the Vaiśeṣikas believe, that there is any other Seer, distinct from seeing, and its conscious possessor.[67]

❖

7. The Absolute rests in the supreme golden sheath. 'Golden' means composed of light, composed of the light of intellectual knowledge (buddhi-vijñāna). It rests in this sheath like a sword in its scabbard, in the sense that this is the place where one can find the Absolute as one can find a sword in its scabbard. It is called the 'supreme' sheath because it lies within all else. But in it lies the Absolute, free from the taint of all defects such as nescience and the rest.[68] The Absolute is called Brahman

because it is greater than all else and the Self of all else. It is also partless and without structure of any kind.

Because it is taintless and partless, it is the pure light that illumines fire and all other luminous principles. The luminosity of these principles depends on the presence of the internal Light of Consciousness in its true nature as the Self or the Absolute. That only is the supreme Light which is not illumined by another, and that is the Light of the Self. The wise, those possessed of discrimination, know the Self as the Witness of the ideas representing material objects, and adopt the standpoint that they themselves are the Self. Because the Self is the supreme Light, it is only those persons who are possessed of discrimination who know it, not others. For the latter (invariably) adopt the standpoint of (identifying themselves with) the empirical perceiver perceiving external objects.

Next the text proceeds to explain the meaning of the phrase 'Light of lights'. Though the sun illumines all below, it does not shine on the Self or Absolute. That is, it does not illumine it. For it is only through the light of the Self that the sun illumines all the not-self. It has no independent power of illumination of its own. The same is true of the moon and the stars and the lightning, what to say of the fire which we can perceive here below.

In short, this world that is manifest before us manifests in the Light of the supreme Lord. He is of the nature of Light. As torches and the like do not burn of themselves but merely conform to the behaviour of the fire that has been applied to them, so do the sun and all other luminous objects in the world shine through the luminosity of the Absolute and not of their own accord.

This being so, it is that Absolute alone that manifests differently in different effects. Hence it follows that the Absolute is of the very nature of luminosity. For what is itself not luminous cannot illumine other things, as is shown by the fact that pots and similar opaque objects are never found to illumine other objects, whereas the sun and other luminous objects do.[69]

❖

8. The opponent has claimed that the Absolute cannot be omniscient in the literal sense of the word, for if His act of knowing is constant and eternal, He will not be a free agent in regard to it. But we are entitled to ask the good man why the eternal activity of knowing should in any way detract from the omniscience of the Absolute. There is no self-contradiction in the proposition 'He who has eternal knowledge, capable of illumining all objects, is omniscient'. It is when knowledge is *not* constant, and a being sometimes has knowledge and sometimes does not have it, that he is not omniscient. But this defect is not present where knowledge is constant and eternal.

Perhaps you will contend that it is not right to speak of free independent cognitive action in relation to an object of knowledge if knowledge is eternal and constant. But this objection is not right. For we find it said of the sun, 'It burns' and 'It illumines', though its heat and light are constant.

Perhaps you will rejoin that we may very well speak of the sun as burning and illumining when it is in contact with objects that can be burnt and illumined, but that in the case of the Absolute there is no contact with any object of knowledge before the rise of the world (at the beginning of the world-period), so that the example fails because it is on a different footing from what it is supposed to exemplify. But this is wrong, for we see that the sun is said to 'shine' even when there is no object for it to illumine. And because it is said of the Absolute that in the absence of any object of knowledge (before the manifestation of the world at the beginning of the world-period) 'It took thought',[70] it can be spoken of as an agent in the same sense as the sun, so that the two are here on an equal footing.

In fact, in regard to the question of having an object, the texts saying that the Absolute 'took thought' (before the projection of the world) are more justified (than the example of the sun could possibly show). Do you then ask what it was that formed the object of the knowledge of the Lord before the rise of the manifestation of the world? It was name and form, we reply, indeterminable either as the principle of reality or as anything different, as yet unmanifest, but about to be manifested. The followers of the Yoga Śāstra maintain that even yogins enjoy direct knowledge of past and future things through His grace. How much more, then, should we attribute the constant and eternal knowledge implied by the projection, maintenance and withdrawal of the whole world-appearance to Him who is eternally and constantly established as the Lord.

The opponent said earlier that the Absolute could not be supposed to 'take thought' before the rise to manifestation of the world, as it would not then be connected with a body or other organs. But this objection is out of place, since the Absolute is knowledge by nature, just as the sun is light by nature, so that in His case it is wrong to speak of dependence on instruments of knowledge. Moreover, it is those afflicted by nescience, such as the individual souls under transmigration, who depend on a body and other instruments to bring about knowledge. This is not so in the case of the Lord, for in His case nothing exists that could obstruct knowledge.[71]

4. The Absolute as Bliss

Śaṅkara was a good deal less exuberant than his later followers came to be in his references to the Absolute or the Self as bliss. This may be illustrated from the case of the famous work called 'The Crest-Jewel of Wisdom', attributed to him but now known to have been composed centuries after his death by some member of his school. Of the 580 verses of the 'Crest-Jewel' almost a tenth refer in one way or another to the topic of bliss, whereas in Śaṅkara's one independent work of guaranteed authenticity, the Upadeśa Sāhasrī, there is only one appearance of the term bliss (ānanda)[72], and the Absolute is regularly described as 'Being-and-Consciousness-only (sac-cin-mātra)' and not according to the later formula 'Being-Consciousness-Bliss (sac-cid-ānanda)'. Nevertheless, the Upanishads do speak of the Absolute as bliss, and this note is not absent from Śaṅkara's genuine texts, as we have already had occasion to notice.[73]

Of the following Extracts dealing further with the subject, No. 1 points to the bliss of the Absolute available in dreamless sleep when nescience is absent. No. 2 shows that, under the influence of nescience, the bliss of the Absolute manifests in fragmentary and temporary form as worldly joy. No. 3 speaks of the bliss in the 'ether of the heart' enjoyed by those who realize the true nature of the Self. Nos. 4-6 explain how the bliss of the Self is permanent, and, unlike that derived from objects, not dependent on activity. No. 7 (a most important passage) declares that the bliss of the Self is not anything experienced like an object. If certain upanishadic passages (of which the later theistic schools of Vedanta were to make much) refer to supernormal joys, these are but references to exalted states of yoga and, as such, within the domain of nescience. The knower of the Absolute is not identified with them or with states of misery either, as he is not identified with the mind or with any external adjunct.

TEXTS ON THE ABSOLUTE AS BLISS

1. But when in dreamless sleep that nescience[74] which sets up the appearance of beings other than the Self has ceased, there is no (apparent) entity separated from oneself as if it were another. At that time, with what could one see, smell or understand? Then one is wholly embraced by one's own Self as Consciousness, of the nature of self-luminous Light. One is then all serene, with one's desires attained, transparent as water, and this is all on account of the absence of any second. For if a second thing is distinguished, this must be through nescience, and as this has now ceased, what is left is one (and homogeneous). It is the Seer, because its seeing, being of the nature of self-luminous Light, is without a break. It is without a second, for there is no second thing over against it for it to see. This is the immortal, the fearless state. This is the world of Brahman, that is to say, the world that *is* Brahman (the Absolute).[75] O King, says Yājñavalkya, at this time (i.e. when the soul passes into the state of dreamless sleep) the supreme Reality, having thrown off all external adjuncts such as the body and the senses, shorn of all relationships, rests in its own Light.

This is the highest state of the principle of Light that undergoes (apparent) embodiment. All other states, from that of the deity governing creation (Brahmā) to that of the meanest clump of grass, involve embodiment, are imagined through nescience, and are secondary because they belong to the realm of nescience (whereas in the state of dreamless sleep the soul passes beyond the state of nescience). But this state (of dreamless sleep) is far higher than the position of the gods and other exalted beings, that is achieved through assiduous performance of the rituals and meditation on their symbolic significance. It is a state of identity with the Self of all, where one sees nothing else, hears nothing else, knows nothing else. This is the highest glory. It is the highest of glories because it is one's natural state, and all other states of glory are wrought (and hence perishable). This is one's highest world, and all other worlds, the fruit of rituals, are inferior. But this state is not within the compass of action, as it is one's natural state (and therefore eternally realized, even though, under nescience, one may not be aware of it). This is one's highest world and also one's highest bliss. It is one's supreme bliss in comparison with all other joys whatever that are promoted by the contact of the senses with their objects, because it is eternal. 'That which is infinite, that is joy',[76] says another text...

On a fraction of this bliss, a fraction set up by nescience and lasting as long as the contact of the senses with particular (pleasurable) objects lasts, all other beings subsist.[77]

❖

2. We begin an enquiry into the meaning of the word 'bliss' in the text, to decide whether it means that worldly joy that arises from the inter-relationship of subject and object, or whether it refers to the natural, eternal Bliss of the Self.

Worldly bliss only blossoms when the inner and outer conditions for it are present. It is introduced (as a topic) here only to give some idea of the Absolute. For it is through this familiar worldly bliss that one can gain some notion of the utter joy and beatitude that come to one whose mind is withdrawn from objects.

Even worldly bliss is a fragment of the Bliss of the Absolute. For when knowledge is overborne by nescience and the latter gains the ascendancy in varying degrees, then the Bliss of the Absolute manifests as temporary worldly joy in all living beings from Brahmā downwards, according to their merits derived from previous actions, the merit from previously performed meditations on themes provided in the ritualistic texts and on the (consequent) availability of objects and other means to enjoyment. This same Bliss of the Absolute is directly experienced by one who is versed in the Vedic wisdom and not smitten by desire, and it manifests in ascending degrees in the 'human Gandharvas' (a class of supremely happy beings mentioned in the text under comment) and other beings in proportion to the weakening of their nescience, desire and selfish activity, each class enjoying a hundredfold more until the bliss of Hiraṇyagarbha[78] is reached at the top of the scale. But when the distinction set up by nescience between subject and object has been abolished through knowledge, then what remains is the natural infinite Bliss alone, one without a second.[79]

❖

3. This knowledge of the Absolute, which was attained by Bhṛgu and taught by Varuṇa, starts with a knowledge of the body and proceeds up from there till it establishes itself as the

supreme non-dual principle of Bliss in the ether of the cave of the heart. The implication is that anyone who follows this path can enter into Bliss and know the Absolute. He becomes firmly established in Bliss, in the Supreme, in the Absolute, because his knowledge is firmly established. That is to say he becomes the Absolute.[80]

❖

4. And there is another reason to show that the Absolute must exist. The Absolute is 'savour' (rasa). How do we know that the Absolute is savour? Because, says the Upanishad, that which is well-made is also savour. Savour, whether sweet or bitter, is well-known in the world as that which brings about joy. The text says, 'A person is happy only when he has enjoyed savour of some sort'. Never do we find in the world that joy arises from something that is non-existent. Knowers of the Absolute (brāhmaṇa), men of enlightenment, are found who have no external instruments of joy and make no effort to procure joy, and yet who are as blissful as if they were extracting joy from external means all the time. The savour they enjoy is the Absolute. Hence it follows that the Absolute must exist as that which yields them the savour they enjoy.[81]

❖

5. But why should it be the Self, in particular, that is the thing to be known, to the contempt of all else? The Upanishad replies in the words 'It is dearer than a son...' A son being a typical example in the world of something dear, to say that the Self is dearer than a son is a way of saying that it is supremely dear above all. It implies that it is also dearer than all other things that are held dear in the world, such as wealth, gold or

jewels. One might raise the question why it should be the Self and not the Principle of Vital Energy or some other good that should be held supremely dear. For the Principle of Vital Energy and the complex of body and organs are more intimate possessions than such evidently external entities as sons or wealth. But the Self as the prime metaphysical principle is more intimate even than those intimate possessions. Whatever in the world is supremely dear is sought after with every effort. And this Self is dearer than anything dear belonging to the empirical world. So it follows that very great efforts indeed should be made to attain it, to the exclusion of efforts to attain any other good, even though the latter may seem to be enjoined as a duty.

But someone might persist and ask why should it be the Self that is sought and the not-self rejected, and not the reverse, when both the Self and the not-self are dear and the acquisition of one implies the rejection of the other. To this the text replies that one who holds the Self to be supremely dear, and who hears another declare that some feature of the not-self such as son or the like is dearer than the Self, should say to him, 'Come, the object of your desire, be it a son or whatever else, will one day die or be destroyed'.[82]

❖

6. In this way, this joy, which is the supreme reality and which is experience of the true nature of the Self, is self-established. It is 'peaceful' in the sense of constituting the cessation of all evil. It is delightful, for the word 'nirvāṇa' is derived from nirvṛti meaning delight.[83] It exists in delight as perfect transcendence (kaivalya). Its nature is unutterable

because it belongs to a unique realm; for this superlative joy is accessible to the yogin himself alone. It is not 'born' (produced, for instance by the contact of the senses with their objects) as the joy arising from objects is (which invariably has a beginning and consequently an end). Those who have realized the Absolute say that this joy is none other than the unborn principle which is the object of our search, and that it is the omniscient Absolute, having omniscience for its nature.[84]

❖

7. Here we embark on some reflection (vicāra). The word 'ānanda' is current in the world meaning 'bliss'. And the Upanishads apply the word 'ānanda' particularly to the Absolute, saying 'The Absolute is Bliss'....[85] The accepted meaning of the word 'bliss' is the joy that is an *object* of experience. And if the Bliss of the Absolute were an object of experience, there would be nothing wrong in calling the Absolute 'Bliss'. You might indeed say that the authority of the Veda itself declares that the nature of the Absolute is Bliss that can be experienced as an object, so that no further enquiry is needed. But that is not right. For we find (other) Vedic texts which contradict this. It is true that the word 'Bliss' is applied to the Absolute. But the notion of determinate cognition (vijñāna) stands contradicted if the Absolute is a perfect unity. And there are texts which declare that it is an absolute unity, such as 'But when for him all this has become the Self, then what could he see and with what?'[86] ...And as we thus find contradictory Vedic texts, we must undertake some critical reflection. Furthermore, there are different views held upon the point by the different philosophical schools in their various

theories of liberation. The Sāṅkhyas and Vaiśeṣikas, for instance, hold to the existence of liberation but declare that no joy is experienced in that state, while others state that unsurpassable joy is experienced.

What, then, is the reasonable view? One might initially suppose that joy was experienced in liberation. For we have such Vedic texts as 'Eating, playing and enjoying himself', 'If he became desirous of the world of the ancestors, it would appear by his mere wish', 'He who is Witness of all and cognisant of all' and 'He attains all desires'.[87] You might argue against us (the exponent of the *prima facie* view maintains) that there can be no determinate knowledge (vijñāna) where there are no factors permitting the rise of any act of cognition, since determinate cognition implies an act composed of several factors. But such an argument (the exponent of the *prima facie* view continues) is vain because we know on the authority of the revealed Vedic texts that there *is* determinate cognition of the Absolute, otherwise we could not explain such texts as (the one at present under comment) 'The Absolute is determinate cognition (vijñāna) and Bliss'.

Perhaps (the exponent of the *prima facie* view argues further) you will say that not even a Vedic text can make fire cold or water hot, its sole function lying in the communication of information. Nor could it inform us (of something outside our possible experience and radically contradictory to our experience and say) that there does exist fire that is cold and water that is hot in places that are inaccessible to us.[88] But these arguments (according to the exponent of the *prima facie* view) will not do either. For we have direct objective knowledge (he says) of the presence of Bliss in our inmost

Self. Texts like 'The Absolute is determinate cognition and Bliss' do not contradict experience in the way that statements like 'Fire is cold' would. And the fact that they do not contradict experience is subject to direct verification. The feeling 'I am happy' itself reveals one's own Self to be of the nature of Bliss, so these texts are in no conceivable contradiction with experience. Therefore the Absolute reveals itself to us as being of the nature of Bliss and determinate cognition. And hence the texts like 'Eating, playing and enjoying himself', which we quoted above as implying that the Bliss of the Absolute is an object of experience, do actually have that meaning.

But this whole *prima facie* view is wrong. There cannot be determinate cognition in the absence of organs and instruments of knowledge. Final liberation, however, implies separation from the body,[89] and, in the absence of a body, there cannot be organs and instruments of knowledge for lack of a seat. So determinate cognition is impossible in liberation on account of the absence of organs and instruments of knowledge. And if determinate cognition could arise in the absence of a body and organs, it would be unnecessary to use organs and instruments of knowledge to attain it at all (which is absurd and contradicts the opponent's own beliefs).

Moreover, if there could be objective knowledge of the Bliss of the Absolute in liberation, this would contradict the perfect unity of the Absolute. Nor will it avail to say that the Absolute perpetually knows itself objectively as Bliss because it is of the very nature of determinate cognition (vijñāna). For this would imply that the ignorant man under transmigration, too, would automatically be perpetually aware of his own nature (and so not in transmigration). The fact is that the liberated man is like a cupped handful of water thrown back into a tank. He is in no way separate from the Absolute that he could have determinate cognition of it as being of the nature of Bliss. The claim, therefore, that the Absolute reveals itself to the liberated man as being of the nature of Bliss is nonsensical.

Perhaps you will claim that the liberated one is other than the Absolute but that he knows the Bliss of the Absolute and also knows his inmost Self, so that he has the experience 'I am of the nature of Bliss'. But this view would contradict the perfect unity of the Absolute, and this in turn would be against all the upanishadic texts. And there is no third possibility.

And there is another point. If the Absolute had perpetual knowledge of its own nature as Bliss, the distinction between 'knowledge' and 'absence of knowledge' would be meaningless. If the knowledge of the Absolute perpetually bears on its own Bliss, then that must be its very nature, and the supposition that it took (active steps to have) cognisance of its own Bliss would be improper. The suggestion that the Absolute took (active steps to have) cognisance of its own Bliss would only be tenable if it were at any time ignorant of it, as when we say (quite meaningfully of someone in the world) 'He knows himself and the other person too'. But when the arrow-maker is *constantly* absorbed in the construction of his arrow, the distinction between awareness of it and unawareness is irrelevant.

One would therefore have to suppose that the Absolute only knew its own Bliss at intervals. But in that case its knowledge would bear on other things when it was not engaged in knowing itself, and this would imply that the Self was subject to modification and hence impermanent.[90] Therefore the statement (in the text at present under comment) 'The Absolute is Vijñāna and Bliss' is a statement of the ultimate nature of the Absolute (in which the word 'Vijñāna' has to be understood as meaning pure Consciousness) and does not imply that the Bliss of the Absolute is subject to determinate cognition.

Nor can it be said that the view that the Bliss of the Self is not the object of determinate cognition stands in contradiction with Vedic texts like 'Eating, playing and enjoying himself'. For such texts merely record empirical facts in the case of one who has realized that he is the Self of all. The liberated one is the Self of all. The text in question refers to whatever is experienced (mysteriously) in the way of eating and the rest by yogins in exalted states and by deities, and affirms, by way of eulogy, that it accrues to the liberated man also, as he is the Self of all.

But, you will ask, will not this make the misery of inferior beings accrue for him too? For example, will he not experience pain whenever it comes, as in lower creatures like plants, just as he experiences the 'eating' and so on (of the advanced yogin)? No, all this is refuted by the fact that the very distinction between the feelings 'I am happy' and 'I am miserable' is only superimposed through illusion generated by contact with external adjuncts such as the body and its organs of knowledge and action, themselves composed of (mere) name and form. And we have already explained the meaning of the (seemingly) contradictory Vedic texts of this kind.[91] Hence all texts affirming that the Absolute is Bliss should be interpreted on the model of 'This is his highest Bliss'[92] (where the Bliss of the Absolute is understood as a non-dual principle, different from the bliss arising from the contact of the senses with their objects or from that in which one has knowledge of any object).[93]

NOTES TO CHAPTER IV

References to Extracts are in bold type

1 Above, 141f.

2 Bṛhad. III.ix.28.

3 N.Sid. III.47 (prose). The formula there is satya-jñānānanda. The transition from the upanishadic 'jñāna' to the familiar 'cit' of 'sac-cid-ānanda' probably occurred long after Śaṅkara's day. Prakāśātman (? tenth century) still adheres to the upanishadic 'jñāna', speaking of 'satya-jñānānanda'. *Vivaraṇa*, 615 and 616, cp. Cammann, 119.

4 Cp. Nyāya Sūtra I.i.3, quoted in Biardeau, *Définition*, 372.

5 lakṣaṇārtha-pradhānāni viśeṣaṇāni na viśeṣaṇa-pradhānāny eva, Taitt.Bh. II.1, trans. Gambhīrānanda, 302.

6 Biardeau, *Définition*, 377.

7 Cp. Īśa 8, Bh.G. II.24.

8 Cp. also Sureśvara, N.Sid. II.24ff.

9 See B.S.Bh. III.ii.21, trans. Gambhīrānanda, 617f.

10 Satyam, jñanam, anantam, Taitt. II.i.1.

11 Taitt.Bh. II.i.1, trans. Gambhīrānanda, 309. The contradictory of Reality is not-reality, of Knowledge is not-knowledge, of Infinity is not-infinity (finitude).

12 lakṣyate na tūcyate, trans. Gambhīrānanda *ibid.*

13 Gambhīrānanda, *ibid.*, 310. Cp. Sureśvara, N.Sid. III.2 (prose), III.9 and possibly also III.26 (prose).

14 Sac, *Taittirīya Bhāṣyārtha Vimarśinī*, II, 24f.

15 Chānd. VII.xxiv.1.

16 It cannot designate the Absolute directly as will be shown later

in the present Extract. But it occurs in the Veda and hence must be presumed to refer to a reality.

17 The term vijñāna is sometimes found in Śaṅkara meaning determinate cognition as opposed to the infinite light of Consciousness, and sometimes meaning immediate knowledge as opposed to derived knowledge.

18 Cp.U.S. (verse) XVIII.53.

19 Cp. Note 99 to Chapter III and the references there given.

20 Taitt. II.4 and Taitt. II.7, texts supervening close upon the definition under discussion.

21 Words cannot designate the Absolute either alone or in combination. **Taitt. Bh. II.1.**

22 sāvaśeṣa, Taitt.Bh. III.1, trans. Gambhīrānanda, 390.

23 Taitt. Bh. III.1.

24 Chānd. Bh. VI.viii.4.

25 For the theory of the elements in more detail, see Vol.II, Chap.VI, section 3, below.

26 M.Bh. XII.233.5 says that at the end of the world-period the element earth will dissolve back into water, the element from which it originally sprang forth.

27 Kaṭha Bh. I.iii.15.

28 The concept here is that of a universal drum-sound comprising the class to which all particular instances of drum-sounds belong, and distinct from the other universals, representing, for example, conch-sounds or lute-sounds, etc., but all encompassed by the wider universal sound-in-general.

29 Bṛhad. Bh. II.iv.9.

30 Bh.G.Bh. II.16 and 17.

31 No ātman or Self, the thesis, in particular, of the Mādhyamika Buddhists.

32 As a clay pot, for instance, is invariably perceived as associated with clay.

33 Chānd. VI.ii.2.

34 E.g. 'He formed the resolution "Let Me create the world".' Ait. I.i.1.

35 Taitt. Bh. II.6.

36 On the Sāṅkhya doctrine, see Vol.IV, Chap.XI, section 3.

37 Chānd. Bh. VI.ii.3.

38 Chānd. VI.ii.2.

39 B.S.Bh. II.iii.9.

40 G.K.Bh. III.27.

41 Bh.G.Bh. XIII.14.

42 E.g. in Extract 6.

43 Śaṅkara uses the same illustration in the course of refuting the Materialists, cp. below Vol.IV, Chap.XI, section 2.

44 The owner or builder of the house, who has built it for an end of his own. **Ait. Bh. I.iii.11.**

45 Reading acaitanya-svarūpo.

46 The comparison with a carpenter occurs also at B.S.Bh. II.iii.40, trans. Gambhīrānanda, 500. Cp.below, Vol.III, Chap.VIII, section 2, Extract 15.

47 On the composition of the sense-organs from the subtle forms of the elements, see Chap.VIII, section 1, below.

48 I.e. sattva, rajas and tamas, the three guṇas of Māyā, for which see Vol.II, Chap.V, section 5, below. References to the guṇas,

unless dictated by the text on which he is commenting, are somewhat rare in Śaṅkara. Cp., however, Bṛhad. Bh. II.i.15, trans. Mādhavānanda, 191, where the guṇas are referred to, as here, by the terms 'sukha', 'duhkha', 'moha', as also at Bh.G. Bh. XIII.19, below, Vol.II, Chap.V, section 5, Extract 1.

49 I.e. will have no independent reality apart from cognitions performed through nescience. The argument amounts to phenomenalism as it stands. Śaṅkara, however, wrote from more than one standpoint. When pressing home the transcendence of the Absolute and the unreality of duality, he could speak the language of phenomenalism. But this did not mean that he thought that, when the soul was identified with its individual body-mind organism and regarded itself as an agent striving for purification and release, it could regard the external world as no more than the sum of the erroneous cognitions of its denizens, against the teachings of the Veda and Smṛti, which speak of an external world presided over by an omniscient, omnipotent Lord.

50 On dreamless sleep, see Note 74 below, and, more generally, Vol.III, Chap.IX, section 2, below.

51 U.S. (prose) sections 86-111.

52 Kena (Pada) Bh. I.2.

53 Bṛhad. IV.iii.7 and IV.iii.23.

54 Bṛhad. III.iv.2.

55 Bṛhad. Bh. III.iv.2.

56 Brhad. III.viii.11 and III.iv.2.

57 It is not enough, with Hume and the philosophers of certain Buddhist schools, to deny the existence of the thinker simply because the thinker can never be thought of as an object. For the very experience of objects implies the existence of a thinker. Cp.Karl Jaspers, *The Way to Wisdom*, 28-38, where the author

deals with the topic much on Śaṅkara's lines and appeals to the experience of the mystics of China, India and the West.

58 Kauṣītaki III.8.

59 Bṛhad. I.v.3.

60 Bṛhad. IV.iii.27.

61 The objector labours under the fallacy of reducing all cognition to empirical cognition. On his own premises, his conclusion is true. If we are wholly engaged in thinking, we do not hear the distant train. In so far as we attend to the sound of the train, thought is suspended, even though the gap may be too short to be worthy of remark.

62 The Vedas exist to teach that knowledge which confers liberation. But the Advaitin is saying that the knowledge emanating from the Self is constant and eternal, which would, on the face of it, render the Veda useless.

63 Professor Hacker, 'Śaṅkara der Yogin', 129, contrasts Śaṅkara's use of the whirling torch simile at G.K.Bh. IV.47-50 and U.S. (verse) XIX.10 with its use here. References to the illusory effect of a whirling torch are common in Buddhist authors of the early Mahāyāna period and not unknown in the Brahminical literature either, cp. Maitrī Upan. VI.24; Vātsyāyana *Nyāya Sūtras Bh.* III.ii.58, and Bhartṛhari *Vākyapadīya* II.291 and III.viii.8. Compare also the references at David Hume, *Treatise on Human Nature*, Book l, part ii, section 3 (ed. Selby-Bigge, 35), Jalālu'ddīn Rūmī, *Mathnawī* ed. Nicholson I.1147, and Ovid, *Metamorphoses,* IV.508f.

64 Bṛhad. IV.iii.7.

65 Ait. Bh. II.i.1, introduction.

66 Bṛhad. IV.iii.23.

67 Bṛhad. Bh. I.iv.10.

68 'The rest' means desire and action. Sac, Notes on Śaṅkara's comm. to Muṇḍ. II.ii.9, p 73.

69 Muṇḍ. Bh. II.ii.9 and 10 (or 10 and 11).

70 Chānd. VI.ii.3.

71 B.S.Bh. I.i.5.

72 U.S. (verse) XVII.63. The joy (sukha) of the knower of the Self is mentioned, *ibid.* VIII.6.

73 See above, Chap.III, section 3, Extract 1.

74 Since (as we have already seen, above, Chap.II, section 1 *ad init.*) Śaṅkara was apt to identify the term nescience with superimposition according to a common usage amongst philosophers of different schools in his day, he was quite prepared to say that it was absent in dreamless sleep, even for the unenlightened man, though in the case of the latter the 'seeds' of nescience remained. See Chap.IX, section 2, below.

75 Not 'Brahma-loka' in the sense of realm or state of consciousness presided over by Brahmā, in which the soul that has attained deferred release awaits final liberation at the end of the world-period, for which see Vol.VI, Chap.XIV, sections 2 and 3, below.

76 Chānd. VII.xiii.1.

77 Bṛhad. Bh. IV.iii.32.

78 See Chap.VI, section 3, below.

79 Taitt. Bh. II.8.

80 Taitt. Bh. III.6.

81 Taitt. Bh. II.7.

82 Bṛhad. Bh. I.iv.8.

83 Śaṅkara explains the etymology of the word nirvāṇa at

Bh.G.Bh. II.72 and V.24-26 in the same way as he does here.

84 **G.K.Bh. III.47.**

85 Taitt. III.6, cp. Extract 3 of present section.

86 Bṛhad. II.iv.14.

87 Chānd. VIII.xii.3, Chānd. VIII.ii.1, Muṇḍ. I.i.9, Taitt. II.5.

88 Water was supposed to be naturally cold according to the physics of the day.

89 This rather difficult point of the 'bodilessness' of the liberated man will be treated of in Vol.VI, Chap.XVI.

90 If the Self were the agent in any act of knowing, it would be subject to change and therefore composed of parts and therefore certain eventually to decompose.

91 Bṛhad. Bh. II.v.15, trans. Mādhavānanda, 273f.

92 Bṛhad. IV.iii.32, cp. Extract 1 of present section.

93 **Brhad. Bh. III.ix.28.**

LIST OF GENERAL ABBREVIATIONS

In principle, works are referred to under their authors' names throughout the Notes, and the abbreviations occasionally used to distinguish between an author's different works should not cause any difficulty. Except for the two entries R.T. and Sac, the following list comprises those abbreviations that are used independently of any author's name. The list excludes the names of Upanishads on which Śaṅkara wrote commentaries, which are listed under his name in the Bibliography and readily identifiable there.

A.B.O.R.I.	*Annals of the Bhandarkar Oriental Research Institute*, Poona
Ā.D.S.	*Āpastamba Dharma Sūtra*
Ā.Ś.G.	*Āgama Śāstra of Gauḍapāda*
Ā.S.S.	Ānanda Āśrama Sanskrit Series, Poona
Ā.Ś.S.	*Āpastambīyam Śrauta Sūtram*, Mysore University
A.V.	*Atharva Veda*
B.B.V.	*Bṛhadāraṇyakopaniṣad Bhāṣya Vārtika* (Sureśvara)
B.B.V.S.	*Bṛhadāraṇyakopaniṣad Bhāṣya Vārtika Sāra* (Vidyāraṇya)
Bh.	*Bhāṣya* (i.e. Commentary)
Bh.G.	*Bhagavad Gītā*
Bh.G.Bh.	*Bhagavad Gītā Bhāṣya* (Śaṅkara)
B.S.	*Brahma Sūtras*
B.S.Bh.	*Brahma Sūtra Bhāṣya* (Śaṅkara)
B.Sid.	*Brahma Siddhi* (Maṇḍana Miśra)
C.P.B.	*The Central Philosophy of Buddhism* (T.R.V. Murti)
G.I.P.	*Geschichte der indischen Philosophie* (Frauwallner)

G.K.	*Gauḍapāda Kārikās*, included in Gambhīrānanda, *Eight Upanishads*, Vol.II
G.K.Bh.	*Gauḍapāda Kārikā Bhāṣya*
G.O.S.	Gaekwad's Oriental Series, Baroda
G.P.	Gītā Press, Gorakhpur
I.H.Q.	*Indian Historical Quarterly*
I.I.J.	*Indo-Iranian Journal*
J.A.	*Journal Asiatique*
J.A.O.S.	*Journal of the American Oriental Society*
J.B.O.O.S.	*Journal of the Bihar and Orissa Oriental Society*
J.O.I.B.	*Journal of the Oriental Institute*, Baroda
J.O.R.M.	*Journal of Oriental Research*, Madras University
J.R.A.S.B.B.	*Journal of the Royal Asiatic Society of Great Britain and Ireland, Bombay Branch*
J.U.B.	*Jaiminīya Upanishad Brāhmaṇa*
M.Bh.	*Mahābhārata* G.P. Mūla-mātra Ed., 4 Vols.
M.K.	*Mādhyamika* (or *Mūlamādhyamika*) *Kārikās* of Nāgārjuna
M.R.V.	*Māṇḍūkya Rahasya Vivṛtiḥ* (Saccidānandendra Svāmin)
M.V.	*Method of the Vedanta* (Saccidānandendra Svāmin)
N.S.	Nirṇaya Sāgara Press
N.Sid.	Naiṣkarmya Siddhi (Sureśvara)
N.Sū.	*Nyāya Sūtras*
P.D.	*Pañcadaśī* (Vidyāraṇya)

P.E.W.	*Philosophy East and West*, Honolulu
P.M.	Pūrva Mīmāṃsā
P.P.	*Pañcapādikā* (Padmapāda)
R.T.	Rāma Tīrtha (17th century commentator)
R.V.	*Ṛg Veda*
Sac.	Saccidānandendra Svāmin (modern author d.1975)
Ś.B.	*Śatapatha Brāhmaṇa*
S.B.E.	Sacred Books of the East Series, Oxford University Press, Oxford (reprinted by Motilal Banarsidas, Delhi)
Ś.Ś.P.B.	*Śuddha-Śaṅkara-Prakriyā-Bhāskara* (Saccidānandendra Svāmin)
Ś.V.	*Mīmāṃsā Śloka Vārtika* (Kumārila Bhaṭṭa)
T.S.	*Taittirīya Saṃhitā*
T.B.V.	*Taittirīya Bhāṣya Vārtika* (Sureśvara)
U.S.	*Upadeśa Sāhasrī* (Śaṅkara)
V.P.	*Viṣṇu Purāṇa*
V.V.S.	*Viśuddha Vedānta Sāra* (Saccidānandendra Svāmin)
W.Z.K.S.O.	*Wiener Zeitschrift für die Kunde Süd- und Ostasiens*
Y.D.	*Yukti Dīpikā*
Y.S.	*Yoga Sūtras* (Patañjali)
Z.D.M.G.	*Zeitschrift der Deutschen Morgenländischen Gesellschaft*
Z.I.I.	*Zeitschrift für Indologie und Iranistik*
Z.M.R.	*Zeitschrift für Missionswissenschaft und Religionswissenschaft*, Münster/Westfalen

BIBLIOGRAPHY

I. Texts of Śaṅkara

Aitareya Upaniṣad Bhāṣya, G.P. Ed., n.d. See Venkataramiah, D.

Bhagavad Gītā Bhāṣya (Bh.G.Bh.), ed. D.V. Gokhale, Poona, 1931. See also Śāstrī, A. Mahādeva.

Brahma Sūtra Bhāṣya (B.S.Bh.), ed. with the *Ratna Prabhā Ṭīkā* of Govindānanda, the *Nyāya Nirṇaya Ṭīkā* of Ānandagiri and the *Bhāmatī* of Vācaspati, by Mahādeva Śāstrī Bākre, N.S. Press, Bombay, 1934. See also S.S. Sūryanārāyaṇa Śastrī.

Bṛhadāraṇyaka Upaniṣad Bhāṣya, ed. H.R. Bhāgavat, Ashtekar Company, Second Ed., Poona, 1928. Also consulted: Ā.S.S. Ed. of the same work, with the *Ṭīkā* of Ānandagiri.

Chāndogya Upaniṣad Bhāṣya, Ā.S.S. Ed., Poona, 1890. Also consulted: H.R. Bhāgavat's Ed., Ashtekar Co., Poona, 1927.

Īśa Upaniṣad. See Saccidānandendra, *Īśāvāsya*. Also consulted: G.P. Ed. of Śaṅkara's *Īśa Bhāṣya*.

Kāṭhaka (usually referred to as *Kaṭha*) *Upanishad*, ed. with Shri Shaṅkara's Commentary and Sanskrit Notes by Saccidānandendra Svāmin, Adhyātma Prakāśālaya, Holenarsipur, South India, 1962. Also consulted: G.P. Ed. of same work.

Kena Upanishad, with the *Pada* and *Vākya* Commentaries of Shri Shaṅkara, ed. with Sanskrit Notes by Saccidānandendra, Holenarsipur, 1959. Also consulted: G.P. Ed.

Māṇḍūkya Upaniṣad and Gauḍapāda Kārikā Bh.(G.K.Bh.), G.P.Ed., n.d.

Muṇḍaka Upanishad, ed. with Shri Shaṅkara's Commentary and Sanskrit Notes by Saccidānandendra, Holenarsipur, 1960. Also consulted: G.P. Ed.

Praśna Upaniṣad Bhāṣya, G.P.Ed., n.d.

Taittirīya Upaniṣad. See Sac, *Taittirīya Upanishad Shikshāvallī* and *Ānandavallī-Bhṛguvallī*, with Shaṅkara's Commentary and Editor's Notes and Commentary. Also consulted: G.P. Ed. of *Taittirīya Bhāṣya*.

Upadeśa Sāhasrī with gloss of Rāma Tīrtha, ed. D.V. Gokhale, Bombay, 1917. Also consulted: *Upadeśa Sāhasrī* with Hindi trans. of Munilāla, Banaras, 1954. See also Jagadānanda, Mayeda and Alston.

Vivaraṇa on the *Adhyātma Paṭala* of the *Āpastamba Dharma Sūtra* in H.R. Bhāgavat, *Minor Works of Śrī Śaṅkarācārya*, 2nd Ed., 1952 (422ff).

(Attributed) *Vivaraṇa* on *Yoga-Bhāṣya* of Vyāsa on Patañjali's *Yoga Sūtras*, Madras Government Oriental Series, 1952.

For TRANSLATIONS of Śaṅkara's work, see under: Alston, Deussen, Gambhīrānanda, Hacker, Jagadānanda, Jhā, Leggett, Mādhavānanda, Mayeda, Nikhilānanda, A. Mahādeva Śāstrī, Thibaut and Venkataramiah.

II. List of other authors and works quoted

('trans.' denotes English translation unless otherwise stated.)

ABHINAVAGUPTA, *Īśvara Pratyabhijñā Vimarśinī*, 2 vols, Bombay, 1919 and 1921.

AITAREYA ĀRAṆYAKA: see Keith, A.B.

AITAREYA BRĀHMAṆA: ed. Aufrecht, Bonn, 1879.

ALSTON, A.J. (trans.), *The Thousand Teachings of Śaṅkara* (*Upadeśa Sāhasrī*), Shanti Sadan, London, 1990.

— , *Realization of the Absolute* (*Naiṣkarmya Siddhi* of Sureśvara), Shanti Sadan, London, 2nd. Ed. 1971.

ĀNANDABODHENDRA: see *Yoga Vāsiṣṭha*.

ĀNANDAGIRI: standard sub-commentaries (ṭīkā) on Śaṅkara's commentaries and Sureśvara's Vārttikas consulted in Ā.S.S. Ed.

ĀNANDAPŪRṆA, *Nyāya Kalpa Latikā*, ṭīkā on B.B.V., Tirupati, Vols.I and II, 1975.

ANANTAKṚṢṆA ŚĀSTRĪ (ed.), *Two Commentaries on the Brahma Siddhi*, Madras, 1963. (Being the *Bhāvaśuddhi* of Ānandapūrṇamuni and the *Abhiprāya Prakāśikā* of Citsukha).

ANNAMBHAṬṬA, *Tarka Saṅgraha*, ed. and trans. Athalye, 2nd ed., Bombay, 1930.

ĀPA DEVA, *Mīmāṃsā Nyāya Prakāśa*, ed. (with comm.) V. Abhyankar, Poona, 1937. Ed. and trans. F. Edgerton, New Haven (Yale), 1929.

ĀPASTAMBA DHARMA SŪTRA: See Cinnaswāmī Śāstrī, Bühler, and Bhāgavat, *Minor Works*.

ĀRYA DEVA, *The Catuḥśataka*, ed. V. Bhattacharya, Calcutta, 1931.

ASHTEKAR: see Bhāgavat, H.R.

ĀTMĀNANDA, Swāmī, *Śaṅkara's Teachings in his own Words*, Bombay, 2nd. Ed., 1960.

AUGUSTINE, St., *Confessions*, trans. Sir Tobie Matthew, Loeb Ed., London, 1923.

— , *De Trinitate*, text and French trans. Mellet, Desclée de Brouwer, 2 vols, 1955.

BELVALKAR, S.K., *Lectures on Vedānta Philosophy*, Part I, Poona, 1929.

— , *The Brahma Sūtras of Bādarāyaṇa*, Poona, 2 vols, 1923 and 1924.

BERGAIGNE, A., *La Religion Védique* (3 volumes), Paris, 1883.

BHĀGAVAT, H.R., *Upaniṣadbhāṣyam* (of Śaṅkara) Vols I and II, Ashtekar Company, Poona, 1927 and 1928.

—, *Minor Works of Śrī Śaṅkarācārya*, Poona, 2nd Ed. 1952.

BHĀMATĪ: See Śaṅkara, *Brahma Sūtra Bhāṣya*.

BHĀRAVI, *Kirātārjunīyam*, ed. with Mallinātha's comm. and Hindi trans., Śobhita Miśra, Banaras, 1952.

BHARTṚHARI, *Vākyapadīya*, complete text ed. K.V. Abhyankar and V.P. Limaye, Poona, 1965.

BHĀSKARA, *Brahma Sūtra Bhāṣya*, Banaras, 1915.

BHATT, G.P., *Epistemology of the Bhāṭṭa School of Pūrva Mīmāmsā*, Varanasi, 1962.

BHATTACHARYA, V.S., *Āgama Śāstra of Gauḍapāda*, Calcutta, 1943, (Abbreviated Ā.Ś.G.).

BIARDEAU, M., *La définition dans la pensée indienne*, J.A., 1957, 371-384.

— , (Contribution on Indian philosophy to) *Encyclopédie de la Pléiade, Histoire de la philosophie*, I, Paris, 1969.

—, *La philosophie de Maṇḍana Miśra*, Paris, 1969.

— , *Quelques réflexions sur l'apophatisme de Śaṅkara*, I.I.J., 1959, 81-100.

— , *Théorie de la connaissance et philosophie de la parole dans le brahmanisme classique*, Paris and the Hague, 1964.

— , *La démonstration du Sphoṭa par Maṇḍana Miśra*, Pondichéry, 1958.

BOETZELAER, J.M. van, *Sureśvara's Taittirīyopaniṣad Bhāṣyavārttika*, Leiden, 1971.

BÖHTLINGK, O., *Sanskrit-Wörterbuch*, 3 vols, St Petersburg, 1879-89, reprinted Graz, 1959.

BUDHAKAR, G.V., '*Is the Advaita of Śaṅkara Buddhism in Disguise*?', Quarterly Journal of the Mythic Society, Bangalore, several parts, *incipit* Vol. XXIV, 1933: 1-18, 160-176, 252-265, 314-326.

BÜHLER, G., (trans.) *Āpastamba Dharma Sūtra*, S.B.E.

BUITENEN, J.A.B. van and DEUTSCH, E., *A Source Book of Advaita Vedānta*, Hawaii, 1971.

CAMMANN, K., *Das System des Advaita nach der Lehre Prakaśātmans*, Wiesbaden, 1965.

CANDRAKĪRTI: see Nāgārjuna.

CHATTERJI, S.K., *Indo-Aryan and Hindi*, 2nd Ed., Calcutta, 1960, reprinted 1969.

CHATTOPADHYAYA, D.P., *History of Indian Philosophy*, New Delhi, 1964.

CINNASWĀMĪ ŚĀSTRĪ (ed.) *Āpastamba Dharma Sūtra*, Banaras,1932.

CITSUKHA, *Abhiprāya Prakāśikā* (Comm. on Maṇḍana's *Brahma Siddhi)*, see Anantakṛṣṇa Śāstrī.

CRESSON, A., *Les courants de la pensée philosophique française*, Vol. 2, Paris, 1927.

CURTIUS, G., *Principles of Greek Etymology*, trans. A.S. Wilkins, London, two vols, 1875 and 1876.

DAKṢIṆĀMŪRTI STOTRA, ed. A. Mahādeva Śāstrī and K. Raṅgācārya with Sureśvara's *Mānasollāsa* and explanatory ṭīkās by Svayamprakāśa and Rāmatīrtha, Mysore Oriental Library Publications, 6, 1895.

DAṆḌIN, *Daśakumāra Carita*, ed. and trans. M.R. Kale, 3rd Ed., Bombay, 1925, reprinted Delhi, 1966.

DARŚANODAYA: see Lakshmīpuram Srīnivāsāchār.

DAS GUPTA, S.N., *History of Indian Philosophy*, Vol. V, Cambridge, 1955.

DE, S.K., *Aspects of Sanskrit Literature*, Calcutta, 1959.

DEUSSEN, P., *Erinnerungen an Indien*, Kiel and Leipzig, 1904.

—, *The Philosophy of the Upanishads*, trans. Geden, 1906, reprinted New York, 1966.

— , *Sechzig Upanishad's des Veda*, Leipzig, 3rd Ed. 1921, reprinted Darmstadt, 1963.

— , *Die Sūtra's des Vedānta*, Leipzig, 1887, reprinted Hildesheim, 1966.

— , *The System of the Vedānta*, Chicago, 1912. Abbreviated D.S.V.

— , and Strauss, O., *Vier Philosophische Texte des Mahābhāratam*, Leipzig, 1906.

DEUTSCH, E., *Advaita Vedānta*, Honolulu, 1969. See also van Buitenen, J.A.B.

DEVARAJA, N.K., *An Introduction to Śaṅkara's Theory of Knowledge*, Delhi, 1962.

DEVASTHALI, G., *Mīmāṃsā*, Vol. I, Bombay, 1959.

— , *Śaṅkara's Indebtedness to Mīmāṃsā*, J.O.I.B., 1951-2, 23-30.

DHARMAKĪRTI, *Pramāṇa Vārttikam*, ed. Dvārikādāsa Śāstrī, Varanasi, 1968. See also Prajñākara Gupta.

DĪGHA NIKĀYA, ed. Rhys Davids and Carpenter, Vol. II, Pali Text Society, London, 1966 (reprint).

DOWSON, J., *A Classical Dictionary of Hindu Mythology*, reprinted London, 1968.

ECKHART, Meister, *Sermons and Treatises*, ed. and trans. M. O'C. Walshe, Vol. II, Watkins, London, 1981.

EDGERTON, F., *Buddhist Hybrid Sanskrit Grammar and Dictionary*, Yale University, 1953, two vols. Reprinted Delhi 1970 and 1972.

FRAUWALLNER, E., *Geschichte der indischen Philosophie*, Vols I and II, Vienna, 1953 and 1956. Abbreviated G.I.P.

— , *Materialien zur ältesten Erkenntnislehre der Karma-mīmāṃsā*, Vienna, 1968.

— , *Die Philosophie des Buddhismus*, Berlin, 1958.

GAIL, A., *Bhakti im Bhāgavata Purāṇa*, Wiesbaden, 1969.

GAMBHĪRĀNANDA, Swāmī (trans.), *Brahma-Sūtra Bhāṣya of Śaṅkar-ācārya*, Calcutta, 1965.

— (trans.), *Chāndogya Upaniṣad with the Commentary of Śaṅkarācārya*, Calcutta, 1983.

— (trans.), *Eight Upaniṣads with the Commentary of Śaṅkarācārya*, Calcutta, two vols 1957 and 1958. (Vol.I comprises Īśa, Kena, Kaṭha, Taitt: Vol.II, Ait., Muṇḍ., Māṇḍ.with G.K. and Praśna.)

GARBE, R., *Die Sāṅkhya Philosophie*, Leipzig, 1917.

GAUTAMA DHARMA SŪTRA, trans. G. Bühler, S.B.E.

GELDNER, K.F., *Der Rigveda*, Harvard, four vols, 1951-57.

GHATE, V. S., *Le Vedānta*, Paris, 1918.

GLASENAPP, H. von, *Entwicklungsstufen des indischen Denkens*, Halle, 1940.

—, *Die Philosophie der Inder*, Stuttgart, 1949 (abbreviated as '*Einführung*')

—, *Stufenweg zum Göttlichen*, Baden Baden, 1948.

GOKHALE, D.V. see under Texts of Śaṅkara (above), *Bhagavad Gītā Bhāṣya* and *Upadeśa Sāhasrī*..

GONDA, J., *Inleiding tot het Indische Denken*, Antwerp, 1948.

—, *Les religions de l'Inde*, Vols I and II, Paris, 1953 and 1956.

GOPĪNĀTH, see Kavirāj.

GOUGH, A.E. see *Vaiśeṣika Sūtras*.

GOVINDĀNANDA: see Śaṅkara, *Brahma Sūtra Bhāṣya*.

GROUSSET, R., *Les philosophies indiennes*, two vols, Paris, 1931.

HACKER, P. Most of Paul Hacker's important articles on Advaita Vedanta were assembled in *Kleine Schriften* (see below). These can now be read in English translation in *Philology and Confrontation*, ed. and trans. Wilhelm Halbfass, State University of New York Press, 1995.

— , *Eigentümlichkeiten der Lehre und Terminologie Śaṅkaras*, Z.D.M.G., 1950, 246ff. (Halbfass, 57ff).

—, *Die Lehre von den Realitätsgraden im Advaita-Vedānta*, Z.M.R., 1952, 277ff. (Halbfass, 137ff).

— , *Jayanta Bhaṭṭa und Vācaspati Miśra, ihre Zeit und ihre Bedeutung für die Chronologie des Vedānta* included in *Beiträge... Walter Schubring dargebracht* (see Schubring) 160-169.

— , *Kleine Schriften*, herausgegeben von L. Schmithausen, Wiesbaden, 1978.

— , *Prahlāda*, Wiesbaden, 1960.

— , *Śaṅkara der Yogin und Śaṅkara der Advaitin*, W.Z.K.S.O. 1968/1969, 119ff. (Halbfass, 101ff).

— , *Śaṅkarācārya and Śaṅkarabhagavatpāda*, New Indian Antiquary, April-June 1947. Preferably consulted in the corrected version in *Kleine Schriften*, 41ff. (Halbfass, 41ff).

— , *Untersuchungen über Texte des frühen Advaita Vāda*, I, Wiesbaden, 1951. (abbreviated 'Texte').

— , *Upadeshasāhasrī, Gadyaprabandha* (Prose Section) übersezt und erläutert, Bonn, 1949.

—, *Vedānta Studien* I, Die Welt des Orients, Wuppertal, 1948, 240.

—, *Vivarta*, Wiesbaden, 1953.

HALBFASS, W. (ed. and trans.), *Philology and Confrontation*, State University of New York Press, 1995. (See above, under Hacker)

HAUER, J.W., *Der Yoga*, Stuttgart, 1958.

HAZRA, R.C., *Studies in the Purāṇic Records*, Dacca, 1940.

HEIMANN, B., *Studien zur Eigenart indischen Denkens*, Tübingen, 1930.

HIRIYANNA, M., *Essentials of Indian Philosophy*, London, 1949.

— , *Outlines of Indian Philosophy*, London, 1932.

HUME, R.E., *The Thirteen Principal Upanishads*, 2nd Edition of 1931, reprinted Madras (O.U.P.), 1958.

INGALLS, Daniel H.H., *Śaṅkara on the Question 'Whose is Avidyā?'* in P.E.W. 1953, 68ff.

— , *Śaṅkara's Arguments against the Buddhists*, in P.E.W., 1954, 291-316.

ĪŚVARA KṚṢṆA, *Sāṅkhya Kārikās* with *Tattvakaumudi* Commentary of Vācaspati Miśra, text and trans. Gaṅgānātha Jhā, ed. H.D. Sharma, Poona, 1934.

IYER, K.A. Subramania, *Bhartṛhari*, Poona, 1969.

JACOB, Col. G.A., *A Handful of Popular Maxims*, in three Parts, Bombay, 1900, 1902 and 1904.

—, *A Concordance to the Principal Upanishads and Bhagavad Gītā*, 1891, re-issued Delhi, 1963.

— see also under Sadānanda and Sureśvara.

JAGADĀNANDA, Svāmī, *A Thousand Teachings* (the *Upadeśa Sāhasrī* of Śaṅkara), text and trans., Madras, 2nd Ed. 1949.

JAIMINI: see under Śabara.

JASPERS, K., *The Way to Wisdom*, London, 1951.

JAYA DEVA, *Gītagovinda Kāvyam*, ed. Nārāyaṇa Rāma Ācārya, Bombay, 9th Ed., 1949.

JHĀ, Gaṅgānātha, *Pūrva Mīmāṃsā in its Sources*, Banaras, 1942.

— , *Chāndogya Upanishad and Śrī Śaṅkara's Commentary* (2 volumes), Madras, 1899

— see also under Īśvara Kṛṣṇa, Kumārila Bhaṭṭa, Śabara, Praśastapāda.

JHALAKĪKARA, B.J., *Nyāya Kośa*, Bombay, 3rd Ed., 1928.

JOHNSTON, E.H., *Early Sāṅkhya*, London, 1937.

JOSHI, L.M., *Studies in the Buddhistic Culture of India*, Delhi, 1967.

JOŚĪ, T.L. (= Jośi, Tarkatīrtha Lakṣmaṇaśāstrī), *Vaidika Saṃskṛti kā Vikāsa* (Hindi trans. from the Marathi), Bombay, 1957.

—, *Dharma Kośa Upaniṣat Kāṇḍa*, Wai (Maharashtra), 1950.

KAṆĀDA: see Vaiśeṣika Sūtras.

KAVIRĀJ, Gopīnāth, *Bhūmikā* (Introduction to Acyuta Grantha Mālā Ed. of Śaṅkara's B.S.Bh.), Banaras, 1937.

KEITH, A.B. (ed. and trans.), *Aitareya Āraṇyaka*, Oxford, 1909.

—, *A History of Sanskrit Literature*, Oxford, 1920.

—, *The Karma-Mīmāṃsā*, Calcutta, 1921.

—, *The Sāṃkhya System*, Calcutta, 1924.

—, (trans.) *Taittirīya Saṃhitā*, Harvard Oriental Series, 2 vols, 1914.

KṚṢṆA MIŚRA (ed. and trans.), *Prabodha Candrodaya*, Sita Krishna Nambiar, Delhi, 1971.

KṚṢṆA YAJVAN, *Mīmāṃsā-Paribhāṣā*, text and trans. Mādhavānanda, Calcutta, 1948.

KULLŪKA: see under Manu Smṛti.

KUMĀRILA BHAṬṬA, *Mīmāṃsā Śloka Vārttika* (abbreviated Ś.V.), Banaras, 1898-1899; trans. Gaṅgānātha Jhā, Calcutta, 1900-1908.

—, *Tantra Vārttika*, ed. Gangādhara Shāstrī, Benares, 1882-1903; trans. Gaṅgānātha Jhā, Bibliotheca Indica, Calcutta, 1903-24.

KUNJUNNI RAJA, K., *The Date of Śaṅkarācārya and Allied Problems*, Brahma Vidyā (= Adyar Library Bulletin) Vol. 24, 1960, 125-48.

—, *Indian Theories of Meaning*, Adyar, Madras, 1963.

KŪRMA PURĀṆA, Bombay, 1927.

LACOMBE, O., *L'Absolu selon le Védanta*, Paris, 1937.

LAKSHMĪPURAM SRĪNIVĀSĀCHĀR, *Darśanodaya*, Mysore, 1933.

LEGGETT, T., *The Chapter of the Self* (translation and exposition of Śaṅkara's *Vivaraṇa* on Praśna I, Paṭala 8 of *Āpastamba Dharma Sūtra)*, London, 1978.

LEHMANN, A., *Aberglaube und Zauberei*, 3rd Ger. Ed., Stuttgart, 1925.

MĀDHAVĀNANDA, SVĀMĪ (trans.), *The Bṛhadāraṇyaka Upanishad with the Commentary of Śaṅkarācārya*, Calcutta, 6th Ed., 1985.

MADHUSŪDANA, see Sarvajña Muni.

MĀGHA, *Śiśupālavadham*, Chowkamba Vidyā Bhavan, Banaras,1955.

MAHĀBHĀRATA: G.P. Ed. (Mūlamātra). Also consulted, critical Ed. of V.S. Sukthankar, Poona, 1933-72. See also Deussen and Strauss.

MAHADEVAN, T.M.P., *Gauḍapāda*, Madras, 1952.

—, (ed.) *Word Index to the Brahma-Sūtra Bhāṣya of Śaṅkara*, Madras, two Parts, 1971 and 1973.

MAHĀNĀRAYAṆA UPANISHAD, ed. and trans. J. Varenne, Paris, 1960.

MAṆḌANA MIŚRA, *Brahma Siddhi* (abbreviated B.Sid.), ed. Kuppuswami Shastri, Madras, 1937. See also Anantakṛṣna Śāstrī, Biardeau, Schmithausen and Vetter.

MANU SMṚTI, with Comm. of Kullūka, Bombay, 1902.

MATICS, Marion L., *Entering the Path of Enlightenment*, trans. of *Bodhicaryāvatāraḥ*, London, 1970. See also Śānti Deva.

MAYEDA, S., *The Authenticity of the Upadeśa Sāhasrī*, J.A.O.S., 1965, No.2, 178-196.

— , *On the Authenticity of the Māṇḍūkya and the Gauḍapādīya Bhāṣya*, Brahma Vidyā (= Adyar Library Bulletin), 1967-8, 74ff.

— , *On Śaṅkara's Authorship of the Kenopaniṣadbhāṣya*, I.I.J., X (1967), 33-35.

—, *The Authenticity of the Bhagavadgītābhāṣya ascribed to Śaṅkara*, W.Z.K.S.O. IX (1965), 155-197.

—, *Śaṅkara's Upadeśa Sāhasrī*, critically edited with Introduction and Indices, Tokyo, 1973.

— , *A Thousand Teachings, The Upadeśasāhasrī of Śaṅkara*, trans. with Introduction and notes, Tokyo, 1979.

MONIER-WILLIAMS, Sir M., *Sanskrit-English Dictionary*, Oxford, 2nd Ed., 1899.

MORICHINI, G., *Early Vedānta Philosophy* (being a short summary of H. Nakamura's work on that subject) in the periodical *East and West* (Rome), 1960, 33-39.

MÜLLER, Max, *Sacred Books of the East* (abbreviated S.B.E.), Vol. XV, Oxford, 1884. Reprinted Delhi.

MURTI, T.R.V., *The Central Philosophy of Buddhism* (abbreviated C.P.B.), London, 1955.

— , *The Two Definitions of Brahman in the Advaita*, in *Krishna Chandra Bhattacharya Memorial Volume*, Almaner, 1958, 135-150.

MUS, P., *Barabadur*, Hanoi, 1935.

NĀGĀRJUNA, *Mūlamādhyamika Kārikās*, ed. with *Prasannapadā* Commentary of Candrakīrti by de La Vallée Poussin, St. Petersburg, 1903-1913.

NAKAMURA, H., *A History of Early Vedanta Philosophy*, Part One, New Delhi, 1983.

— , *The Vedānta Philosophy as was Revealed in Buddhist Scriptures*, in Dr. Maṇḍan Miśra (ed.), *Pañcāmṛtam*, Delhi, 1968, pp 1-74.

—, *Vedanta Tetsugaku No Hatten (Development of Vedānta Philosophy)*, in *Indian Philosophical Thought, Vol. III*, Tokyo, 1955.

— see also Morichini, G.

NARENDRADEVA, *Bauddha-Dharma-Darśana*, Patna, 1956.

NIKHILĀNANDA, *The Māṇḍūkyopaniṣad with Gauḍapāda's Kārikā and Śaṅkara's Commentary*, Calcutta, 4th ed., 1955.

OLDENBERG, H., *Die Lehre der Upanishaden und die Anfänge des Buddhismus*, Göttingen, 1923.

— , *Die Weltanschauung der Brāhmaṇa-Texte*, Göttingen, 1919.

ÖPIK, E.J., *The Oscillating Universe*, Mentor Books, N.Y., 1960.

OTTO, R., *Mysticism East and West*, N.Y., 1932.

PADMAPĀDA, see PAÑCAPĀDIKĀ

PADOUX, A., *Recherches sur la symbolique et l'énergie de la parole dans certains textes Tantriques*, Paris, 1964.

PAÑCAPĀDIKĀ (abbreviated P.P.), a work attributed to Padmapāda, ed. S. Shrīrāma Shāstrī and S.R. Krishnamūrthi Shāstrī, Madras, 1958. For trans. see Venkataramiah.

PANDEY, S.L., *Pre-Śaṅkara Advaita Philosophy*, Allahabad, 1974.

PĀṆINI, *The Ashṭādhyāyī of Pāṇini*, ed. and trans. S.C. Vasu, two vols, 1891, reprinted Delhi, 1962.

PARAMĀRTHA SĀRA: ed. with the *Vivaraṇa* of Rāghavānanda by S. N. Śukla, Banaras, 1933. For trans., see S.S. Śāstrī, below.

PASSMORE, J., *A Hundred Years of Philosophy*, Pelican Books, Harmondsworth, 1968.

PATAÑJALI, *Yoga Sūtras* with Comms. of Vyāsa and Vācaspati, Bombay, 1892.

—, (trans.) J.H. Woods, Harvard, 1914, reprinted Delhi, 1972.

— : see also Śaṅkara for (attributed) *Vivaraṇa* on Vyāsa's Comm. (Bhāṣya) to *Yoga Sūtras*.

POTTER, Karl, *Bibliography of Indian Philosophies*, Delhi, 1970.

PRAJÑĀKARA GUPTA, *Pramāṇa Vārtika Bhāṣyam*, ed. Rāhula Sāṃkṛt-yāyana, Patna, 1953.

PRAKĀŚĀTMAN, *Vivaraṇa*, ed. S. Shrīrāma Shāstrī and S.R. Krishna-mūrthi Shāstrī, Madras, 1958. See also Cammann, above.

PRAŚASTAPĀDA, *Praśastapāda-Bhāṣya* (or *Padārthadharma Saṅgraha*), with *Nyāyakandalī* of Shrī Dhara, Banaras, 1895. Eng. trans. Gaṅgānath Jhā, Banaras, 1916.

PŪRVA MĪMĀṂSĀ SŪTRAS: see under Śabara.

RADHAKRISHNAN, Sir S., *Indian Philosophy*, London, two vols, 1927.

—, *The Principal Upanishads*, London, 1953.

RĀGHORĀM, B. Shivprasād: (Publisher) *Hundred and Eight Upanishads*, Banaras, 1938 (Sanskrit text only).

RĀMA DEVA: see Jaiminīya Upanishad Brāhmaṇa.

RĀMĀNUJA, *Śrī Bhāṣya*, ed. Vāsudeva Śāstrī Abhyaṅkar, Bombay, 1914.

RATNAPRABHĀ: see Śaṅkara, *Brahma Sūtra Bhāṣya*.

RENOU, L., *Grammaire et Védanta*, in J.A., 1957, 121-132.

RENOU and FILLIOZAT, *L'Inde Classique*, two vols, Paris and Hanoi, 1947 and 1953.

ṚG VEDA, Rig Veda (Abbreviated R.V.): see also Geldner.

— , *Ṛg Veda Saṃhitā*, with Comm. of Sāyana, Vedic Research Institute, Poona, 5 vols 1933-51.

RITTER, H., *Das Meer der Seele*, Leiden, 1955.

RŪMĪ, Jalālu'ddīn, *Mathnawī*, trans. R.A. Nicholson, London, Vol.I, 1926.

RÜPING, K., *Studien zur Frühgeschichte der Vedānta Philosophie*, Wiesbaden, 1977.

ŚABARA, Jaimini's *Pūrva Mīmāṃsā Sūtra Bhāṣya*, Calcutta, two vols, 1873 and 1887. Trans. Gaṅgānātha Jhā, G.O.S., 3 vols, 1933, 1934 and 1936. See also Frauwallner.

SACCIDĀNANDENDRA SVĀMIN (abbreviated as Sac.) All Sac's works are published by the Adhyātma Prakāśa Kāryālaya, Holenarsipur, Karnataka, India, unless otherwise stated.

—, *Brahmavidyā Rahasya Vivṛtiḥ*, 1969.

—, *Gītā-Śāstrārtha-Vivekaḥ*, 1965.

—, *Intuition of Reality*, 1973.

— , *Īśāvāsya Upaniṣad* with Śaṅkara's Bhāṣya and author's Sanskrit *ṭīkā* (written under the lay name of Y. Subrahmanya Śarmā), 1937.

—, *Māṇḍūkya Rahasya Vivṛtiḥ*, 1958.

— , *The Method of the Vedanta* (abbreviated M.V.), London, 1989 (Translation by A.J. Alston of *Vedānta Prakriyā Pratyabhijñā*, q.v.).

—, *Misconceptions about Śaṅkara*, 1973.

—, *Śaṅkara's Clarification of certain Vedantic Concepts*, 1969.

— , *Śuddha-Śaṅkara-Prakriyā-Bhāskara* (abbreviated Ś.Ś.P.B.), quoted from Sanskrit Ed. in 3 parts, 1964. Available in English, 3 parts 1965-1968, subtitled *Light on the Vedantic Method according to Śaṅkara*.

—, *Sugamā* (Sanskrit exposition of Śaṅkara's Adhyāsa-bhāṣya), 1955.

—, *Taittirīya Upanishad Shikshāvallī,* ed. with Shaṅkara's Commentary and editor's Sanskrit notes, 1961.

—, *Taittirīya Upanishad Ānandavallī-Bhṛguvallī,* ed. with Shaṅkara's Commentary and editor's *Bhāṣyārtha Vimarśinī* sub-commentary, 1962.

—, *Vedānta Prakriyā Pratyabhijñā*, 1964. For an English translation of this work, see *The Method of the Vedānta*, previous page.

—, *Viśuddha Vedānta Sāra*, 1968. (Abbreviated V.V.S.)

SADĀNANDA, *Vedānta Sāra*, ed. with two commentaries, Col. G.A. Jacob, 5th revised Ed., 1934.

—, text of *Vedānta Sāra* with Eng. trans. Nikhilānanda Svāmin, Calcutta, 1947.

SADĀNANDA YATI, *Advaita Brahma Siddhi*, Calcutta, 1888-90.

ṢAḌVIṂŚA BRĀHMAṆA, ed. K. Klemm, Gütersloh, 1894. Trans. W.B. Bollée, Utrecht, 1956.

SAHASRABUDDHE, M.T., *A Survey of Pre-Śaṅkara Advaita Vedānta*, Poona, 1968.

SĀṄKṚTYĀYANA, Rāhula, *Darśana Dig-Darśana*, Allahabad, 2nd Ed., 1947. (Hindi).

ŚĀNTI DEVA, *Bodhicaryāvatāraḥ*, ed. P.L.Vaidya, Darbhanga, 1960. See also M.L. Matics.

SARVAJÑA MUNI, *Saṅkṣepa Śārīrakam* with the Commentary of Madhusūdana, Banaras, 1924.

Sarvajñātman and Sarvajñātma Muni: alternative forms of the above name.

ŚĀSTRĪ: sometimes interchanged with Shāstrī, q.v.

ŚĀSTRĪ, A. Mahādeva, *The Bhagavad-Gītā with the Commentary of Śaṅkarācārya*, Madras, 1897. Reprinted, Madras, 1977.

—, *Dakshiṇāmūrti Stotra of Śrī Śaṅkarāchārya*, Madras, 3rd Ed., 1978. Contains Sanskrit text and Eng. trans. of the *Mānasollāsa Vārttika* attributed to Sureśvara. See also entry under *Dakṣiṇāmūrti*

Stotra above for Sanskrit edition of text and commentaries.

ŚĀSTRĪ, Maṅgaladeva, *Bhāratīya Saṃskṛti kā Vikāsa*, Part II, *Aupaniṣada Dhārā*, Banaras, 1966 (Hindi).

ŚĀSTRĪ, Rāmānanda Tivārī, *Śrī Śaṃkarācārya kā ācāra darśana*, Allahabad, 1950 (Hindi).

ŚĀSTRĪ, S.S. Sūryanārāyaṇa, *The Paramārtha Sāra of Ādi Śeṣa*, Bombay, 1941.

— and C.K. Rājā, *The Bhāmatī: Catussūtrī*, Adyar, Madras, 1933.

ŚATAPATHA BRĀHMAṆA, trans. Eggeling, S.B.E. (in 5 parts).

SCHMITHAUSEN, L., *Maṇḍana Miśras Vibhrama Vivekaḥ*, Vienna, 1965.

SCHUBRING, W. (Festschrift) *Beiträge zur indischen Philologie... Walther Schubring dargebracht*, Hamburg, 1951.

SHARMA, L.N., *Kashmir Śaivism*, Banaras, 1972.

SHĀSTRĪ : sometimes interchanged with Śāstrī, q.v.

SHASTRI, Hari Prasad: see Vālmīki and Vidyāraṇya.

SILBURN, L., *Instant et Cause*, Paris, 1955.

SOGEN, Yamakami, *Systems of Buddhistic Thought*, Calcutta, 1912.

ŚRĪ HARṢA, *Śrī Harṣa's Plays*, ed. and trans. Bak Kun Bae, Bombay, 1964.

SRĪNIVĀSĀCHARĪ, P.N., *The Philosophy of Bhedābheda*, Madras, 1934.

STAAL, J.F., *Advaita and Neoplatonism*, Madras, 1961.

STCHERBATSKY, Th., *The Conception of Buddhist Nirvāṇa*, revised and enlarged edition by Jaidev Singh, Bhāratīya Vidyā Prakāśana Edition, Banaras, n.d.

—, *Buddhist Logic*, Vol. II, Leningrad, 1930.

—, *Central Conception of Buddhism*, London, 1923.

—, *La théorie de la connaissance et la logique chez les Bouddhistes tardifs*, Paris, 1926.

STRAUSS, O., *Indische Philosophie*, Munich, 1925. See also Deussen.

SŪRA DĀSA, *Sūra Sāgara*, ed. Vājapeyī, Vārāṇasī, 2 vols, 1953 and 1956.

SUREŚVARA, *Bṛhadāraṇyaka Bhāṣya Vārttikam* (abbreviated B.B.V.) ed. with Ānandagiri's ṭīkā in the Ā.S.S. Ed., three vols, Poona, 1892-1894. See also Ānandapūrṇa.

—, (Attributed) *Mānosollāsa*. Commentary on *Dakṣiṇāmūrti Stotra*, q.v.

—, *Naiṣkarmya Siddhi* (abbreviated N.Sid.), ed. with Jñānottama's Commentary, by Col. G.A. Jacob and revised by M. Hiriyanna, Bombay,1925. Trans. by A.J. Alston as *The Realization of the Absolute*, Shanti Sadan, 2nd Ed. 1971.

—, (Attributed) *Pañcīkaraṇa Vārttika* in *Panchīkaraṇam of Shree Shankarāchārya*, Edited with six commentaries, Gujarati Printing Press, Bombay, 1930.

—, *The Saṃbandha Vārttika*, text and Eng. trans. T.M.P. Mahadevan, Madras, 1958.

—, *Taittirīya Bhāṣya Vārttika* (abbreviated T.B.V.), Ā.Ś.S. Ed. with ṭīkā of Ānandagiri, 1911. For Eng. trans. see Boetzelaer, above.

TAITTIRĪYA ĀRAṆYAKA, Ā.S.S., Poona, Vol. I, 1926.

TAITTIRĪYA BRĀHMAṆA, ed. Rājendralāl Mitra, Calcutta, 1870.

TAITTTIRĪYA SAṂHITĀ: see Keith, above.

THIBAUT, G., *The Vedānta Sūtras with the Commentary of Śaṅkarācārya* (= Brahma Sūtra Bhāṣya, B.S.Bh.), Eng. trans., Parts I and II.

TROṬAKA (or Toṭaka), *Śruti Sāra Samuddharaṇa*, ed. Kevalānanda Svāmin, Ā.S.S. Ed., Poona, 1936.

UDDYOTAKARA, *Nyāya Vārttikam*, ed. Dvivedin and Dravid, Benares, 1916-7.

UI, Hakuju, *Vaiśeṣika Philosophy according to the Daśapadārtha-śāstra*, Chinese Text with English translation and notes, Banaras, 1962.

UPĀDHYĀYA, Baladeva, *Śrī Śaṃkarācārya*, Allahabad, 1950. (Hindi).

—, *Śrī-Śaṃkara-Dig-Vijaya*, Sanskrit text with Hindi trans., Hardwar, 1944.

UPĀDHYĀYA, B.S., *Bauddha Darśana tathā anya Bhāratīya Darśana*, 2 vols, Calcutta, 1954 (Hindi).

UPĀDHYĀYA, Rāmajī, *Bhārata kī Saṃskṛti-Sādhanā*, Allahabad, 1967. (Hindi).

VĀCASPATI MIŚRA: see under Texts of Śaṅkara, *Brahma Sūtra Bhāṣya, Bhāmatī sub-commentary*. See also Īśvara Kṛṣṇa.

VAIŚEṢIKA SŪTRAS, with Comm. of Śaṅkara Miśra, ed. and trans. A.E. Gough, Benares, 1873, reprinted New Delhi, 1975.

—, ed. Jīvānanda, Calcutta, 1886.

VALLABHĀCĀRYA, *Aṇu Bhāṣya*, text and *Bālabodhinī* commentary, two vols, Bombay, 1921 and 1926.

VĀLMĪKI, *The Ramayana of Valmiki* (trans. H.P. Shastri), three vols., London, 2nd revised Ed. of Vol. I, 1962.

VĀSIṢṬHA *Dharma Sūtra*, trans. G. Bühler, S.B.E.

VĀTSYĀYANA, *Nyāya Sūtra Bhāṣya*, Poona, 1939. Eng. trans. Gaṅgānāth Jhā, Poona, 1939.

VENKAṬANĀTHA, *Tattva Muktā Kalāpaḥ* with *Sarvārtha Siddhi* and *Bhāva Prakāśa*, Mysore, Vol. II., 1940.

VENKATARAMIAH, D., *The Pañcapādikā of Padmapāda*, G.O.S., Baroda, 1948.

— , *Aitareyopaniṣad with Śaṅkarācārya's Bhāṣya*, text and Eng. trans., Bangalore, 1934.

VETTER, T., *Maṇḍana Miśra's Brahmasiddhiḥ, Brahmakāṇḍaḥ* only, annotated German trans., Vienna, 1969.

— , *Zur Bedeutung des Illusionismus bei Śaṅkara*, W.Z.K.S.O. 1968/69, 407-423.

—, *Erkenntnisprobleme bei Dharmakīrti*, Vienna, 1964.

VIDYĀRAṆYA, *Bṛhadāraṇyaka Bhāṣya Vārttika Sāra* (B.B.V.S.), Acyuta Grantha Mālā Ed., Banaras, two vols, 1941 and 1943.

— , *Panchadashi* (= Pañcadaśī, abbreviated P.D.), text and trans. by H.P. Shastri, 2nd revised Ed., London, 1965.

VIJÑĀNA BHIKṢU, *Sāṃkhya Pravacana Bhāṣya*, ed. R. Garbe, Cambridge, Mass., 1895.

VIMUKTĀTMAN, *Iṣṭa-Siddhi*, ed. Hiriyanna, G.O.S., Baroda, 1933.

VIṢṆU PURĀṆA: G.P. Ed. with the Hindi trans. of Śrī Munilāla Gupta, 1937.

VIVARAṆA: see Prakaśātman.

VYĀSA: see Patañjali.

WARDER, A.K., *Outlines of Indian Philosophy*, New Delhi, 1971.

WOODS, J.H: see Patañjali.

YĀJÑAVALKYA SMṚTI, with Mitākṣarā Commentary and Hindi trans., Umesh Chandra Pandey, Banaras, 1967.

YAMAKAMI, S: see under Sogen, Y.

YĀSKA, *Nirukti*, Calcutta, 4 vols, 1882-91.

YOGA VĀSIṢṬHA, with the Commentary of Ānandabodhendra, two vols, Bombay, 1937.

YOGA SŪTRAS: see Patañjali.

YUKTI DĪPIKĀ, ed. Ram Chandra Pandeya, Banaras-Delhi, 1967.

The Śaṅkara Source-Book

A Conspectus of the Contents of the Six Volumes

Volume I — Śaṅkara on the Absolute

I. SOURCES OF ŚAṄKARA'S DOCTRINE: HIS LIFE & WORKS

1. A Doctrine of Transcendence
2. Vedas: Saṃhitās, Brāhmaṇas, Upanishads
3. The Smṛti: Viṣṇu worship and Śiva worship
4. The Bhagavad Gītā
5. The Brahma-Sūtras and their Background: Bhartṛprapañca
6. The True Tradition: Gauḍapāda, Draviḍa, Brahmanandin, Sundara Pāṇḍya
7. Doctrine of Illusion before Śaṅkara: Māyā Vāda and Avidyā Vāda
8. Śaṅkara's Date, Life and Works
9. Śaṅkara's School

II. THE DOCTRINE OF NESCIENCE

1. The Nature and Results of Nescience
2. Nescience as Non-Comprehension and False Comprehension
3. The Self and the Not-Self: Non-Discrimination and Mutual Superimposition
4. The Standpoint of Nescience and the Standpoint of Knowledge

III. KNOWLEDGE OF THE ABSOLUTE

1. The Absolute is already known in a general way
2. The Absolute is not known as an object
3. The Path of Negation
4. Going beyond the Mind

IV. THE ABSOLUTE AS BEING, CONSCIOUSNESS AND BLISS

1. The Definition of the Absolute as 'Reality, Knowledge, Infinity'
2. The Absolute as the Self-Existent Principle
3. The Absolute as the Self-Luminous Principle
4. The Absolute as Bliss

Volume II — Śaṅkara on the Creation

V. THE ABSOLUTE AS CREATOR AND CONTROLLER

1. The Absolute as Creator and Controller of the World
2. The Absolute as the Lord
3. The Absolute as the Material and Efficient Cause of the World
4. The Absolute as Inner Ruler
5. The Absolute as the Lord of Māyā

VI. THE WORLD AND ITS PRESIDING DEITIES

1. Sat-kārya Vāda
2. Name and Form: Indeterminability
3. World-periods and Theory of the Elements
4. The Presiding Deities

VII. THE ACOSMIC VIEW

1. The Creation-texts as a Device to teach Non-Duality
2. Nothing can come into being
3. The Argument from Dream

Volume III — Śaṅkara on the Soul

VIII. THE SOUL AND ITS ORGANS AND BODIES

1. The Soul as the Self viewed under External Adjuncts
2. The Organs and Bodies of the Soul
3. The Light that illumines the Soul
4. The Soul and the Lord are not distinct

IX. THE 'STATES' OF THE SOUL AND THEIR TRANSCENDENCE

1. Dream
2. Dreamless Sleep
3. Turīya

CONTENTS OF THE ŚAṄKARA SOURCE BOOK

Volume IV — Śaṅkara on Rival Views

X. REFUTATION OF INADEQUATE BRAHMINICAL DOCTRINES

1. Refutation of Liberation through Action
2. Refutation of Liberation through Knowledge and Action Conjoined
3. Refutation of Bhedābheda Vāda
4. Refutation of the Pāśupatas and Pāñcarātras
5. Refutation of Sphoṭa Vāda

XI. REFUTATION OF NON-VEDIC WORLD-VIEWS

1. Dialectic (tarka): its Purpose and Rules
2. Refutation of Materialism
3. Refutation of the Sāṅkhyas
4. Refutation of the Vaiśeṣikas
5. Refutation of the Buddhist Schools
6. Refutation of the Jainas

Volume V — Śaṅkara on Discipleship

XII. ADOPTING THE PATH

1. The Wheel of Transmigration
2. The Injunction to Adopt the Path
3. Preliminary Qualifications for the Path
4. Spiritual Qualities to be cultivated on the Path

XIII. THE VEDA AND THE TEACHER

1. The Self can only be known through the Veda
2. The Veda, the Smṛti and Reason
3. The Approach to the Teacher
4. The Teacher and the Texts

Volume VI — Śaṅkara on Enlightenment

XIV. THE INDIRECT PATH

1. Meditation in the Context of the Vedic Ritual (upāsanā)
2. Realization of Identity with Hiraṇyagarbha
3. The Path of the Flame
4. Supernormal Powers on the Indirect Path

XV. THE DIRECT PATH

1. Adhyātma Yoga
2. Devotion (bhakti)
3. Communication of 'That Thou Art'
4. Meditation (dhyāna) and Repeated Affirmation (abhyāsa)
5. Meditation on OM

XVI. THE ENLIGHTENED MAN

1. Enlightenment is not a change of state

Available from Shanti Sadan

The Method of the Vedanta

A Critical Account of the Advaita Tradition

by Śrī Swāmī Satchidānandendra

translated into English by A J Alston

This monumental study of Advaita Vedanta was written in Sanskrit by the South Indian Swāmī Satchidānandendra (1880-1975). The translation represents the first large-scale critical history of Advaita to appear in the West. Mandana, Padmapada, Vimuktatman, Vachaspati and Prakashatman are all presented in long chapters, Sarvajnatman, Anandabodha, Shri Harsha and Chitsukha more briefly. Each author is represented solely by extracts from his own works, with the author's comments. Unusually detailed attention is given to Śaṅkara's predecessors.

The Method of the Vedanta is a panorama to show how later Advaita gradually broke up into mutually opposed schools and adopted more and more of the methods of the Logicians, thereby losing the firm anchorage in the Upanishads preserved by Śaṅkara and Sureśvara.

'It is a work which could only have been written by a follower of Śaṅkara who has devoted his life to the study of his writings and those of other Advaita Vedāntins. Even for a Western scholar who makes a special study of Advaita Vedānta it would be difficult to obtain such an intimate knowledge of the Advaita Literature unless he would be prepared to study for many years at the feet of Advaita masters....We must be grateful to Alston for having undertaken this difficult task and for having made this important work more accessible to the Western reader.'

Professor J W De Jong, Indo-Iranian Journal

1005pp hardback ISBN 07103-0120-0

THE THOUSAND TEACHINGS OF ŚAṄKARA
Upadeśa Sāhasrī

translated into English by A J Alston

The *Upadeśa Sāhasrī* is the one independent work accepted by all authorities as undeniably written by Śaṅkara, most of whose known writings are concerned with commenting on and interpreting the words of the great classical texts of the Upanishads, Brahma Sutras and Bhagavad Gita. It gives an unconstrained exposition of Advaita Vedanta by India's greatest philosopher. The practising student of Yoga will find in this classic a wealth of insight and a powerful aid to spiritual self-examination (*viveka*). Includes transliterated Sanskrit text.

438pp Paper 0-85424-041-1

REALIZATION OF THE ABSOLUTE
Naiṣkarmya Siddhi of Sureśvara

translated into English by A J Alston

Sureśvara was an enlightened disciple of Śaṅkara and a brilliant exponent of Advaita Vedanta in its purest form. His *Naiṣkarmya Siddhi* establishes the Upanishadic doctrines on a strictly rational basis. At the same time, it introduces the reader to the course of discipline and meditation required for practical realization of his identity with the Absolute. Sureśvara called the work 'a compendium containing the essence of the entire Upanishadic teaching'. Transliterated Sanskrit text and explanatory notes are included.

285pp Cloth 0-85424-021-7

THE HEART OF SHRI SHANKARA

by Śrī Swāmī Satchidānandendra

translated into English by A J Alston

A translation of a work first published in 1929 under the title *Refutation of Root Ignorance* or *The Heart of Shri Shankara*. It considers the philosophical view that there is a root-ignorance that creates the phenomenal world and which in some sense really exists. The Swami sets out to show that this view arose among Advaitins after Shankara and is contrary to his true teaching.

226pp A4 comb-bound. 0-85424-050-0

THE CREST JEWEL OF WISDOM
Viveka Chūḍāmaṇi

A classic of Advaita Vedanta

The commentary by Hari Prasad Shastri demonstrates the practical validity of the teachings of Adhyatma Yoga, while the translation by A J Alston puts the verses into approachable English, faithful to the Sanskrit original, which is included in romanised script. The text covers some sixty key Vedanta topics ranging from the qualifications of the enquirer to his final enlightenment.

336pp Paper 0-85424-047-0

Classical texts translated by Hari Prasad Shastri

ASHTAVAKRA GITA

AVADHUT GITA

DIRECT EXPERIENCE OF REALITY
Aparokshānubhūtī

PANCHADASHI
A 14th Century Vedāntic Classic

THE RAMAYANA OF VALMIKI
in three volumes

TEACHINGS FROM THE BHAGAVAD GITA

TRIUMPH OF A HERO
Vīra Vijaya of Swami Mangalnāth

VERSES FROM THE UPANISHADS
with commentary

WORLD WITHIN THE MIND
Teachings from the Yoga Vāsishtha